FIRST EDITION

Published in the United States of America
By Diamond Books
An Imprint of Eakin Publications, Inc.
P.O. Drawer 90159   ★   Austin, Texas 78709-0159

ISBN 0-89015-768-5

The
Blood
Covenant

Rena Chynow

WITH Dean M. Shapiro

DIAMOND BOOKS Austin, T

To the memory of
Mark and Lillian Chynoweth, Duane Chynoweth,
Jenny Chynoweth, Ed Marston, and
all the other victims, living or dead,
of this tragic story.

I was alone in the house that November morning in 1987, standing at the kitchen sink, staring out the window; not really looking at anything, just staring.

It had been over two weeks since Dan Jordan's murder. I must have been thinking about Dan's kids and widows, mulling over in my mind the details I had been able to gather of the incident. Although my heart went out to his families, I had not felt any personal loss. Dan's claim to the "priesthood" was, to me, a sad joke. And I felt, now that he was gone, maybe some of his followers would wake up and realize they had been deceived, and make a fresh start. On the other hand, Dan's murder could be proof that the group we had all pulled away from was finished with their inner fighting and power struggles, and might now begin knocking off the rest of the defectors. That put my family next on their "list" of traitors . . . next in line for execution.

I had escaped from that part of my past. I had worked very hard to block it out, to forget. My family and I had been victims. Our sincere desire to serve God was used against us by a man who gradually turned power-hungry. We had finally pulled away, gone through the painful process of self-deprogramming, and completely changed our lives. That part of the past was like a bad dream and we were different people now. But could I continue to completely disassociate myself from the past?

As I stood there, staring out the window, suddenly the realities of the situation struck home — and this time I couldn't suppress the thoughts that now came flooding over me. I couldn't pretend Dan's death and the other deaths before his had no effect or bearing on my new life. There was no guarantee the murders would now stop, or that my family would be left alone. But what could we do? It seemed our only option was to hope the police would finally catch "them" before they could kill any more people.

I thought of "them." Just a handful of kids, for they had been kids last time I saw any of them, some eight years or so before. I wondered about their lives and how far off track they had been led. I thought again, as I had many times before, of my own dead sister's children. We had heard of their abuse at the hands of the older half brothers, yet felt completely helpless to do anything to stop it. I knew that the oppression I had been subjected to when a part of that group paled in comparison to the horrors they had been put through. But we had no way of knowing how to find them, and even if we could, how could we help them? Those kids were trained to not trust or believe anyone, to kill anyone who said anything against their present lifestyle or beliefs. Could they ever be convinced that the things they had been brainwashed into believing were all false? Could any of them be salvaged? Was there anything I could do?

These were not really new questions. Occasionally, I would find myself thinking of the past, if only briefly, before repressing it all again. But this time, as I thought of my sister's children, it occurred to me that maybe there was something I could do to help. If any of those kids were trying to break free, maybe I could make that transition less painful than it had been for me. Maybe I could show them that a normal life is possible. I could somehow show that the real world out there is not completely full of "evil people," as they have been taught, and explain how things got so completely mixed up. If I could tell my story, maybe, somehow, I could help just one of them . . .

I was so excited by this thought, I dropped everything and began trying to figure out how to start. Where does one begin? How to explain it? A thousand thoughts were flying around inside my mind when I remembered I had kept a diary for years. Maybe that would be the place to start.

I went to my cedar chest, dug down to the very bottom, and found the worn and ragged homemade notebooks that contained my childhood. With a pounding heart, I began to read.

It took me three agonizing days to get through that diary. I walked around in a daze, like a zombie. All kinds of emotions raged inside. Is that young girl me? Did I really act and feel that way at one time? How could I have blocked out all of my childhood so completely? I wept for that girl, for her family, and for the sacrifices they made in God's name that led in such a completely different direction than planned.

Reviewing the diary was such an emotional and painful experience, I had to immerse myself in other activities and let the trauma I was feeling subside. A month later, I again read the diary and was amazed to find that my subconscious had already tried to repress and erase those same words read only the month before.

What to do now? Did I really need to drag out the past? Would the possible benefit to others outweigh the pain of telling and reliving the story? What about the emotional effect on my children — they who know next to nothing about their natural father? And what about my husband, the man who has loved me in spite of my past, taught me so much, given his name to my children, and shown me that the real world "out there" isn't all full of bad people? How would this affect us?

At first John, my husband, was hesitant. "If it's that painful, don't put yourself through it" was the message I got. My mother, brothers, my friend Sandy, and my lawyer all said, "Do it!" My attorney put it this way; "Look, write about it. If nothing else, it will be good therapy. After all, if you haven't dealt with the past yet, well it's time you did."

Thus began the journey back . . .

Acknowledgments

I would like to thank John D. O'Connell, my attorney and friend, who urged me to "get it all out"; my mother Thelma Ray Chynoweth, for her strength, love, and for sharing many details about the past even though they were painful; my agent Lloyd Jones and my publisher Tony Seidl, for believing in this story; my in-laws Carl and Helen and my stepdaughter Sandy, for their acceptance, love, and support; also Verlan M. LeBaron, Jr., Dick Forbes, Tony LeBaron, my brothers Glen, Victor, Mark, Duane and Johnny Chynoweth, Ramona Marston, Celia LeBaron, Silvia E. LeBaron, Lillian Chynoweth, Sgts. Burmester and Carroll, Lt. Roque and O. Gary Shaw, for sharing vital information and background; my dear friend Jim Coate; and all the other friends and family who were supportive of my efforts.

My special gratitude goes to my husband John, who has stood by me and been my pillar of strength through thick and thin. And thank you to my wonderful co-writer Dean M. Shapiro, for his persistence and diligence in wading through mountains of documents, my diaries, newspaper clippings, etc., and dragging other details from my reluctant subconscience that were vital to the completeness and accuracy of this account.

The following is a list of important individuals discussed in the book. For further explanation of Ervil's wives and children, his own brothers and sisters, or the family of Bud Chynoweth (Rena's father) see family tree charts.

Allred, Owen — brother of Rulon C. Allred

Allred, Dr. Rulon Clark — naturopathic doctor of Utah; patriarch of a fundamentalist polygamous sect; close to Verlan LeBaron and therefore targeted for murder in 1977

Castro, Fernando — original member of Quorum of Twelve Apostles enticed by Ervil to join his side after split from Joel; in the end remained loyal to Joel and reported Ervil's activities to Joel

Chynoweth, Duane — Rena's brother, married to Laura Chaparra Amador first (marriage dissolved) then married Lucy; murdered in 1988 by order of Ervil

Chynoweth, Glen — Rena's brother; wife, Kathy

Chynoweth, Mark — Rena's brother; married to Lillian; murdered in 1988 by order of Ervil

Chynoweth, Rebecca (Becky) — daughter of Ervil and Delfina; married to Victor Chynoweth; murdered by order of Ervil, 1977

Chynoweth, Victor — Rena's brother; married to Nancy and Rebecca (Becky) (Ervil's daughter)

Evoniuk, Leo — a convert to Ervil's following while both were jailed in Mexico; later made a high priest and carried on Ervil's commands after his death; presumed murdered in 1987

Forbes, Dick — special investigator, Salt Lake County Attorney's Office

Forbes, Paul — brother of Dick; sergeant with Murray Police Department

Jensen, Carol — wife of Earl Jensen

Jensen, Earl — high-ranking official in Church of the Firstborn; his daughter (Christina) was one of Ervil's wives

Johnson, Benjamin F. — confidant of Joseph Smith; claimed the mantle of "true priesthood" was passed to him by Smith; great-grandfather of Ervil LeBaron

Jordan, Daniel Ben — original member of Quorum (Council) of Twelve Apostles, Church of the Firstborn; close confidant to Ervil but later broke away; murdered in 1987

Kunz, Rhea — Verlan's mother-in-law; unsuccessfully targeted to be murdered by Ervil's order so that Verlan would be lured to funeral

LeBaron, Abel — son of Alma, Jr.

LeBaron, Alma D. III — son of Alma, Jr.

LeBaron, Conway — cousin of Ervil who helped him establish Church of the Lamb of God

LeBaron, Ivan — son of Joel

LeBaron, Jeannine — wife of Joel

LeBaron, Kathy — wife of Joel

LeBaron, Nephi — son of Alma, Jr.

LeBaron, Pauline — wife of Conway

LeBaron, Sammy — son of Alma, Jr.; member of Quorum of Twelve Apostles

LeBaron, Verlan M. — son of Verlan

McCaughey, Steve — attorney defending Vonda White and Ed Marston

Marston, Ed — son of Nephi and Anna Mae Marston; family friend of Chynoweths and Ervil follower; murdered in 1988 by order of Ervil

Marston, Nephi — father of Ed and Ramona Marston, killed in auto accident, 1968; husband of Anna Mae, who later married Ervil

Marston, Ramona — daughter of Anna Mae; wife of Dan Jordan; assisted in murder of Rulon C. Allred

O'Connell, John — Rena's attorney

Ray, Louis and Susan Bell — parents of Thelma Ray Chynoweth (Rena's mother)

Rios, Eulalia — wife of Nephi Marston; killed in auto accident, 1968

Rios, Gamaliel — staunch follower of Ervil; murdered in 1983

Rios, Raul — staunch follower of Ervil; charged in connection with Joel LeBaron's murder; murdered in 1983

Silver, Stephen — church member who headed the English program at Los Molinos school; original member of Quorum of Twelve Apostles

Simons, Robert — a practicing polygamist in Utah who had no following but whom Ervil called a false prophet; murdered in 1975 by order of Ervil

Smith, Joseph — founder of Church of Jesus Christ of Latter Day Saints (Mormon Church)

Strothman, Jack — friend of Robin and Dave Sullivan; convert to Church of the Lamb of God

Sullivan, Betty — wife of John

Sullivan, Bonnie — wife of Lloyd

Sullivan, Dave — nephew of Lloyd Sullivan

Sullivan, Don — son of Lloyd; follower of Ervil who later defected

Sullivan, John — nephew of Lloyd; follower of Ervil who later defected

Sullivan, Lloyd — member of Church of the Lamb of God who later defected and reported to Verlan on Ervil's murder plots; died in 1978 of heart attack

Sullivan, Noreen — wife of Don

Sullivan, Robin — nephew of Lloyd Sullivan

Van Sciver, Robert (Bob) — attorney for Mark and Victor Chynoweth

Vest, Dean Grover — an Ervil follower who defected; murdered in 1975 by order of Ervil

Widmar, Siegfried — a counselor to Joel LeBaron's First Presidency

Widmar, Weiner — son of Siegfried

Yocom, David — Salt Lake County assistant attorney

Zarate, Andres — son of Benjamin Zarate; a follower of Ervil who carried on with the Mexico faction after Ervil died

Zarate, Cuthberto — brother of Andres; son of Benjamin

Brief Ancestry of Ervil LeBaron

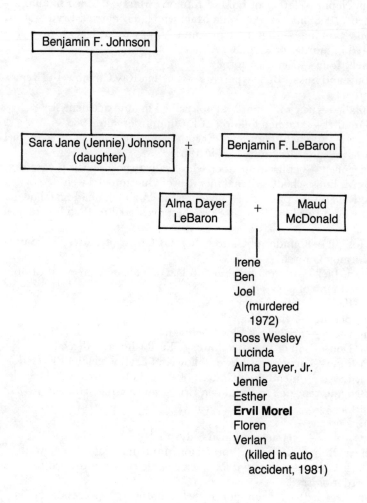

Benjamin F. Johnson

Sara Jane (Jennie) Johnson
(daughter)   +   Benjamin F. LeBaron

Alma Dayer
LeBaron   +   Maud
McDonald

Irene
Ben
Joel
  (murdered
  1972)
Ross Wesley
Lucinda
Alma Dayer, Jr.
Jennie
Esther
Ervil Morel
Floren
Verlan
  (killed in auto
  accident, 1981)

The Wives and Children of Ervil LeBaron

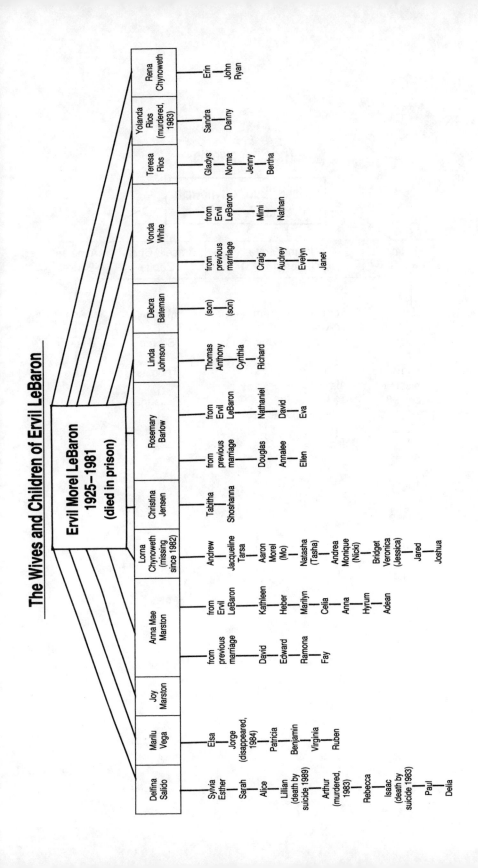

The Chynoweths

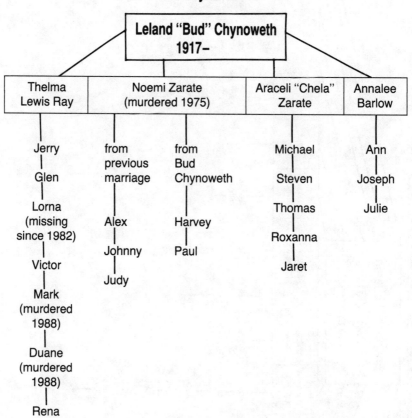

Leland "Bud" Chynoweth
1917–

Thelma Lewis Ray	Noemi Zarate (murdered 1975)		Araceli "Chela" Zarate	Annalee Barlow
Jerry	from previous marriage	from Bud Chynoweth	Michael	Ann
Glen			Steven	Joseph
Lorna (missing since 1982)	Alex	Harvey	Thomas	Julie
Victor	Johnny	Paul	Roxanna	
Mark (murdered 1988)	Judy		Jaret	
Duane (murdered 1988)				
Rena				

Prologue

As the phone rang at Duane's Appliance in Houston, Texas, Thelma Ray Chynoweth answered it. The caller said he had a used washer and dryer to sell, and if Duane was interested he could pick them up at 6010 Rena Street at 4:00. Thelma said she would give the message to her son, and the caller hung up.

Shortly afterward, Thelma, who managed the store with Duane, went home, leaving Duane to mind the shop alone. She was sixty-nine years old and had gotten into the routine of taking an afternoon nap. She promised Duane she would be back as usual to watch the store while he went out on calls. As 4:00 approached, however, Thelma still had not arrived. She was nearly always prompt, but on that particular day she overslept and was running late. Lucy, Duane's wife of eleven months, had planned on going with him and bringing his four daughters by a previous marriage. However, since Thelma wasn't there yet and he needed to hurry, Lucy stayed behind to keep an eye on the shop while he was gone.

Having been a single father for a few years before his recent marriage, Duane centered his life around his children. He took them everywhere with him. Rarely did he go out on a service call or pickup without one or more of them in tow. But, since his mother was late, Duane took only his second-oldest daughter, Jenny, with him. The other three little girls stayed with Lucy to keep her company, and they cried at being left behind. Duane and Jenny climbed into Duane's 1986 GMC pickup truck and he drove toward the address given over the phone. By the time Thelma showed up, Duane and eight-year-old Jenny had left.

Duane's destination was in an upper middle-class subdivision and he arrived, as scheduled, at 4:00. He backed his truck up the driveway, getting it as close to the garage as he could go, and shut off the motor. He and Jenny sat there a few minutes, chatting while they waited for someone to arrive. A few minutes later, another pickup pulled in front of the driveway and stopped.

Duane climbed out of the cab as a suit-clad young man with a short beard got out of the other truck. The man walked up the driveway toward Duane, who introduced himself and asked about the machines to be picked up. Showing no expression on his face, the man reached into his coat and pulled out a .45-caliber pistol. Three shots rang out and struck Duane in the head. He fell forward onto the lawn, a murder victim at the age of thirty-one.

On hearing the shots from the passenger side of the truck, Jenny let out a scream. The gunman heard her and stepped over Duane's body to investigate. Seeing the terrified girl sitting there screaming, he reached in through the open door and fired two more shots. Jenny was hit in the face by both bullets and died instantly. The killer calmly turned around, walked down the driveway, climbed into his own truck, and drove off, leaving two victims in his wake.

★   ★   ★

Mark Chynoweth had been sick over the weekend. When Monday came his wife Lillian tried to persuade him to stay home and rest, but Mark was determined to go to work. There was too much to do at the shop, he told her. So, despite not feeling well, Mark got up, dressed, and drove to his appliance store in the 2100 block of Blalock Street in Houston.

Arriving at Reliance Appliance, he parked his truck, got out, unlocked the door to his shop, and flipped on the lights. Another work week was just beginning.

That particular Monday started out no different from any other. There were workers to oversee, phones to answer, service calls to schedule, deliveries to make, bills to pay, and all the other details that routinely go along with running a small business. Mark stayed in the shop all day, attending to these matters, while Lillian came and left several times. Around 3:30 that afternoon, while Lillian was there, her younger brother Paul dropped by to see them. Paul had his camera with him and took a picture of Mark and Lillian standing together. The three of them chatted for a few minutes and Paul offered to take Mark's oldest child, Brandon, out for a bite to eat. Lillian kissed Mark goodbye and walked out the door with them.

Mark sat down at the computer on his desk, picking up where he had left off on some bills he had begun earlier. Looking up at the clock on the wall he noticed it was nearly 4:00. At the same moment, a well-dressed man walked into his office. Mark glanced his way, and a horrified look came over his face as he saw that the man was armed. Mark instinctively flung his left arm up in front of his face as the man opened fire. The first bullet pierced his arm, lodging in his left eye, and the force propelled him backward, along with the chair he was sitting in. The gunman walked over to him, pumped three more bullets into his chest, and calmly walked out. By the time the police arrived, Mark Chynoweth, age thirty-six, was dead.

★   ★   ★

Two hundred and fifty miles away, in the Dallas suburb of Irving, Texas, Edward T. Marston, another appliance store owner, waited impatiently in the driveway of a home to make a pickup. He had been called to arrive at 4:00, and it was getting close to 4:30. Finally, a pickup truck pulled up and a man got out. Ed stood there waiting as the man walked closer to him.

As the man got within an arm's length, Ed stretched his hand out and started to introduce himself. Instead of shaking hands, the man pointed a pistol at him and fired two shots. Ed was hit in the head and chest and collapsed in the driveway. The gunman fled. Emergency units arrived and raced Ed, unconscious but still breathing, to the nearest hospital. Later that evening, Ed Marston died on the operating table, a murder victim at age thirty-two.

★   ★   ★

Who were these victims and why were they murdered? What was the fatal thread that wove them all together? Their tragic deaths on June 27, 1988, were the fulfillment of a bloody prophecy made by a man who had died seven years earlier. And they were all close to me. Duane and Mark Chynoweth were my older brothers. Jenny Chynoweth was my niece. Ed Marston was the stepson of my former husband and a close family friend.

From the early 1960s to the early '80s, my family had been among the followers of Ervil Morel LeBaron, a man the media has dubbed "The Mormon Manson." Although the Manson analogy may be accurate, the "Mormon" part is not entirely. The Church of the Lamb of God, which Ervil led, and the Church of the First-born of the Fulness of Times, which Ervil led previously with his brother Joel, were not sanctioned by the Mormon church, but they were rooted in original Mormon precepts. Polygamy, or the right of a man to take multiple wives, was one of the original principles of Mormonism that was later disavowed by them. It was primarily this issue that led the LeBaron family and others to split away from the Mormon church and start their own.

I was the last and youngest of Ervil's thirteen wives. We were married in 1975, when I was sixteen and he was almost fifty, and I bore two of his nearly sixty children. During our five-year marriage and for many years afterward, I had to live with some ghastly memories. I killed a man in cold blood, acting on my husband's orders which he claimed were "commands from God." I spent a year and a half running from the law, five months in jail awaiting trial for murder, and many years afterward trying to block out my past.

Ervil died in prison on August 15, 1981, while serving a life sentence for masterminding the murder he had me commit for him, one of many deaths he ordered. But the senseless killings did not end with his death. Seven years later they were still going on. Between 1972 and 1988, twenty to twenty-five people have been killed or simply "disappeared," either on his direct command or under orders he left before he died.

Ervil never committed any of the murders himself. He didn't have to. He had loyal followers like us to carry out his "God-given" commands. Like Charles Manson, he stayed behind the scenes, targeting his victims and sending us, his hard-core disciples, out as his executioners.

The cult founded by Ervil LeBaron and passed on to some of his youngest children has continued the violent legacy he began in 1972, when he had his brother Joel murdered in a power struggle for control of their church. His failure to be acknowledged as the leader of that church after his brother's death led to more violence and bloodshed. Now that Ervil is dead, some of his own sons have become avenging angels of his will. The blood-stained hand of Ervil LeBaron has reached beyond his grave.

For the past three years my family and I have been in hiding. My name is on a "hit list" Ervil drew up shortly before his death. What was my "crime"? What were the "crimes" of my murdered brothers and Ed Marston, whose names were also on that list? What were the "crimes" of some of the other victims? The answer is that we were traitors, defectors from Ervil's flock. We committed the unpardonable sin of breaking away from him. In so doing we, in effect, signed our own death warrants.

The story I have to tell is shocking, yet true. It has attracted international media coverage. Other books have been written about Ervil LeBaron and there may be more to come, but until now, no one has ever come forward and told the story from the "inside." I was there during those turbulent years. I was a witness to many events that other people have written about or reported on in the visual media. I have letters Ervil wrote to me from prison and copies of his writings from previous years. In addition, I have the diary that I kept between the ages of thirteen and nineteen. All of these written records, plus my own recollections, have enabled me to piece together a very complicated story.

In the pages that follow, I will attempt to explain why my family and others followed Ervil and why we continued to follow him, even when he ordered us to commit terrorist-type acts of violence. I hope to show how he started out as a dynamic visionary leader, then gradually deteriorated into an irrational fanatic who resorted to violence and murder to fulfill what he said was "God's will." By telling this story, I hope to help others — especially those still under his influence who continue to follow his beliefs and who pose threats to the lives of others. I also hope to help the men, women, and children whose lives were traumatized by his actions — people whose experiences have been similar to my own.

The average person probably cannot comprehend how we could allow one man to exercise so much control over us, over our lives. So much control, in fact, that his will could overrule our own consciences. He ordered the firebombing of a village in which two people were killed and thirteen others wounded. His followers committed other murders, acting on his orders, even when some of those being murdered or conspired against were his own brothers, wives, and children. What was it about him that could compel such obedience from otherwise passive, law-abiding individuals?

The truth is that the church my parents joined was one which originally advocated peace and love. Ervil and Joel LeBaron represented these virtues to us when they first came into our lives in the early 1960s. I was very young at that time, but this is what attracted my mother and my older sister (and later my father, three of my brothers, and me) to their church and its doctrine. Prior to that, we were all raised in the Mormon church but found it to be lacking in certain key scriptural areas affecting our daily lives and our relationship to God. The LeBarons seemed to have the answers to all the questions we had about our church. They made us feel as though they — and we as their disciples — had a divine mission to fulfill on earth. We were convinced that we were "God's chosen people." Joel and Ervil's doctrine promised great blessings from God to those willing to sacrifice and follow them. All others who had the chance but rejected this doctrine would be cursed and damned for eternity.

Their teachings appealed to us, since they embodied every aspect of human goodness we ourselves believed in. We were willing to make whatever sacrifices of personal comforts and material goods it took to attain that exalted level of godliness they promised us. Unfortunately, like so many other breakaway churches throughout history, the spiritual purity of our founding principles gave way to fanaticism. An overzealous leader became irrational when he saw his efforts to enforce God's law over the people thwarted. Irrationality led to violence when peaceful means failed to achieve the desired goal.

My family followed Ervil when he split from his brother Joel after disputes they had over the enforcement of laws governing the membership. We continued to follow him for another ten years, during which time his interpretation of the doctrine turned to violence and bloodshed. We accepted his teachings for a long time, even when people were being killed, believing it was the fulfillment of God's will. Only much later did we realize it wasn't God's work at all, but the twisted workings of a once-brilliant mind gone mad.

Once we came to this realization, we faced the awesome task of trying to straighten out our lives. We had to deprogram and divorce ourselves from the violent aspects of his teachings that had gotten us into so much trouble. When the break finally came, I found out just how hard self-deprogramming could be. It was a gradual and painful process. I spent countless hours on my knees, praying for guidance and forgiveness while trying to forget my past and the horrible deeds I had done in Ervil's name. I ended up completely shutting out the past because I couldn't deal with the guilt and anger. It took many years of slow awakening to reach the point where I could look back and finally talk about it.

Now, thanks to the love and support I've gotten from my family and friends, I can.

CHAPTER 1

To understand Ervil LeBaron, his church, and the whole issue of polygamy, one must go back many years, to the founding of the Mormon church itself. It began around 1830 in Palmyra, New York, when a farmer named Joseph Smith claimed he had revelations from the angel Moroni. This angel led him to the golden tablets that became the basis for the *Book of Mormon*. Smith founded the Church of Jesus Christ of Latter Day Saints, better known as the Mormons, and gathered up a group of followers who believed in the message he brought them.

The Mormons believe in the divinity of Jesus Christ but they also found their roots in the patriarchs and prophets of ancient Israel. Joseph Smith incorporated the principles of the faith into his numerous writings, the principal one being *Doctrine and Covenants*, or *D&C* for short. The Mormons held to many values espoused by the ancient Hebrew patriarchs. Hard work, devotion to God, and solid family relationships were among those values, but the practice that caused the most controversy — and trouble — was polygamy. They believed that it was as much their right to have multiple wives as it was for the biblical patriarchs, and that God's special blessings were bestowed on them for it. Because of this practice, Joseph Smith and his followers were persecuted almost from the start. They were physically assaulted, jailed, and had their property destroyed. They were harassed so often that life became intolerable for them where they were.

Driven from one town to another in a desperate westward retreat, Smith and his church settled in Illinois and named their new community Nauvoo. Although the name of their settlement was the Hebrew word for "beautiful," the mood surrounding them was anything but that. The polygamous lifestyle they practiced led to a popular outcry from neighboring townspeople that finally erupted in violence. On June 27, 1844, an angry mob stormed the jail where Joseph Smith and his brother were being held and they were murdered.

Knowing that they could no longer remain safely in Illinois, 16,000 Mormon pioneers hastily packed up and continued to trek westward under their dynamic new leader, Brigham Young. After many months spent crossing the Great Plains and the treacherous passes of the Rocky Mountains, they stood on a cliff overlooking the valley of the Great Salt Lake in July 1847. Uttering his famous words, "This is the place," Young led his people down into the valley and they settled around what is now present-day Salt Lake City.

Within a short time the Mormon settlers had transformed a desert wasteland into a fertile farming community. They named their colony Deseret, meaning "land of honeybees" from the *Book of Mormon,* and it grew and prospered under Young's leadership. Far from the hostility of outsiders who had harassed and persecuted them everywhere else they had attempted to settle, the Mormons flourished in their isolation, free to follow their religion unhindered — including their sacred practice of polygamy. Their numbers grew rapidly as more and more children were born to the multiple wives of the men, and other converts from elsewhere joined them. By 1860 there were more than 40,000 people in the colony and a decade later the population had more than doubled.

However, there were outside political developments brewing that would have a profound impact on the Mormon church and polygamy. One by one the territories surrounding Deseret were petitioning Congress to admit them into the Union as states. Deseret had applied for statehood as early as 1849 but, because of its laws allowing and encouraging polygamy, the petition was denied by Congress. To make matters worse, for nearly forty years the federal government passed laws disenfranchising the Mormons. Polygamy was declared to be a crime, and economic sanctions were enforced against the territorial government, despite the fact that only about ten percent of the Mormons were practicing polygamists. Finally, in November 1890, the Mormon hierarchy succumbed to the pressure. They issued a manifesto officially renouncing polygamy and declaring it illegal. On January 4, 1896, Deseret became the forty-fifth state under its territorial name, Utah.

But the official church declaration against polygamy by the Mormon leaders did not end what had already become a deep-rooted practice and belief for many. A number of dissident Mormon fundamentalists continued the practice, despite being denounced, criminally prosecuted, and eventually excommunicated by the mainstream Mormon hierarchy. One of those was Benjamin F. Johnson.

Johnson, a confidant of Joseph Smith and the brother of two of Smith's wives, claimed that the Mormon founder had passed a mantle of the "true priesthood" on to him. Johnson later passed that mantle on to his grandson, Alma Dayer LeBaron, born in 1886. Dayer defied the anti-polygamy laws of Utah and was driven out of the state in 1920 for taking a second wife. He took his wives, Maud and Onie, across the Mexican border to the village of Colonia Juárez, about 150 miles southwest of El Paso, in the state of Chihuahua. There, unmolested by a tolerant Mexican government and surrounded by other self-exiled polygamous Mormons, they tilled the land and raised their families. Onie left Dayer soon after their arrival but Maud stayed on, bearing him two daughters and seven sons.

Of those seven sons, the two that emerged above the others were Ervil and Joel. Later newspaper articles and books written on the LeBarons compared the two to Cain and Abel. They were as different as two men could possibly be. Joel was usually quiet, soft-spoken, reserved, and pious. He had what some of his followers called "a saintlike quality" that awed people and drew them to him. Like Ervil, he had an abundance of charisma but it came across in a more gentle way. He felt the call to prophecy early in life and had a gift for making those who came to him with their troubles walk away feeling good. He would hug them and pat them on the back, giving them reassurances that everything would be all right when, in effect, he had actually done nothing to solve their problems. He never told anyone they were wrong, therefore not making any enemies. All of his followers were taught he was infallible and immortal, and Joel did nothing to discourage these beliefs on their part.

Ervil, on the other hand, commanded a strong presence: six foot four inches, 240 pounds; square jawline and wide chin; a thin straight mouth and imposing Roman nose; brown hair thinning, giving way to a broad forehead accented with thick eyebrows and piercing blue eyes. When he spoke he leaned forward, and it appeared as though he was penetrating your mind with his eyes. You almost felt like he was reading your innermost thoughts when, in actuality, he was hardly seeing you at all. He was merely caught up in what he was saying. Aside from his dominant physical stature, however, Ervil was also a well-versed, self-taught theologian. He could talk for hours at a time and was an authority on the Bible and other Mormon scripture. His powerful rhetoric and self-assured manner of expressing his thoughts contrasted sharply with the low-key, soft-spoken Joel.

Except for Verlan, who would later assume leadership of the Church of the Firstborn after Joel's death, the other LeBaron brothers were relatively insignificant in the church. Ben LeBaron claimed to be a prophet and visionary and often did bizarre things which later landed him in mental institutions. He died in a car accident in 1978 near Little Rock, Arkansas. Ross Wesley LeBaron, who also claims the gift of prophecy, is in 1990 still living in the Salt Lake City area and is in his mid-seventies. A former polygamist who now lives alone with a herd of goats, Wesley frequently calls radio talk shows and claims that Christ will return to earth in a flying saucer. The other brothers, Alma, Jr., and Floren, remained relatively aloof from the fracas surrounding their other brothers while staying loyal to the church founded by Joel.

Ervil was born on February 22, 1925, in Colonia Juárez, Chihuahua, Mexico. As children, he and Joel, who was nearly two years older, were as close as two brothers could be. They played together, worked together, and got into trouble together with their pranks. Their youngest brother, Verlan, described many of their escapades in *The LeBaron Story*, a book he self-published just before his death in 1981. But, despite being from a large family and having brothers and sisters to play with, the LeBaron children did not have a particularly happy childhood.

Their lives were clouded by hostility and tension. They were taunted, harassed, and often beaten up by the other children of Colonia Juárez because their father was one of the few villagers still practicing polygamy. Many of these children were the sons and daughters of polygamists themselves, but that didn't seem to matter to them. Their parents had come to accept the revisionist Mormon position on marriage, making the LeBarons and one or two other families outcasts. They were ostracized from a society in which they had sought and been initially granted asylum. Other villagers wouldn't allow the LeBaron children to play with their own children, and they were not invited to many social functions. The strain proved too much for one of the LeBaron daughters, Lucinda, who at age sixteen underwent a mental breakdown that would end up confining her to institutions for most of the rest of her life.

Eventually, Dayer would take his family and transplant them from this hostile environment into a colony he founded, one that bears his name today. But, while the LeBarons were still in Colonia Juárez, some significant events would take place in Ervil's life. The family still considered themselves Mormons at this time, despite being at odds with the mother church over the issue of polygamy and other fine points involving the priesthood doctrine. They were fundamentalists, but Mormons nonetheless. In the early 1940s, Joel and Alma LeBaron, Jr., went on L.D.S. missions among the native and predominantly Catholic Mexicans (whom the Mormons call "Lamanites"), in the region between Veracruz and Mexico

12

City. Ervil joined them shortly afterward, but not before going to his father to receive what he considered a proper ordination. Over the years the wording of the priesthood ordination had been changed, and Ervil didn't trust it. Knowing that his father had been ordained properly, he wanted the priesthood conferred on him the same way. After getting his father's blessing, Ervil joined his brothers on their mission.

The three brothers were beginning to enjoy some success in converting Lamanites to their fundamentalist beliefs. However, church authorities stepped in and began cracking down on their missionary work. The LeBaron brothers returned to Colonia Juárez and were excommunicated from the Mormon church shortly afterward for advocating polygamy.

It was around this time that the oldest LeBaron son, Ben, began claiming he was "The One Mighty and Strong" in fulfillment of a prophecy in Section 85 of Joseph Smith's *Doctrine and Covenants*. Issuing pamphlets and publicly announcing that he possessed the gift of prophecy, Ben staked his claim to the mantle of the priesthood Benjamin Johnson had passed on to Dayer LeBaron, perhaps hoping Dayer would bestow the mantle on him before his death.

Ben's pronouncements and claims attracted very few followers, but one of those few was Ervil. Upholding Ben's claims to the true priesthood, Ervil put all of his resources and efforts behind trying to have Ben acknowledged as such. Ben, who was plagued with bouts of mental illness from an early age, claimed to have had "visions" as early as nine years old. In his later years he did a number of bizarre things that would result in confinement in mental institutions. In a widely publicized incident in Salt Lake City in the late 1940s, Ben stopped traffic at a busy intersection so he could do about 200 push-ups in the middle of the road, claiming afterward that it proved he was "The One Mighty and Strong." At other times he would throw his head back and roar like a lion. These stunts added nothing to his credibility, nor did they win him any new followers.

After a few years of touting Ben as the heir to the true priesthood, Ervil became disillusioned. In his book, Verlan said, "After years of labor, he [Ervil] saw that Ben did not fill the bill. Although Ervil had passed through a heavy and tragic deception, he did not lose his desire to serve in the Lord's cause, but kept seeking to find it." Later he did find it, in the person of Joel — the brother and close companion of his earliest years.

In 1944, Alma Dayer LeBaron bought 200 acres of land twenty miles south of Colonia Juárez and founded Colonia Le-Baron. Dayer and his sons set about planting crops and orchards, raising livestock, and working long hours to make their ranch as prosperous and self-sustaining as possible. It started out with just the family and in later years became a gathering place for other fundamentalists.

Shortly after Dayer set up the ranch, Ervil contracted a serious case of malaria that rendered him unable to work. Since there was a lot of work to do to get the ranch functioning properly, Dayer had no patience with Ervil's inability to do his share. He kicked Ervil out of the house and sent him to live in an isolated adobe shack out on the property. Ervil stayed in that shack for about a year or two, battling the disease. His mother would bring food to him, and he spent all of his time studying. He was determined to do God's work, despite his ill health, and he would read everything he could get his hands on — especially the Bible and Mormon literature. Having a very sharp mind, he retained much of the knowledge he picked up during those years — knowledge that would come in handy later in his life.

According to the story told by the family, a few days before his death in February 1951, Dayer called his wife Maud, Joel, and Ervil to his bedside. While Maud and Ervil held his paralyzed hands over Joel, Dayer conferred a blessing upon him. He told Joel, in effect, that he was passing the mantle and authority of the priesthood on to him, just as Benjamin Johnson had passed it on to him many years earlier. Dayer placed all earthly affairs in Joel's hands and made him promise to build on the foundation that he (Dayer) had begun. It was a scene reminiscent of the Old Testament in which the dying patriarchs conferred the birthrights on their favorite sons.

After Dayer's death, his work was carried on primarily by Joel and Ervil. From the time they were officially excommunicated from the Mormon church until the mid-1950s, a time span of nearly fifteen years, the LeBarons were essentially without a church. In September 1955, Joel traveled to Salt Lake City with a special mission in mind. On the twenty-first, accompanied by Floren and Wesley, he walked into the secretary of state's office in the State Capitol with notarized official papers in his hand. With these papers he incorporated the Church of the Firstborn of the Fulness of Times.

Soon after that Joel went into a canyon in the mountains and claimed to have had a series of "visions" reaffirming his worthiness to wear the mantle of the priesthood. During these visions, Joel claimed to have been visited by Abraham, Moses, Jesus Christ, Joseph Smith, and a number of other prophets. He printed copies of the church's articles of incorporation, held a few baptisms, and a short time later returned to Mexico to explain his new church to the citizens of Colonia LeBaron.

Joel set himself up as the "Grand Head of the Melchizedek Priesthood" and asserted his claim to being "The One Mighty and Strong." According to Verlan's account, when word got back to Ervil in Mexico that Joel had founded a new church, Ervil was fearful. He had spent several fruitless years supporting Ben's claims to the priesthood and now Wesley was also making similar claims in Utah. Scorn, ridicule, and even outright hatred had already been heaped on the LeBaron family as a result of these claims, and Ervil feared more to come because of what Joel had done.

Also, according to Verlan, Ervil decided to put Joel to the test when Joel returned to Mexico. The two of them sequestered themselves for several hours, during which time Ervil debated Joel on scripture and questions relating to the priesthood he didn't think Joel would be able to answer satisfactorily. However, not only was Joel able to respond, he succeeded in weakening Ervil's arguments and finally convinced Ervil that he was indeed a prophet. From that moment through the next dozen or so years, Joel had no more loyal or enthusiastic a follower than the brother he had been so close to in his youth. Soon after Ervil's conversion to Joel's new church, Maud and other family members were also baptized.

Growth was very slow for the church over its first five or six years but, by the early 1960s, membership began to escalate. Colonia LeBaron had expanded beyond Dayer's original ranch and was now a small village containing other American and Mexican families. All or most of the villagers became members of the Firstborn Church. Joel then set about establishing the ruling hierarchy of the church. In 1961, Ervil was appointed Joel's second in command or "Patriarch of Israel." Two counselors to Joel's "First Presidency" were soon appointed, and a Quorum (Council) of Twelve Apostles was chosen. Among the original quorum members were brothers Verlan and Alma and a man who would later play an important role in my own life, Daniel Ben Jordan.

The structure of the Church of the Firstborn was rooted in priesthoods of the Old Testament. Joel held the Melchizedek Priesthood, which descended from the priest who blessed Abraham after he slaughtered the rival kings. This was the highest priesthood, whose succession included Moses and Jesus Christ. Joel claimed that he would be the one to return the mantle of the priesthood to Christ when he returns to earth to establish His kingdom.

As "Patriarch of Israel," Ervil held the Aaronic Priesthood, which descended from Aaron during the time of Exodus and continued through John the Baptist. Just as John had prepared the world for the coming of Christ, Ervil, as patriarch, felt it was the sacred duty of his office to prepare the world for the Second Coming. This was to be done through the implementation of "civil law" or "The Law of Liberty," which will be explained later.

In gathering up converts to their church, Ervil and Joel claimed that the Mormon church had fallen into apostasy and no longer represented the word of God. They charged that the 1890 manifesto renouncing polygamy had no legitimate authority from God because it did not contain the words, "Thus sayeth the Lord," as all previous Mormon revelations had done. They also taught that the wording of the bestowal of the priesthood had been wrongly altered and many men were receiving invalid ordinations. Joel and Ervil, on the other hand, claimed to have received the fullness of the priesthood through the proper method of ordination — through men who truly had the priesthood to bestow. They felt that God had taken the priesthood from the Mormon church for its unwillingness to live by the laws He decreed, polygamy being among them.

Polygamy, which had been sanctified in the Bible and the doctrines of Joseph Smith, could not be nullified for reasons of secular political expediency, Joel and Ervil argued. Sacred doctrine could not be renounced by the will of a temporal authority, in this case the United States government and its component states. They took the position that, by renouncing polygamy, the established Mormon church was also renouncing the priesthood as God had sanctified it. Consequently, the two brothers made many of their converts from among those who were equally disenchanted with the mainstream church and its doctrines. The men who followed them were allowed to take plural wives after they proved themselves worthy of the privilege. They had to be in good standing in the priesthood, pay tithing, and have a recommendation from their bishop, but once these and other requirements were met they could enjoy the blessings of plural marriage.

The women believed strongly enough in the LeBarons' teachings to acquiesce in their subservient roles. In most cases, the wives felt they were fulfilling God's will and were happy to be part of these "extended families," even though it often consigned them to poverty and other material sacrifices. They felt it was necessary to sacrifice in order to receive great blessings. (While I was married to Ervil, most of his other wives and I thought of each other as "sisters.")

Despite being illegal in this country, polygamy can be justified by its adherents. It is a societal support system that realistically addresses the needs of women who might otherwise remain single, divorced, or widowed. Where polygamy is practiced, there is no prostitution or illegitimacy. Having plural wives makes it possible for a man to have more children than are normally produced in a monogamous household. It was a practice that was sanctioned for the biblical patriarchs who eventually succeeded in populating ancient Israel. It was a practice that enabled the Mormon pioneers to multiply and survive. And it was a practice that swelled the ranks of the churches to which my family would belong.

CHAPTER 2

I was born in Ogden, Utah, on April 10, 1958, the youngest of seven children to Thelma Lewis Ray Chynoweth and Leland Harvey "Bud" Chynoweth. My mother liked the name Serena and wanted to call me that, but she felt it was too long when combined with my last name. She settled on Rena. My oldest brother, Jerry, died when he was seven years old. My other brothers and sister, in order, were Glen, Lorna, Victor, Mark, and Duane.

Glen, seventeen years older than I, was married when I was only around three or four years old. He and his wife Kathy lived with us for a while. At that time he drove a cement truck and later worked at Hill Air Force Base, where my father also worked. Unlike the rest of us, he stayed in the established Mormon church.

Lorna was fourteen when I was born. Because of the vast differences in our ages, we were never close. Vic was older than me by eleven years. He was the rowdy, boisterous one who was always getting into fights at school and other kinds of trouble. A born salesman, he developed a knack for making money. The businesses he would go into later on would play a key role in financially supporting Ervil's church.

Mark was a superb musician. I spent many hours as a child listening to him play the piano, and most of us were confident he would grow up to be a concert pianist. However, as he got into his teens he dropped the piano in favor of the electric guitar and organ and formed some rock groups. Like Vic, Mark would also play a key role in Ervil's church, but his contributions would be on a doctrinal level in the priesthood.

Duane was the closest to me in age — only sixteen months separated us. He was quiet and introspective, good at sports and anything mechanical, but not at academics. It was not until he was an adult that he was diagnosed as being dyslexic. Today there would have been therapy that could have helped him with the problem, but in those days little was known about this type of learning disability. Duane was my "guardian angel," watching over me and getting me out of many scrapes in my early years. Once, during a vacation in Yellowstone, he rescued me from being drowned in a fast-moving river. The funny thing is that at the time I didn't feel like I was in any danger. I sometimes resented his intrusions but, in retrospect, it's clear I really needed a guardian angel.

Like most of those around us, we were raised Mormon early in life. Mom was a homemaker and sometimes taught Sunday school at the Mormon church our family attended. She was born in 1918 in Mancos, Colorado, the fourth of six children to Louis and Susan Bell Ray. Grandma Ray was the daughter of a Mormon bishop, and Mom was brought up in a religious household. For many years she had been content to accept the official teachings of the church, but there were some aspects of the doctrine that troubled her. She kept her doubts to herself, thinking they would resolve themselves one day.

My father, the oldest boy in a family of ten children, was born in 1917 to Harvey and Roxy Chynoweth in the small town of Henrieville in southern Utah. His father was a rancher and the bishop of the Mormon church there. He, too, was brought up in a religious home, but despite this, Dad later rebelled against this upbringing and refused to attend church for many years. As a result, he was regarded as the "black sheep" of the family.

Dad and Mom met while attending high school in Tropic,

Utah. They secretly married in 1936 before Mom graduated and tried to keep it a secret, but the news came out in the local newspaper. Like most girls of her time who married that young, Mom was expected to drop out of school. She was determined to finish, however, and she did. Later they moved to Logan in northern Utah and Dad trained as an aircraft mechanic at the state university there. During World War II he served in the army, but he was stationed in the U.S. and never saw combat duty. After completing his courses at Utah State, he transferred to Hill Air Force Base in Clearfield, just outside of Ogden. He worked his way up, and by the time I was born he was the chief aircraft inspector on the base.

On the surface we appeared to be just a normal, average, middle-class American family. We owned a five-bedroom house in Layton, Utah, a suburb of Ogden. The house had two baths, three fireplaces, and an acre of land facing the snow-capped peaks of the Wasatch Mountains. We had a boat, a camper, and many of the other trappings of middle-class life. On weekends we would often go fishing or swimming or do things together that many other families did. On vacations we would pack up the camper and go on long trips to Yellowstone National Park, the Grand Tetons, and other scenic places. There was plenty of activity in our lives, and I remember happiness.

However, underneath the surface, our home life wasn't as it appeared. Dad had a drinking problem and he became verbally abusive when he drank. Mom would pray that God would help him overcome his alcoholism, and though she was in anguish over the problem, there was nowhere she could turn for help. Alcoholics Anonymous and other support groups like it didn't exist in our community then. Because of the Mormon strictures against alcohol, no one even wanted to admit the problem existed.

It was around that time that Mom found what she perceived to be the answer to a lot of her problems — domestic, as well as spiritual. One day, when I was about three years old, her brother (my Uncle Vern) brought two important-looking men into our house: Joel and Ervil LeBaron. These two brothers headed a church they had founded on fundamentalist Mormon doctrine about six years earlier. As Mom listened to them preach their doctrine in our living room, she began finding what she thought were the answers to the many spiritual uncertainties she faced. So much of what the LeBaron brothers said made sense to her, and she and Lorna, then seventeen, secretly joined their Church of the First-born. They began attending meetings in Salt Lake City, about forty miles away, and studying the doctrine the LeBarons taught. The more Mom studied and learned, the more flaws she began seeing in the established Mormon precepts, and the further she pulled away from the church in which she had been raised.

Needless to say, Dad was not thrilled with Mom's newfound devotion to the LeBarons and their renegade church, and it only made things worse between them. Nonetheless, despite Dad's objections, Mom continued attending the meetings. She wanted to be a part of this new religion that offered the hope of eternal life and celestial blessings for obeying the higher laws of God her former church had renounced.

Shortly after Mom and Lorna joined the church, Lorna came home with the news that Ervil had asked her to marry him. Mom was the only one she told about it, and Lorna asked what she should do. Mom said she didn't want to influence her one way or another. Whatever was decided, it would have to be her own decision — hers and God's. In making that decision, Lorna had to take into serious consideration the life that would await her.

At the time, Ervil had three other wives. He had been married to a fourth woman, but she had left him some time ago. He was nineteen years older than Lorna. He spent much of his time on the road, preaching and trying to raise money and converts for the church. She would not be seeing as much of him as would a wife in a normal, monogamous marriage, and she would have to share his affections with others. Furthermore, she would be living in another country with a different language, different customs, and a lower standard of living than she was accustomed to, without all the modern conveniences of American life. It would not be an easy situation for anyone to accept, let alone a young girl who was about to turn eighteen.

Lorna prayed and prayed over her dilemma and finally reached the conclusion that marrying Ervil would be fulfilling the

Lord's will. When she told this to Ervil he wanted to marry her right away, but she wanted to finish high school first. He agreed and they set a wedding date for the first Sunday in June 1961. Mom, still the only one in the family who knew of her decision, was supportive. Secretly, the two of them began planning the wedding.

Lorna had seen a picture in a fashion magazine of an elaborate Grecian-style wedding dress that draped across both shoulders and fell in elegant folds across the bodice into a full-length draped train. Mom gasped in disbelief when Lorna showed it to her.

"What do you think I am, a magician?" Mom said.

"It was just an idea, Mom. Whatever you can come up with will be fine," Lorna replied.

But Mom had seen how badly Lorna wanted that dress and she was determined to oblige her. After all, her oldest daughter was going to be marrying a very important man and Mom wanted to make the occasion special. She first had to figure out how to get the money together to buy the fabric she would need. Mom prayed over it and, miraculously, the next day she found four dollars in the washing machine. Giving the money to Lorna, Mom sent her into town to buy some taffeta. Mom worked hard on the dress in the free time she had while Dad was at work and my older brothers were in school, and at night she kept her handiwork hidden to keep Dad from finding out what she and Lorna were plotting.

On the day of the wedding, Mom and Lorna prepared to go to their regular Sunday meeting in Salt Lake City. However, for some inexplicable reason, Dad refused to let Mom go. In desperation, Mom called Uncle Vern to take Lorna and she smuggled Lorna's wedding dress out to his car wrapped in a blanket. Uncle Vern drove Lorna to her wedding and brought her home a few hours later as if nothing had happened.

A few weeks later, Lorna told Dad she had been offered a job at the Grand Canyon and she packed and left. She then went with Ervil to Mexico, where she joined the rest of his family in Colonia LeBaron. Several months later, when Dad began asking if Lorna was coming home to go to college, Mom finally told him the truth: she was married to Ervil LeBaron and living in Mexico. Dad was aghast on hearing this news, and the rift between he and Mom widened even further.

Mom had moved into Lorna's old room and was considering getting a divorce. When she asked Ervil's advice, he seemed to think it would be the best thing. However, when she asked Joel, he advised her to stay with Dad and try to work it out. Since Joel was the spiritual leader of the church and the "higher authority," Mom obeyed his advice.

Somewhere along the way Dad began to realize that he was losing Mom, and a radical change came over him. He quit drinking and smoking — cold turkey — and began studying the scriptures. He, too, found answers in the teachings of the Church of the First-born. When I was in first grade he began joining Mom, Duane, and me at meetings in Salt Lake City. Dad joined the church and began doing what he could to financially support the missionary work.

One of my earliest memories of Ervil was the day Dad bought him a yellow Ford station wagon and Ervil took us all for a ride up a nearby canyon. With Mom sitting in the front seat next to him, Ervil gave a continuous lecture on how he felt one should drive. He rambled on and demonstrated how to let off the gas gradually and lightly touch the brakes, how to take corners and dips, and he insisted that one of the back windows should always be rolled down slightly while the air conditioner was running so the hot air could be pushed out. Mom just nodded, half-smiling, not saying a word. I got tired of it and wanted just to go home. Mom would later say she thought it was funny getting a lecture on driving from one of the worst drivers she had ever seen.

Our home life improved dramatically as a result of Dad's conversion. He began making improvements on and around the house, doing jobs he had put off doing for years. Our house, which Dad and Mom had begun building themselves, was still unfinished. What should have been our family room was anything but that, being filled with car parts, engine blocks, and tools in the absence of a garage. After Dad's conversion, however, the family room was finished and he even added a nice, homey fireplace to it. He also did work on the yard and got rid of much of the junk that had been lying around for as long as I could remember. At last we were a happy, together family.

In 1964, while I was still in first grade, Dad took vacation time around Christmas. Mom, Dad, Mark, Duane, and I loaded up the truck and camper and went south to visit Lorna in Mexico. She was expecting her first child, and it had been quite some time since we had seen her. We brought along clothing, furniture, and other items for her and the baby. We drove for three days and crossed the border at El Paso, Texas. Continuing southward, across the hot, dry desert of the Mexican state of Chihuahua, we finally reached Colonia LeBaron.

We spent a week in "The Colony," as it was called, visiting with family and observing the conditions there. Uncle Vern was living there then, as was Grandpa Ray, his and Mom's father. I remember thinking to myself how different life was from what we were used to. Growing up in the relative comforts of American life, it's easy to take for granted that you get water by simply turning on a faucet. In this place, water had to be drawn from wells and carried by hand in buckets. Electricity was nonexistent and kerosene lamps served as lighting. Indoor plumbing, another convenience we take for granted, was also nonexistent. I had never even seen an outhouse before, let alone had to use one, but in Colonia LeBaron that's all there was. The roads in and around the town were unpaved, dusty, and full of bumps and ruts.

Most of the children of the village ran around barefoot in old, shabby clothes. Boards or sheets of plastic were nailed up over the windows of the crude wood and adobe shacks, and most of them had dirt floors. Clothes were washed by hand in big galvanized tin tubs, and they were pressed with old-style flatirons that had to be heated on the stove. All the females had to wear dresses, even on the coldest days, making Mom and I feel like aliens in our pants. The whole experience was one of culture shock for us all.

To call it poverty would have been an understatement, but no one called it that. "Sacrifice" would have been more appropriate. The villagers, all followers of Joel and Ervil, were convinced that they were God's chosen people. They were giving up all the comforts and trappings of a materialistic world in order to live according to God's will and prepare for the rewards of the hereafter. Everything but the very basic necessities of life were sacrificed. These people, we thought, were living like this so that monies could be used to bring people into the knowledge of God. In our own way, we felt compelled to do what we could to help the others. We believed that to "love thy neighbor as thyself" would find its own reward in God's eyes.

Over the next few years we made several more trips to The Colony, each time bringing more clothes, furniture, and other household items for Lorna and the other brethren. We felt we were making an important contribution to a community founded upon and rooted in beliefs we all shared. We were part of an organization, a "celestial family," that was going to bring about the restoration of all things good and positive. This, in turn, would usher in the millenial reign of Jesus Christ.

I was repeatedly told that Ervil and Joel were important men with an important job to do. They were commanded by the Lord, the supreme authority over us all, to gather up all the righteous men and women and take them into the "wilderness" (Mexico), where they were to serve the Lord by living according to His commandments and higher laws. We were led to believe that we were the "chosen few" who would survive the upheavals that would bring about the fall and destruction of "Babylon" (the United States), and our reward would be an eternal crown. We were to become as perfect and spiritually pure as possible so that, when Jesus returned to earth to establish His Kingdom and a thousand years of peace, we would be worthy of welcoming Him.

In 1966, when I was eight years old, we too moved to the "wilderness" and began living our lives according to "God's plan," preparing for His return.

CHAPTER 3

Duty and devotion to the LeBarons' principles compelled us to follow them to Mexico. They were touting our neighbor to the south as the "new Zion" for all the good people who wanted to be spared God's wrath when the United States was struck down by His hand for its sins. In 1966, Dad took early retirement after twenty-six years on his job, put the house up for sale, and we headed for Colonia LeBaron.

The thought of leaving the house I had grown up in was hard to accept. I asked Mom and Dad several times why we couldn't just pick the house up and take it with us. I had seen houses being moved on big trucks before and wondered why we couldn't do the same. Despite my feeble protests, we left it behind.

We drove our truck and camper and a trailer full of possessions to Colonia LeBaron and stopped there only long enough to pick up Lorna and her two children, Andrew and Tarsa. Our destination was Ensenada, Mexico, on the Pacific Coast in the state of Baja California. Joel and Ervil and the Church of the Firstborn had just established a second colony in Baja California for spreading the gospel among the less-educated Mexicans. The name of the colony

26

was Los Molinos ("The Mills," in Spanish). But we didn't feel like we were "worthy" enough to settle in the colony immediately. We had to "purify" ourselves first and be sure that we could "love our neighbors as ourselves." We imposed this condition on ourselves, thinking everyone else was far ahead of us spiritually. So we chose Ensenada, a popular beach resort sixty miles south of the American border and about one hundred miles north of Los Molinos.

After driving day and night for several days, we arrived in Ensenada in the pre-dawn hours of a foggy, drizzly November day in 1966. As soon as it turned daylight, Duane and I snuck out of the camper while our parents were still sleeping off the long drive. It was our first look at the town that would be our new home. We were parked in the lot of a motel near the beach. We could hear the waves from the nearby ocean breaking on the shore, but we couldn't see them because of the thick early morning fog. Following the sounds, we soon found ourselves alongside the Pacific Ocean.

Visibility was only about twenty feet, but our first glance at this massive body of water was an awesome sight I'll never forget. I was only eight years old at the time and felt dwarfed by such vastness. The smell of the salt water, the sound of the waves crashing on shore, and the cries of the seagulls were memorable, but there were other sights around us that were even more memorable. Duane and I began to notice some large dark forms lying still in the sand, and we walked up to them to investigate. They were dead seals and porpoises — scores of them, as far as the eye could see. At first we thought this area was a bad spot and if we walked on down the beach we wouldn't see any more. We were wrong. They were all around us, everywhere we went on that beach. I was horrified at the sight of all these corpses and tried to look away as we walked around them, but I kept stealing glances at them nonetheless.

When we got back to the camper, still shaken from the sight of all those dead marine animals, Mom and Dad were awake. We told them what we saw and asked for explanations. Mom, seeing how upset we were, tried to comfort us but she didn't have any answers. A few days later we learned an offshore oil spill had been the culprit.

For our first few weeks in Ensenada, we lived out of the

camper, parking it wherever it was most convenient. The town had only a few paved streets and it was hard getting around in the beginning. There were a lot of new and different things we had to get used to, living in another country. The largest grocery store in town was only about one-third the size of the average grocery store back home. It was full of strange foods we'd never heard of, labeled in a language we had not yet mastered. What little American food they did have was a lot more expensive than we were used to paying. The laundromat we used was close to the main store, and nearby was a bakery, a confection shop, and a *tortilleria*. While Mom was doing laundry, Duane and I would head for the bakery or the confectionery shop across the street. But, as we were soon to discover, what might look pretty didn't necessarily taste too great. Through trial and error, we did find some things that were tasty.

Finally, we found a house to rent. It was much smaller than we were used to. The house belonged to an American who rented it to us partially furnished. There were three bedrooms and one bath, but the owner used one of the rooms to store his antique furniture, forcing us to make do with only two bedrooms. There were four of us at the time, plus Lorna and her two kids, so living conditions were cramped.

The house was made of cinderblocks painted pink, with a five-foot cinderblock fence on both sides. Another cinderblock fence, this one about six or seven feet high, ran along the back of the house. There were broken Coke bottles imbedded in the cement on top of it to prevent people from climbing over. The front yard was small but well-tended with bougainvillea vines climbing a trellis next to the front door. Rose bushes and other plants grew along the fence that had some ornate wrought-iron latticework woven into it. Elsewhere in that tiny front yard was a round pool about four feet in diameter and about two feet deep, covered with glazed, brightly colored tiles. We were never quite sure if it was meant to be a pool or not. It was too large to be a birdbath. Maybe it was a goldfish pond; we just didn't know.

One of the things we didn't discover until after we moved in was that there was no water pressure. We had two fifty-gallon drums for water storage and at night a small trickle from the outside faucet eventually would fill the barrels. We had to dip buckets into the barrels and carry water into the house to flush the toilets and wash dishes. When we wanted to take a bath we used a galvanized tin washtub that sat in the bottom of the shower stall. There was no hot running water, so heating the water in buckets on the stove was the only way to take a warm bath. Sometimes, between 10:00 and 11:00 P.M., it was possible to get a shower by standing against the wall under the faucet and letting the water trickle down. The only problem was that it was ice cold.

Of course, other conveniences were noticeably absent as well. Only one gas heater in the living room was supposed to somehow warm the whole house. Winters along the Mexican Pacific coast were nowhere near as cold as they were in Utah, but our first winter there was unusually wet and chilly. We had to sleep under several layers of blankets and, occasionally, on the living room floor close to the heater.

Although the house was a big step down from what we were used to, by Mexican standards it wasn't too bad. Poverty is a relative thing, and to the native Mexicans around us, we appeared to be living like royalty.

Our presence in the neighborhood caused quite a stir. We were not only the new kids on the block, but we were *Americanos,* as well. We became objects of curiosity. Avenida Mar, or Ocean Avenue, as our street was called, was actually a fairly nice neighborhood — again, judging by Mexican standards. Most of the kids there, being from families better off than the norm, attended private Catholic schools. However, Mom managed to find two different schools for Duane and I that weren't Catholic.

On my first day at school I was put back in first grade, which was humiliating. Back in the States I would have been in third. Mom said not to worry, though. She was confident that after I learned Spanish I would be placed in the grade I should be. Her words gave me little comfort, though, and my pride was wounded. Once I learned the language, I did adjust rather quickly. For Duane, however, the shock was greater. He was placed in second grade instead of fifth where he should have been. That was rough on him, and it only added to the difficulties he'd always had with school.

Other members of our church lived nearby, and one of them had a son named Mike who was Duane's age. They went to the same school and became good friends. They would ride off together on their bikes and often cut school together.

Our first month or so was, obviously, our biggest transition period. It took us some time to get used to such a drastically different lifestyle and the cultural differences between Mexico and the U.S. Nearly everything was different from what we had been used to. I think we found it harder to adjust to the poverty all around us than to adjust to our own radically changed lifestyle.

As if we weren't having enough problems trying to cope with unfamiliar surroundings, torrential rains hit shortly after our arrival. It rained continuously for several days, and the town experienced some severe flash flooding. A river was created where none had existed previously, and all the homes in its path were washed away. The town was literally cut in half. People were stranded and couldn't get from one side of town to the other. We were close to the flood zone and faced the very real possibility of having to evacuate. Fortunately, though, the rain stopped and the "river" receded, putting us out of danger. The water from this temporary river emptied into the ocean, and after the rains stopped we ventured out to see the damage. All along the beaches, for miles in either direction, the sand was littered with debris — the wreckage of people's homes. Everywhere we looked were pieces of furniture, lumber, shingles, big chunks of roofs and walls, and many other household items. Villagers swarmed the beach, trying to find salvageable items to sell or use in rebuilding their homes.

Around Christmas, Mark, who was then about fourteen, joined us. He had stayed in Utah to finish the school semester when the rest of us moved. Always the outspoken one, Mark made no bones about his hatred for our new home. He hated school, he hated the town, and he seemed to hate everything there was about what he called "beaner-land." He stayed around the house and sulked and wrote letters to his girlfriend in Utah, telling her he was going to run away and come back to her. However, one of those strange twists of fate that change people's lives was soon to happen to him. Mom claimed it was just a case of God looking out for us.

Duane and his friend Mike were going to play hookey one morning, taking a different route along a side street, when they heard a band playing. They stopped to investigate and found a couple of guys trying to make music. After telling them they knew a good organ player, the musicians asked Duane and Mike to bring him over. They raced home and broke the good news to Mark. This little event changed Mark's life and his whole attitude toward Mexico. He became the organist and lead singer of this group that called themselves "The Believers," after the Monkees' hit song, "I'm a Believer." Mark promptly gave up all thoughts of returning to Utah as the excitement of being the leader of a band at age fourteen began to sink in.

Mark and his group were highly sought after and his reputation as a musician grew. They were invited to do gigs in local bars where Mark, though underage, was still allowed to play. For a while they had a regular weekly live spot on the local rock and roll station. The girls went crazy over him, and it seemed like everyone in town knew who he was.

One cold night during our first winter, Lorna and Ervil and their two kids were staying with us. Mark was sleeping out in the camper but he got too cold and came in about 1:00 A.M. He curled up on the floor in front of the heater and tried to get back to sleep. Mom had been up and about, checking on Lorna and Ervil, who were both sick. Mom felt kind of dizzy herself, but she didn't pay much attention to her own condition. She passed by the mirror in the bathroom and noticed that her upper lip was black but, again, she didn't think too much about it. Then, noticing Mark curled up on the floor, she found a sleeping bag and threw it over him.

This woke Mark up. Just as he did, he saw Mom lunge through the swinging door to the kitchen and heard a loud crash. He jumped up, raced into the kitchen, and found Mom sprawled on the floor looking up at the stove and mumbling incoherently about the gas. Mark flipped on the light and found he was standing in a black fog from the waist up. Thinking fast, he dragged Mom outside into the cold night air and rushed back into the house to see about the rest of us.

I remember someone shaking me and prying my eyes open, saying "Yeah, she's got it, too." I was half-dragged, half-carried outside where, along with the others, we stood in the cold and shivered. We had all come within minutes of being asphyxiated.

The next morning the cleanup began. Every wall and ceiling in the house was covered with black soot. Every stitch of clothing and every pot and pan had to be scrubbed. The wall behind the heater was the blackest of all, with a pattern spreading out and upward like a peacock's tail. It was arduous, painstaking work, but we were thankful to be alive. Mom said we had all been spared because Ervil, one of God's chosen, was staying in our house.

Toward the end of the summer of 1967, we moved into a larger house not far from our first one but too far for a nine-year-old to walk. I had to say goodbye to the friends I had made and soon found friends in our new neighborhood.

Our new house had four bedrooms, a bath, a combination kitchen-dining area and, instead of a living room, it had a wide hall that ran from one end of the house to the other. In the back was a smaller house that was like a maid's quarters, with an outhouse behind it. Dad fixed it up and Lorna moved into it with her kids.

This house was a beehive of activity. There always seemed to be extra people in it. Other church members would stop by on their way to or from Los Molinos, and many of them stayed for extended periods of time. Greg, a young man around Mark's age who played bass in Mark's band, stayed with us a few months. A lady named Sylvia Spencer stayed with us while recuperating from a Caesarean section, even though we hadn't known her prior to that. Esther, who was married to one of the LeBaron brothers, also stayed with us soon after losing her first child. Another young girl had an emergency apendectomy and stayed with us until she was well enough to travel again.

Every weekend it was like a tidal wave hitting our house. Church members from San Diego and elsewhere would come in to town, and the Chynoweth place was always *the* place to go. I took it all in stride, only too happy to have other people around, but it got to the point where Mom would shudder and dread the sight of a car driving up. Mom usually kept her cool, but at least once I recall her saying in an exasperated tone of voice, "Oh, just once I'd like to sit down to a meal with just my own family!"

Birthdays had always been special to me, even though several of them were spent on the road traveling to Chihuahua to visit Lorna and attend church conferences. I would proudly tell everyone we met that it was my birthday, and would occasionally be rewarded with some small gift or trinket. Gas station attendants would give me free glasses or a dime or maybe just a "happy birthday." Whatever I got, it was still important to me.

My tenth birthday was coming up in April 1968 and I was eagerly looking forward to it. I counted the months until they became weeks, then counted the weeks until they became mere days. I was going to be ten on the tenth! But a few days before my birthday, Nephi Marston, the ex-husband of one of Ervil's wives and father of Ed and Ramona Marston, was killed in an auto accident. Killed along with him was his wife, Eulalia Rios, and four other church members. Our house was crawling with people like never before. Instead of having a birthday party for me, we had a funeral. Over the years to come, other unfortunate things would happen to me on or around my birthday, until it reached the point where I finally stopped celebrating them.

Still, the memories I have of the two years we lived in Ensenada are good ones. Of course, during that time we attended church meetings, and Ervil and Joel and other church officials came and went frequently, but our church activities are not among the most memorable recollections I would have of that time. What I remember best were the happy childhood activities I enjoyed with the other kids in this foreign country and culture. It was definitely an adventure.

CHAPTER 4

After almost two years in Ensenada, we were ready to make our next move. This time it would be to Los Molinos, the Church of the Firstborn colony founded by Joel and Ervil. This was where, according to them, the saints would gather in preparation for the "Last Days," and we were ready to join them.

Los Molinos was about one hundred miles south of Ensenada. Mom and Dad went down to check it out first. They came back describing it as a very bumpy, dusty ride and the community, they said, wasn't much of anything. The nearest town was Colonia Vicente Guerrero, a few miles to the north. Los Molinos was a crude little town with hills to the north, salt flats to the south, mountains and a highway to the east, and the Pacific Ocean about a mile to the west. It was flat, arid country with no trees to speak of — only low bushes and cactus fences. Joel and Floren LeBaron had put up the fences, thinking they would keep their goats in.

Moving there was a letdown, compared to the busy, active life we had led in Ensenada, a much larger town. But we all thought we were doing the right thing and obeying God's will. Our sacrifices would have their own rewards, we confidently felt.

34

Dad had hunted around the lumber yards in San Diego for used lumber we could take down with us. He found some used, heavy-duty, orange-colored plywood which he precut and labeled. When we got to Los Molinos we set the camper off the truck and built a lean-to off of it. Dad helped get the lean-to up and left us to put up the outhouse ourselves. Mark assembled the outhouse, only to find that he'd nailed it up backwards. The bench part wouldn't fit inside. Until we got it fixed, we had to walk half a mile to use someone else's outhouse.

If we thought we were roughing it before, we were wrong. Los Molinos was a desolate, barren place when we arrived. There were about a dozen old trailers, a handful of crude shacks, about three or four houses, and a two-room combination church/school building. No one had electricity, indoor plumbing, or running water. Until we got our own well dug, we had to walk half a mile with buckets to get our water from someone else's well.

I slept with Mom in the camper when Dad wasn't around. My bedroom was under the overhang of the camper until Dad came back from California with two wooden, homemade camper shells and nailed them together, upside-down to right-side-up. He added a door with a lock on the front, a piece of plywood on the back, and a floor. Inside was a mattress, a chest of drawers, a clothes rack, and a mirror. It was for me — my own little house. And I loved it.

Duane and Mark had a harder time of it. They slept in the lean-to and in the mornings they would wake up to find gophers had tunneled up through the "floor" during the night. The plywood on the floor would be shoved up and dirt mounds could be seen. It was cute at first, but fixing the floor constantly and shoveling out dirt got to be a real pain in the neck.

We were about a mile from the beach and the wind blew almost constantly. When it didn't, the air was thick with tiny, pesky gnats that flew into our eyes, noses, and mouths. We couldn't even enjoy the beach because the water was ice cold. We were used to warmer waters at Ensenada, but here a cold current washed close to shore. We used to joke that we could bottle the water at Los Molinos and sell it for ice. Mark was affected the worst by this. He had taken up surfing while at Ensenada, but now he had to brave icy water if he wanted to continue doing it here. He did, for a while, but soon thought better of it.

I recall it now as being very adventurous and I don't remember complaining. It was kind of fun and challenging, and definitely different. We called our home the "orange crate," which seemed appropriate. Dad had found an old Servel gas refrigerator which wasn't working properly. Verlan LeBaron told him to stand it on its head for a few days and, sure enough, it worked after that. We set it up next to the camper under the lean-to.

One of the biggest inconveniences, as I mentioned, was not having our own water supply. Mom decided to "witch" for a spot to dig a well. Of course, we kids were skeptical, but Mom was sure of herself. She said her father used to do the same thing: Take the Y-section of a green branch and walk around with it, waiting for it to point downward toward an underground water source. She couldn't explain why, but she knew that it worked. We watched her, slowly pacing back and forth like a sleepwalker, holding the upper two branches in her hands with the bottom part pointing straight out in front of her. I was embarrassed for her and I kept looking around, hoping no one else was watching.

After a while, Mom called to us and we went over to where she was. She said she could feel something in the spot she was standing. I wanted to feel it for myself, so she showed me what to do and where to walk. I was amazed to discover that the stick did indeed appear to pull downward a little when I reached the spot she had indicated. Mark and Duane tried it too. We remained doubtful, but Mom ordered the boys to begin digging. Amidst much grumbling the work began. The soil was hard as a rock and progress was slow. After two or three days, the hole was only six feet deep. At this point, a church member named Paul who was in town to see his wives had heard about our well and came by to offer his "expertise."

He took two coat hangers, straightened them out, then bent one end down, holding the wires like long-nosed pistols. As he walked along, the wires which were pointed forward would cross each other, only to straighten out as he went on further. It was like magic, but actually it had more to do with magnetic pull. He used this to explain the underground geology of the area, saying that sweetwater veins run northeast to southwest and saltwater veins run southeast to northwest. The spot Mom had scouted was where a sweetwater and saltwater vein intersected. If we dug in the exact place he indicated, we would strike sweet water, he said. Mark and Duane, who had already spent a few days digging the first hole, were not too excited about having to start a new one. But they dug anyway and, sure enough, they hit sweet water. We now had our well.

Another time, Mom came in with an armload of mushrooms she'd found under the iceplants that carpeted the ground all around us. She was excited about the prospects of cooking up some mushroom soup, but we kids were a little more fearful. "How do you know they're not poisonous?" the boys asked.

"We'll put a silver dime in the soup," Mom replied. "If it turns black, they're poisonous . . . I think."

"What do you mean, you *think*?" they countered.

"Well, that's how my mother said you could tell," Mom answered.

The boys looked at each other. "Oh, great! That sounds fool-proof," Mark said sarcastically.

But Mom's enthusiasm won out over our skepticism. We ate her soup and lived. So, for the next few days, we had a mushroom-filled menu. Then one day they were gone just as quickly as they had appeared.

Los Molinos had a new two-room schoolhouse when we arrived and, since the community had provided the building, the government had an obligation to provide the teachers. Professor Lorenzo taught first and second grades in one classroom, while Professor Marichi taught third, fourth, and fifth grades in the other. During recess we played baseball, at which I was only fair. I could hit and catch a little, but I had trouble throwing. Nonetheless, I did once manage to catch a fly ball at third base and made a perfect throw to the second baseman for a double play. Soon after that, baseball fizzled out and volleyball was the new "in" thing. Then blow darts, then stretch (a game played by throwing knives into the ground).

Blow darts started out innocently enough. One of the boys showed up at school one day with a hollow pipe through which he would blow beans at a target. Duane and his friends took the idea and "improved" on it. They devised darts that had nails imbedded in them, with tips so sharp they became lethal weapons. The teachers panicked and banned *all* blow darts from school. "Stretch" came along to replace this game.

To play stretch, two people stood facing one another and threw knives toward each other's feet. The object was to get the knife stuck in the ground less than twelve inches from your opponent's foot, forcing him to "stretch" his foot to that point. Then he would do the same to the other player. The one who stretched the other one beyond his reach was the winner. Again, it was one of those games that started out harmlessly enough and got worse. The boys began with butter knives but soon graduated to real knives, and finally Duane showed up at school with a bayonet. That was the final straw for the teachers. They called the parents in for a closed-door meeting and protested. Duane and some of his pals were eavesdropping outside a window and heard one of the teachers say, "Next they'll be bringing cannons to school."

Of course, Duane and his buddies were not about to disappoint the teachers. They spent a day or two mulling over the right design and finally showed up at school one morning with a "cannon" in tow. It was just an old drive shaft from a car wired to the front axle, wheels, and handle of a toy wagon, but the teachers were not at all amused by Duane's sense of humor. Imagine their expressions on coming out of the school to call the kids to class and seeing this cannon-like object pointed at them. The other kids thought it was hysterical. After all, this was a very small town and there wasn't a lot to do for entertainment. So we used our imaginations and improvised.

Duane had two close friends, Ricky and Manuel, and the three of them were practically inseparable that first year of school. They were the best in sports and the first ones to introduce the new trends to the rest of us. This was the late 1960s, and long hair on guys was "in." So of course, Duane and his friends had to sport the latest styles. Most of the parents, products of strict upbringings themselves, were fighting their sons about this. One Sunday evening, Mom sat Duane down and told him there was no more putting off getting his hair cut. He had fought it long enough and lost. He sat through the ordeal rebelliously as Mom cut away and, when she was through, he looked at himself in the mirror. Seeing himself shorn of his long hair, he turned on her and shouted, "I hate you!" as he stormed off to sulk in his room.

The next morning Duane told Mom he wasn't going back to school until his hair grew back. They argued about it. Then there was a knock on the door and Mom opened it to see a very short-haired, dejected-looking Ricky standing there, waiting for Duane to walk with him to school. When they saw each other, the look of amazement on their faces was priceless. I remember Mom saying afterward, "I have never been so happy to see Ricky as I was that day." She still swears that there was no conspiracy between her and Ricky's mother. Just a coincidence.

I was even responsible for one craze that swept the small town — stilts. Mom helped me make them one day, and I spent the rest of the day learning how to walk in them. The next day at school I was showing them off. Before you knew it, everyone wanted a pair. Within a week every two-by-two or two-by-four that wasn't securely nailed down was being used for some kid's stilts. Naturally, Duane and his pals had to outdo everyone else and, by week's end, my stilts were already the shortest and most outdated ones in town.

Halfway through my first school year in Los Molinos, Professor Marichi advanced Duane and me from third grade to fourth. We had Spanish school in the morning, went home for lunch, and came back for English school in the afternoon. The majority of the Anglo kids had never had anything but Spanish schooling because most of them were born and raised in Mexico. They spoke English because it was their parents' native tongue, but they had no formal training in it. A man named Stephen Silver headed the English program, while Mom and a few other parents assisted.

The school library was small and extremely limited. It consisted of discarded or slightly outdated textbooks and spelling books surplused by the California public school system. One of the colonists had made quite an effort to get those books, and that year

I put them to good use. I zipped through all the spelling books from second- through eighth-grade level and read every other book I could get my hands on. I also took a high school punctuation course.

School was enjoyable for me — most of the time. The hardest part was interacting with the other girls there, especially a girl named Jill and her sidekick, whose name I can't remember. Jill was about a year or so older than me, and I really wanted to be friends with her. I soon found that was out of the question. She had blonde, almost white hair and was very pale. Her red nose was constantly peeling, and she had beady little pale-blue eyes. I had never met anyone so full of hatred and anger before and haven't since. Before I knew what she was like, I thought it was something that I had done wrong and I was deeply hurt by her verbal attacks on me. Her albino-like face would twist up and she would spit out my name as if it were a horrible curse word.

I tried fighting back and verbally sparring with her, but I was no match. Finally, after being beaten and further humiliated, I decided I would just give her the cold shoulder. Eventually, she would get tired of me not fighting back and would leave me alone. It was a hard and painful lesson to learn.

Around this same time we moved into the still-unfinished house Dad and Mark and Duane had been building, using the lumber from the "orange crate" for our roof. By this time, we had a gas-powered generator to run our wringer-washer once a week, so we didn't have to wash by hand like the other villagers. We had a gas-powered pump to get water up from our well, and Dad had built a water tower. At last we had running water in the house.

I was now about eleven years old and experiencing the first stirrings of puberty. I began wearing a training bra and noticing the boys and men around me. The first crush I had was on Steve Silver, even though he was probably twenty years older than me. Steve had dark blonde hair and wore horn-rimmed glasses. He was the director of the afternoon English school and a superb teacher. About ten years earlier, he had been one of a group of nine Mormon missionaries who, while working in France, left the Mormon church after embracing the principles of the Church of the Firstborn. Dan Jordan was also a member of that group, along with three other men (including Steve) who later served on the original Quorum of Twelve Apostles of the CFB. Steve and most of the other ex-missionaries made their way to Colonia LeBaron soon after their ship arrived back in the U.S. Steve eventually went on to Los Molinos.

Steve was a gifted writer who edited CFB newsletters and drafted rebuttals to pamphlets and tracts put out by Mormon opponents of the Firstborn Church. He was well-traveled, articulate, and an important man in our congregation. Not only was he a superb teacher, he was also patient, witty, and charming. Those were the qualities I was attracted to, and I thought he was perfect — until one night he came crashing down from his pedestal.

By this time, Dad had given up his job in San Diego and, along with Mark, was now working full time building houses and managing the church affairs. Joel had appointed him bishop and stake president, and Steve was named treasurer. One night after I had just gone to bed, I heard Dad and Steve finish up one of their meetings. I crept over to my window so I could watch Steve leave and admire him as he walked past. He came around the corner whistling softly to himself, then suddenly stopped right in front of my window about ten feet away. He looked both ways and, apparently thinking no one was watching, unzipped his pants and took a leak right in front of my window. It was weeks before I could look him in the eye, and my fantasy about becoming one of his wives was permanently shattered.

Not long afterward, Steve disappeared, leaving his wives and all his possessions behind. I asked Mom what happened to him and she said something about him having a serious illness. It wasn't until much later that I found out he'd absconded with funds from the church treasury. Dad had loaned him money to build his house and was never to be repaid.

However, the modified A-frame house Dad and Mark built for Steve was soon to become ours. Some newly arrived church members, the Batemans, came over to look at the A-frame and decided they wanted *our* house. So Dad agreed to sell our house to them and we moved into the A-frame. (It would later turn out that we were twice burned on the same deal. The Batemans never paid us for that house.)

Dad and the boys worked quickly to finish the exterior of the house and get the roof tar-papered and shingled. Mom and I climbed ladders and lifted sheets of plywood to the overhead beams, nailing them down to make the downstairs ceiling and the upstairs floor. My room was upstairs next to the boys' room, with only a sheet in between to ensure privacy. Until we got the landing and staircase finished, we had to be very careful where we walked, otherwise we would make quicker descents to the downstairs than intended. In order to get to the ladder leading down, we had to walk along a beam and swing over to the ladder. None of us ever fell doing this. We were used to it. Later on, Dad and Mark put up a spiral staircase which Mark, then eighteen, designed himself.

The rest of the house took shape a little at a time. The framework for the kitchen cupboards was put up but never finished. Mom hung little curtains across everything to cover them up, and the drawers were actually cardboard boxes cut down to fit the slots. Nearly everything was makeshift, yet despite that, we still had the nicest place in town.

Around this same time, Dad took his second wife. He married a Mexican woman named Noemi Zarate, whose large family had many members in our church. Noemi had three children from her previous marriage and needed a place to live, so Dad converted part of the shop he had built into living quarters for her and the kids. We welcomed these new members to our "family," and Mom treated Noemi's children as if they were her own. Later on, they would be.

We had a windcharger to power the house. It looked like an airplane propeller with a little rudder behind it to catch the wind from whatever direction it happened to be blowing. As I mentioned earlier, the wind blew almost constantly from the nearby ocean and it turned the prop which, in turn, charged up the twelve big batteries Dad had in the shop. This innovation made us the first ones in town to have electricity.

Of course, Dad and Mark's work did not go unnoticed. It wasn't long before they were being called upon to design and build other people's homes. Mark soon discovered his own genius for designing floor plans. He had designed the A-frame for Steve and had persuaded him to go for a modified A with an eight-foot flat roof to give them more room inside. Dad used his own money to pour the foundation and put up the framework for Steve's house, with assurances he would be repaid.

Dad was a kind-hearted, trusting soul who always wanted to do the right thing. He was never deceitful. Generous to a fault, Dad paid a heavy price for his generosity. When he was appointed bishop, he took his high calling very seriously and wanted to do the best job he could in that capacity. However, he was never given any sort of instruction as to what his functions as bishop would be. So, he dove into the Mormon scriptures and was able to learn and define what his role should consist of. One of them was to supervise the collection of tithes. He began teaching what the scriptures said about tithing, its purpose, and the blessings that come with its practice. But when he went out to collect, he was greeted with a few unexpected responses.

One day he asked a man named Homer Babbitt why he hadn't tithed lately. Homer promptly answered that he was "all paid up." Dad was taken by surprise and asked him to elaborate. Homer replied, "Well, some years back, Joel came to me and said that if I would give him $2,000, I would receive great blessings and be exonerated from any further tithes — ever." Joel, it turned out, had been collecting the tithes himself instead of letting the bishops do it, and he was pocketing the money. Dad was shocked when he learned of this, but we later found out that this was a common practice of both his and Ervil's. Many of the other colonists had also been told they were "paid up for life" because of some monetary favor they had done for Joel.

Joel and Ervil and some of the other men in positions of power with the church were always desperate for money. When you have multiple wives and twenty-five to fifty kids to provide for, coming up with the money to do it could be a real problem. That could explain the seemingly brazen fashion in which they solicited money. Joel, in particular, was real slick. He could justify collecting tithes directly from the people rather than relying on the bishop to do it, in keeping with the scriptures. Joel had a way of making the people feel honored to be donating to him in person. It would be like a Catholic giving a donation to the pope rather than to the parish priest. Which would you feel more honored to do?

Dad had a difficult time dealing with this. When he collected tithes, he divided up the money and apportioned it fairly among the families of Joel, Ervil, and Verlan. It was done in such a way that would take into account their needs and ensure they had enough to meet those needs. The money that was left would go to help other families, plus meet the needs of the village and the missionary program. But when Joel and Ervil collected the tithes themselves, Dad's distribution plan would get thrown off track. He would have fewer money sources from which to try and draw the needed amounts.

Dad had other functions as bishop. The scriptures defined the bishop's role as that of an organizer, so Dad set about appointing a Youth Council and put them in charge of presiding over youth meetings. He did likewise with the women. These meetings were held essentially to reaffirm the gospel and teach the tenets of the church to the women and young people, encouraging them to take active roles in the religious life of the community.

I remember very well those youth meetings. We would open with a prayer, sing a few hymns, hold class for an hour, then have refreshments and games before disbanding. It was a very exciting time for me, feeling like we were part of the "Youth of Israel," the name we chose for our group. Our theme song was, "Hope of Israel," and the chorus went like this

> *Hope of Israel, rise in might*
> *With the sword of truth and right.*
> *Sound the war cry, watch and pray*
> *Vanquish every foe today.*

That song summed up the way we felt. We were the young army of Israel, fighting for truth and right. We held the future of the world and the responsibility of defending those principles against the evil around us. We were raising a standard for all nations to see. We were taught, and we confidently believed, that we were going to play an important role in ushering in the "Milennial

Reign of Christ." Such an exalted status also implied a great responsibility. If we were going to be an example of piety to the world, then we had to be examples to ourselves. We studied the Ten Commandments, the principles of civil law, and other doctrines that would prepare us for the day we would welcome Christ's return and help Him establish His kingdom.

It soon became apparent just how much work needed to be done to educate the youth in preparation for the great event. I was amazed at how ignorant many of the kids were, and these were kids raised in our religion. One might assume that their fathers would have begun educating them at home, but that was not the case. Many of these fathers were busy trying to support their multiple families and simply didn't have the time. A lot of them worked in San Diego or elsewhere or were out in the field doing missionary work, and they only got home to their families on the weekends. Perhaps they should have educated the women to teach the kids while they were away, but even this wasn't being done. A whole generation was being raised ignorant of the gospel and the principles of the Church of the Firstborn. "God's Chosen People" were an uneducated, brutish lot, blindly following the precepts of a church they knew little or nothing about.

CHAPTER 5

Around the time we moved from Ensenada to Los Molinos, one of our people discovered welfare. It wasn't long before many of our group's plural wives were on it. They maintained residences in San Diego, usually in projects or other government-subsidized housing.

At first, Joel, Ervil, Verlan, and the other leaders of the church tried to keep it a secret. For a religious leader to have his wives on welfare wasn't exactly something they wanted publicized, but it couldn't remain a secret for long. The wives talked and gave each other encouragement to file. After all, they were not married in the strictest legal sense of the word and they had no written documentation to show that they were. Their husbands were simply unequal to the task of providing for their multiple wives and children, and money to do that had to come from *somewhere*. So the federal government became the unwitting benefactor of a polygamous lifestyle it had long before declared illegal. Later Joel and Ervil would justify the fraud by saying they were entitled to benefit by the riches of the "Gentiles."

In order to collect, however, the women had to lie, claiming they were dumped by a husband or boyfriend and needed welfare for themselves and the children to survive. When they became pregnant, they would have to tell the case workers they didn't know who the father was or make up a story about a fictitious boyfriend that the agency wouldn't be able to track down and file paternity claims against. My sister Lorna, with her steadily growing flock of Ervil's kids, was among that group of women who moved from Mexico back to the U.S. and started collecting welfare. Around the time she would be getting her check, Ervil would show up. She would always share her "bounty" with him and other family members. For a change, she had a roof over her head and food for her children. Ervil was relieved and happy to have the families provided for.

In the meantime, in Los Molinos, the opposite was happening. Groups of Mexicans were moving there from Colonia LeBaron and elsewhere looking for work. They had been told by Ervil, or maybe Joel, that a new colony was forming in Baja and they flocked to Los Molinos hoping to be in on a construction boom. Of course, when they arrived they were disappointed. There simply was no work at the time, and they had to live on handouts. Working church members would donate boxes of used clothing and other items to them. The intent was a good one, but just giving things to people takes away their pride and incentive and causes resentment and waste. All around the colony, scattered across the fields and in the trash, were the clothes that had been given to the Mexicans. The message was clear: give us work, not welfare.

As bishop, Dad saw the crisis developing and he called the men together. They discussed what could be done to benefit everyone — the Mexicans looking for work and the men who worked in the U.S. during the week and needed homes for their wives and children. Dad set up a building fund for the men and women who worked in the U.S. and helped them figure out budgets that would enable them to contribute. In this way, the Americans could have their homes and the Mexicans building them could be paid for their work.

Dad's plan worked at first and, for a year or two, there was a "building boom" in the village. He and Mark really put their hearts and energies — and their financial resources — into this project. When the men whose houses they were building ran short of money, Dad would dip into his own pockets to pay the laborers. He was confident he would be repaid because, after all, this was a community of Christians.

He was wrong. First he had been burned by Steve Silver, then the Batemans, then by another family, the Tracys. Dad put up ninety-eight percent of the money for a community building near the schoolhouse that was supposed to serve as extra classroom space and a meeting house. No one ever repaid us for that either.

Time after time, the Chynoweths blindly gave so much to receive so little in return. We knew that God would be pleased with our charitable works and felt we would be blessed for so doing. But, though God may have been pleased, those around us were not. Quite the opposite. They became resentful and accused us of thinking we were "superior" to everyone else.

This upset me tremendously. We felt they should be as charitable and giving as we were. It wasn't an unreasonable expectation. We were supposed to be a community of God's chosen people, examples to the world of the type of people Jesus would want to serve Him in His earthly kingdom. We were trying to exemplify the principles He Himself set forth, principles we all supposedly believed in. We hung in there because we had so much faith that the basic principles of the church were solid. Mom and Dad felt it was part of their mission to help educate, organize, and elevate those around us.

Looking back now, twenty years later, I can see that we were indeed superior to those around us in almost every way. What we believed in, others, apparently, did not. We had humbled ourselves and gave of ourselves, trying to uplift God's people. We were sincere in what we were attempting to do. Mom used to always say, "Where much is given, much is expected." Yes, we did have more than most of the others, but we also gave more because of that fact. By the time we left Los Molinos, several years later, we had nothing left. Every penny we made on the sale of the house in Utah was gone. We had been manipulated out of all our money and cheated on land deals. We built homes for others and were never paid back. We rescued countless damsels in distress and paid off others' bad debts, and there was no return on such service.

Still, it would take us awhile before we realized what was happening to us. We lived in Los Molinos for about four years. This was a very eventful time, both in our personal lives and in the church itself. The first rumblings of a split between Joel and Ervil began to manifest themselves around this time, and later developments would eventually consume the entire community — dividing the church membership against itself. Other developments had a direct effect on my family.

Since Dad was often the only man in town during the week, he was constantly being called upon to help the wives whose husbands were in San Diego working. If a car wouldn't start, someone sent for Bud to get the old wreck running again. If someone needed a ride into Guerrero for groceries or a doctor or butane gas for their stoves, they called Bud. If they ran out of money, they borrowed some from Bud. It got so bad that Dad couldn't get any of his own work done. He finally called a meeting with the weekend husbands and told them they were responsible for providing their wives with the things they needed to survive during the week. He made it clear that his job as bishop did not entail getting cars to start, being an errand boy, or serving as a banker.

It wasn't long before some of the women began taking more than just a passing interest in Dad. Being the only man around during the week must have made him fair game in their eyes. Some of them began coming on to him, despite the fact they were married. One of them was Betty, mother of my biggest antagonist in school, Jill. It was obvious that Jill had inherited her personality. Betty was very cool, almost hostile, toward me and Mom and the boys, as if we posed some sort of a threat to her.

I first noticed her little coquetry one day while Dad was working in the yard and she came over to see him about who knows what. She was a bleached blonde, in her late-forties, with all her eyebrow hairs plucked out and redrawn on her forehead an inch above where they should be. And she was full of smiles and giggles, talking to Dad while she'd been cold to the rest of us. Of course, I was a little too young to see the full picture of what was happening, but Mom caught it right away. She went up to Dad and said, "Bud, she's after you." Dad merely snorted, "That's ridiculous," and walked off shaking his head.

When I heard this I was horrified. What if Betty should marry my Dad? That would make Jill my stepsister. A chill went down my back at the thought, and I took off after Mom to question her about it. Mom isn't a jealous person and, in accepting the teachings of Joel and Ervil, she had reconciled that she should willingly share her husband with other women. When I confronted her and asked, "Mom, Dad isn't going to marry that woman, is he?" Mom simply answered, "That's up to God, not us."

"But, Mom, that would make Jill my stepsister. And what about the mean way Betty treats us?" I said, citing specific examples.

Again, Mom, being the forgiving soul she is, alibied for Betty. She said there were probably good reasons for her aberrant behavior and added, "She is probably a good person once you get to know her." So Mom was prepared in her own mind to let the Lord do as He saw fit. If it meant sharing her husband of thirty-plus years with another woman totally different from herself, then that's the way it would be.

Another woman was after Dad also. Her name was Irene. A jolly, stocky woman with a whole thundering herd of children, Irene was also the town gossip. Not only could she talk a mile a minute, she was also very skilled and devious in extracting information from people. She was the one to go to for the latest dirt on someone else. The only problem was, the price you paid for getting that information was often at the cost of telling her something personal you hadn't intended to tell — something that could be used against you. Mom, of course, frowned on this sort of thing, believing that gossip was a tool of the devil. But it went on around her anyway, with Irene as the spearhead.

Irene and Betty were the best of friends. One day they sent for Dad and told him they were going to divorce their husbands and marry him. But there was one condition: he had to get rid of Mom first.

I wasn't there, so I don't know what Dad's reaction was. But I can well imagine him backing out the door after hearing this. That weekend, when their husbands returned, he went to them and told them what happened. Shortly thereafter, Betty moved to San Diego and Irene went on an "extended vacation" somewhere. Dad's dilemma was quietly and effectively resolved.

On the weekends, Los Molinos was a busy place. When the husbands and working-age sons came down from their jobs in San Diego, the colony doubled or tripled in size and there was a lot of excitement in the air. I had a cheap pair of opera binoculars that I would look through whenever a dust cloud up the road signaled someone's arrival. I would rush upstairs and look out my bedroom window, trying to make out who it was, and when I found out I would rush back downstairs and announce it.

Saturdays were set aside for washing clothes, cooking, baking, cleaning, and other chores. And there were tons of clothes to be washed in the old wringer-washer, then rinsed and hung. The constant wind dried the clothes faster than a dryer would. Mom would make bread and I would bake a cake. I also swept, mopped, dusted, and did other household chores. Dad and Noemi would tend the garden and bring in these wonderful vegetables they had grown in rich, seaweed-fertilized soil. Our diet consisted of whatever happened to be growing at the time, plus canned meat or fish we bought from the store. It was nothing to complain about. The vegetables we ate, especially the tomatoes, were so fresh that even today I have trouble eating store-bought produce.

Saturday nights were the social highlights of the week. We would get dressed up and go over to the church for the dance. Before we had a piano, the only music we had was from an accordion and it was I who usually played. It was a twelve bass accordion with leaky bellows you had to pump really hard to keep the sound up. I learned to play waltzes, polkas, and square dances from people visiting the village. So, for most of the dances, I was the music player and this kind of cramped my style. Often I would play the whole night, which didn't give me much opportunity to get out and dance and enjoy myself. Occasionally, someone would show up who could also play and I was only too happy to turn the instrument over to them. That way I could dance with one or more of my admirers.

"Courting" was the accepted custom which usually preceded

a marriage. Once a girl was fifteen or sixteen, she was considered eligible to be married. The man or men interested in her would go to her father and ask permission to court his daughter. This usually meant going to church, dances, or other functions together. Couples in the colonies didn't "date" like they do in the States. There was no giving of rings or going out for movies and hamburgers. We didn't have those kinds of luxuries. Courtships were usually very short, most lasting only a few months, and they almost always ended in marriage. When a man was courting, it was automatically assumed he intended to marry the girl, but there was nothing beyond kissing and hugging and holding hands during this phase. Premarital sex was, of course, taboo. Courting was a carefully regulated ritual that seemed to work best for our purposes.

In a community where polygamy is the norm, competition for the girls is intense and it begins early. Single men would be openly competing with married men. The men who were in good standing in the priesthood were deemed worthy of having as many wives as they felt they could support. Consequently, the older men with status and prestige and positions in the church, and the young, often more handsome and virile single men, were after the same girls. At the dances and other social functions, it was not at all uncommon for the girls to be courted by both single boys in their teens or early twenties and married men in their thirties, forties, or fifties. Sometimes the competition even came from within the same family. Alma LeBaron was after me, as were his sons — Sammy, Abel, and Nephi. Another time, I was approached by a visiting father and son on successive days.

It happened in February 1971, a few months before my thirteenth birthday. A church conference was held in the recently built larger church building, and members from the U.S. and Mexico were there. Joel and many of the leaders from the LeBaron colony in Chihuahua were there, as were Ervil and Dan Jordan. I was in the choir at the time and had a few numbers to perform for the morning session of the conference's first day. I was sitting with the rest of the choir in the first three rows of seats facing the podium when I noticed an older man with light brown, almost blond, hair and glasses staring at me. I tried to look away from him, but the girl next to me kept nudging me and I would look up. Every time, he would still be staring at me.

As soon as the session was over, he made a beeline for me and introduced himself. His name was Siegfried Widmar and his thick accent told of his German birth. As I was soon to find out, he was one of the two counselors to Joel's First Presidency and an important figure in the governing structure of the church. He took hold of my hand and asked me all kinds of questions — what my name was, who my father was, and other things I don't remember. I was uncomfortable and embarrassed by having this much older man holding onto my hand and looking at me that way, but what could I do? It would have been unbecoming for me to break free of him and run, so I answered his questions and got away as soon and as gracefully as I could.

The next day, after the morning meeting, I was standing around outside with my friend Elsa LeBaron, Ervil's daughter by his second wife. This good-looking, blond young man asked us how far it was to the beach, and we started talking to him. Finally, we decided to take him there and got permission to ride with him in his car. After we introduced ourselves, I found out he was Werner Widmar, Siegfried's nineteen-year-old son who was living in Los Angeles. We talked and shared a few laughs and had a really good time, and then he asked me out. On successive days, I had been approached by a father and son.

I had to tell Werner that my parents didn't let me date yet. The inevitable next question was, "Well, how old are you?" I thought that once he found out I was only twelve, that would be the end of it. But he surprised me by asking when my birthday was. I told him and he said, "It's on a weekend, isn't it?" It just happened to be, and he told me he would come down for it.

I was so excited! A gorgeous guy who could have gotten just about any girl he wanted was interested in *me*! I didn't see him again before he left, but I was confident he would be back in a few months for my birthday. I fantasized how romantic it would be as I counted down the weeks and days ahead.

After the conference was over, I found out that both Siegfried and Alma LeBaron had asked Dad's permission to court me. Dad was shocked. "You mean Rena? Are you serious? Why, she's only twelve years old!"

I guess that kind of put a damper on their desires toward me, and I was glad of that. Werner was the only one I could think of.

On the weekend of my birthday, Mom and Dad planned a trip to San Diego. Normally, I would have loved to go. But I had better things to anticipate, or so I thought. I was certain Werner would show up. I stayed home and watched and waited. My game plan was to pretend to be surprised, so I nonchalantly went about my business and didn't watch the road from my window.

For two days I listened for the sound of a car stopping in front of the house. Whenever one did, I would drape myself over a chair with a book in my hand or sit down at the piano and start to play. When the knock came on the door I would say, "Come in." I imagined how I would have shown surprise at seeing him and how we would ride off into the sunset together.

But he didn't come. When the weekend was over, I rationalized that he must have had a good reason for not coming and he would surely be down next weekend. Then the one after that. Finally, the realization hit me that he wasn't coming at all. I had deluded myself all those months.

From that time on, I swore off birthdays. The more I anticipated a birthday, the more disastrous it became. Three years earlier I was eagerly looking forward to celebrating my tenth birthday, only to have it marred by a funeral. When I turned twelve, I was lying in bed with a fractured skull. I had gotten hit with Mark's surfboard and bled from the ear and had to wear a neck brace for a month. Now this. Stood up by someone I had fallen in love with and had so many great fantasies about.

These bad experiences made me superstitious about my birthday. I reached the point where I refused to tell anyone when it was. I would hope the day would slip by unnoticed and unmarred by catastrophe and, to this day, I still feel uneasy about them. I'm always relieved when they're over.

CHAPTER 6

The church conference of February 1971 marked a turning point in our lives and the lives of everyone in the Church of the Firstborn. The initial eruption from that time would send out aftershocks that continue to be felt to this day among those of us who followed Joel and Ervil. It was the climax of a great schism between them, one that divided their followers into two opposing camps.

Before describing the events that led to the split, some explanation of Ervil's beliefs is necessary. The "Laws of God," as Ervil taught them, existed in varying degrees — each one progressing upward toward the attainment of the highest level of celestial glory. The first of these laws was the "civil law" which was based on the Ten Commandments. Civil law, or "The Law of Liberty," was not administered by the church since it contained punishments for transgressions. Church punishments did not extend beyond excommunication or disfellowship, so The Law of Liberty was under the jurisdiction of the Civil Government of God.

Ervil knew that many people would not voluntarily live by the Commandments. A fear of the consequences had to be held over their heads. The Ten Commandments were "Commandments of

God" with punishments prescribed for their infraction. They were not ten suggestions to take or leave at will. They ensured the respect of the rights of God and other human beings and would bring peace to the human family. Ervil often quoted Benito Juarez (a great Mexican president and statesman contemporary with Abraham Lincoln), who said, "With individuals as with nations, the respect of the rights of others is peace." Hence the enforcement of the Ten Commandments by civil authority under direction from God. People who couldn't respect the rights of God and man out of love for God or man, then, could do it out of fear of God. If they failed to do so, they would have to pay the consequences and face retribution. Ervil proved this by quoting Bible scriptures found following the Ten Commandments.

He also claimed revelations in which God told him the time had come for the civil laws to be obeyed before the people could progress to the next stages — the "laws of love." He wanted everyone to love God and one another, but he was realistic enough to know that these levels of love are individual attainments and are not enforceable. To "love thy neighbor as thyself" is the second level of law.

The third level is to "love the Lord thy God with all your heart, might, mind, and strength." It was an absolute requirement for the establishment of the Kingdom of Christ. It was what Jesus taught, and it was the condition He had established as a prerequisite for His return. He would not return until there was a pure people who, because they kept the civil law (Law of Liberty), and respected the rights of God and man, had learned to love their neighbor because that neighbor also kept the laws and was lovable. Some would even be unselfish enough to love the Lord their God with all their heart, might, mind, and strength and be willing and anxious to sacrifice everything — even life itself — for the cause of God. This law was considered the "celestial" level of law.

Since the earliest years of the Church of the Firstborn, Joel and Ervil had worked closely together to develop it and teach its doctrines. When Joel officially appointed Ervil to his patriarchal office in 1961, Ervil took his high calling very seriously. For the next few years he dutifully went about proving his worthiness to hold the highest office in the church next to that held by Joel himself. However, Ervil's attainment of knowledge was an ongoing process. He was constantly studying the scriptures. The more he studied them, the more clearly he saw what his role would be in preparing the way for the Second Coming and the implementation of Jesus' civil government.

Ervil realized that his most important responsibility as patriarch was to teach and enforce civil law. He had to straighten out the House of God. That process had to begin "at home," among the other CFB members, since they were supposed to be God's chosen people. They had to be prepared and ready to accept Christ on His return, and in order to do that they had to be pure in mind, body, and spirit themselves. They were a long way from that point, Ervil believed.

For a number of years, Ervil had maintained his right to enforce civil law in the community through the Ten Commandments. He wanted Joel and everyone else to acknowledge his right to punish by force any transgressions of God's civil laws — the law the Church of the Firstborn subscribed to. However, his efforts toward that end got no support from Joel. Joel's approach was to talk about a problem but do nothing about it. Ervil would chastise someone about not living according to God's law, and that person would go running to Joel, who would say something like, "Don't worry about it. He's just being a little overzealous."

The situation can be likened to two parents trying to raise their children two entirely different ways. While one parent would try to impose discipline and punish the child for doing something wrong, the other parent would come along behind him and tell the child, "It's all right to do what you did. You're forgiven." The discipline of one parent would be negated by the softness of the other. Consistency between parents must be maintained in order to bring children up properly. The same principle applies to religious leaders: consistency must be maintained between them also when ministering to the congregation. Small wonder why Ervil felt resentment toward Joel. In trying to make everyone love him and not rock any boats, Joel was undermining the job Ervil was striving to accomplish. Joel didn't believe in punishments, and he opposed

Ervil when Ervil advocated their use.

According to scripture, the Melchizedek Priesthood existed to administer the law of love. Since this was a higher law than the civil law, Ervil felt that Joel should not be dispensing those blessings until his (Ervil's) work of preparing them to receive those blessings was done. He asked Joel to stand back and allow him to finish doing his job of teaching the civil law to the people, and only after they had learned and accepted the law and were living according to it could Joel then step in and teach them the laws of love.

Ervil's plan may have worked if he and Joel were pulling together. Perhaps if he had gone about it more tactfully and diplomatically, Joel might have cooperated, but that simply wasn't Ervil's style. Tact and diplomacy were not his strong suits. Neither was patience. He saw what needed to be done, he believed strongly in it, and he had no patience with those who saw otherwise, including his own brother. He insisted on the right to implement his program, rather than politely request to do so.

This may have been where Ervil went off the deep end. When the people opposed him and Joel also failed to wholeheartedly support his efforts, it became clear to Ervil that it might take the shedding of blood to get the people to accept civil law. He began to see that those who resisted most strongly might have to be eliminated as an example and so they wouldn't contaminate the others who were sincere in wanting to live under God's laws. This is what he believed, and he found plenty of justification for it in the scriptures.

Citing passages from the books of Ezekiel and Isaiah, Ervil predicted there would be a bloodbath prior to the Second Coming, one that would cleanse the earth of all those unworthy of receiving Christ. When that time came, his office — that of the patriarch — would supersede the office of the Melchizedek priesthood, in much the same way as his patriarchal predecessor, John the Baptist, paved the way for the first coming of Christ.

In Ezekiel 9 and 10, a story is told of soldiers being dispatched throughout Jerusalem to kill everyone who had sinned against God and were, therefore, deemed unworthy of living. However, before the soldiers used their swords, a scribe went out into the city with an ink horn and pen, marking a cross on the foreheads of the virtuous people who deserved to live. Ervil considered himself the scribe with the ink horn, the one who had the power to determine who was and who wasn't worthy of living. He even told my brother Mark, when he was about eighteen or nineteen, that Mark bore the special sign on his forehead, showing him to be one of those chosen to be spared from the slaughter. That "cleansing" process, Ervil said, would have to begin from "within our own house." We had to purify ourselves — God's chosen people — before we could set an example for the world. Jesus' civil government could only take effect when civil law was in effect, and those laws required an obedience to the Ten Commandments. The laws had to be universally, not selectively, enforced, and they had to apply to *everyone*.

Ervil had always been better versed in the scriptures than Joel, and toward the end of the 1960s he began making public statements about enforcing civil law. Some of these statements were made without Joel's knowledge or consent, and they often questioned Joel's policies as they applied to enforcement of the laws. Joel was patient and forgiving and initially made little effort to make Ervil toe the line. By his failure to take a strong stand against Ervil's statements, Joel came across as a weakling and Ervil was further encouraged to continue on this path. Many of those who were calling on Joel to muzzle Ervil began to perceive Joel as lacking in leadership ability, and they drew closer to Ervil and his teachings.

It was around this time that Ervil made one of his most infamous statements to a Sunday school class in Colonia LeBaron. "I know as sure as I know God lives that my program is the only one that will establish the kingdom," Ervil said. "I know that there are men in high positions who disagree. It will be either them or me. I also know that blood will run to solve our problems."

This statement has always been cited by Ervil's detractors in an effort to show his "violent nature." The media has taken a fancy to calling it "blood atonement." While it isn't my intention to defend the violent actions Ervil later took, I do want to show this statement in the context in which it was said. In trying to *peacefully* establish God's kingdom on earth, Ervil encountered so much opposition that he concluded violence and bloodshed would be the only alternative. It didn't mean he intended to kill people who disagreed with him — at least not at that point, anyway. It just seemed to him that such a result of violence was inevitable.

There were a number of other incidents involving Ervil from the early 1960s on that really shattered people's faith in him. One in particular involved Anna Mae Marston, the wife of Nephi Marston, a longtime friend of Ervil's and a follower of the LeBarons since the mid-1940s. Anna Mae was a staunch Mormon who continually berated her husband for accepting the LeBaron doctine. Finally, Nephi prevailed upon Ervil to call on her and try to convert her. Ervil went to their house in Salt Lake City and, upon opening the door for him, Anna Mae reportedly fell in love with Ervil on first glance. Whatever happened after that is open to conjecture, but Ervil was able to persuade her to move to Colonia LeBaron and she did, leaving Nephi to arrange the logistical details of the move.

After moving to Mexico, Nephi continued to work in the States. According to Verlan LeBaron's book, *The LeBaron Story*, one morning Nephi left for work and wasn't able to return for about a month. When he returned, his children — David, Ed, Ramona, and Fay — ran to greet him and carried packages of things he had bought them into the house. As he leaned over to kiss Anna Mae, she told him, "I can't kiss you. I married Ervil while you were away."

The incident sent a shock wave through the community. Ervil had already been married to three other women, two of whom were still married to him, but that wasn't the problem. Anna Mae was still legally married to Nephi when she secretly wed Ervil. To Ervil, however, that didn't matter. Man-made laws were meaningless, and her civil marriage meant nothing to him. That was how he could justify marrying her before she could get her marriage to Nephi annulled. Obviously, he must have convinced Anna Mae of that as well. Largely as a result of this incident, church rules were drafted specifying that a divorced woman could only remarry after a six-month period had elapsed.

Nephi was, of course, crushed by this sudden turn of events, but he eventually resigned himself to accepting the situation. Later he married other wives and, as I mentioned earlier, he was killed in a car accident just before my tenth birthday.

In the mid- to late-sixties there were other incidents in which Ervil's actions may have superseded his authority. Earl Jensen, whose daughter was one of Ervil's wives, was a high-ranking church official who had been a great source of support for Ervil when he and Joel were pulling together in the same direction. But, as Earl began to see the direction Ervil was heading in, he refused to go along with what Ervil was saying and demanding. Without authorization from Joel or even discussion with him on the matter, Ervil told Earl he was relieving him from his high office. Joel immediately reinstated Earl and no harm was done, but it was indicative of the types of things Ervil was doing at the time.

Ervil also had a habit of meddling in the affairs of families in the community. He would counsel people on marriage and divorce as though his word came in the form of revelations directly from God. This was especially true in families that included young girls approaching marriageable age. He would try to tell the parents who the girl should marry, and sometimes it was him. Among the families he was feeding these lines to were the Jensens. He finally prevailed on Earl and Carol Jensen to let him marry their daughter, Christina, who was then only fourteen. He claimed she had come to him as a divine revelation, and it was difficult for two devout parents to argue with that kind of logic coming from the patriarch of their church. He and Christina got married shortly after he married my sister Lorna.

Many years later, he would use the same lines on me. From the time I was twelve years old, Ervil began telling me that I was destined to marry him, and that it was God's will. I believed him at first, and he constantly reminded me of it in the years to come. I accepted it as God's will initially and later went through different stages in my feelings toward him. I even went out with other people before I finally married him.

Ervil also "marriage brokered" with his own family members, especially his daughters. To him they were simply bargaining chips. Like a medieval king trying to cement alliances with other nations, Ervil would offer his daughters in marriage to those whose favor he wanted to curry, thus making their husbands beholden to him. If boys courted his daughters and he didn't feel they were worthy of them, he would warn them off, occasionally threatening violence. His daughters served as his chattel for snaring those who were most influential in the church.

At one point he tried to have Lillian, his fourth daughter by his first wife, married to his second cousin, Conway LeBaron, in order to win him over. Later he gave her in marriage to Mark, who had proved himself "worthy" by his loyalty. His fifth daughter, Becky, became my brother Vic's second wife, again in an effort to win someone over. Vic was making good money at the time and was one of Ervil's chief financial backers. Two of his daughters and three of his stepdaughters were married to Dan Jordan, his right-hand man.

According to Verlan's account, Joel differed sharply with Ervil's activities among the families of the community, believing that marriage should be an individual choice into which no one should be coerced. But, as usual, he did nothing to curb Ervil, and so Ervil continued doing it.

In describing the changes that came over Ervil in the late 1960s, Verlan wrote in his book of an incident he said took place between he and Ervil in Las Vegas. When Verlan confronted Ervil with the complaints many of the church members had against him, Ervil answered emphatically, "If anyone takes a stand against me I will absolutely see that he is put down." Verlan interpreted that to mean that he (Verlan) was being warned to back off and not oppose what Ervil was doing.

As the 1960s drew to a close, Joel began making plans to step down from the First Presidency of the church and appoint Verlan to replace him. Ervil had been informed and appeared to be in agreement with the plan, but he made it obvious that he would be holding Verlan's feet to the fire if this came to pass. The implication was clear: if Verlan failed to perform well in this capacity, Ervil would begin taking steps to depose him.

Finally, however, Ervil went too far. He told Verlan privately that Joel had interfered too much with his (Ervil's) efforts to enforce civil law and he had removed Joel from his office of the presidency a month earlier. Word got back to Joel and, on the eve of a conference in November 1969, Joel called Ervil into a private meeting where only the three brothers were present. There in the back bedroom of the home of one of Joel's wives, Joel looked at Ervil and said, "Ervil, I am now releasing you from the patriarchal office."

Ervil was in disbelief, but for once Joel remained firm. Ervil began to cry and Joel and Verlan were emotionally touched too. The decision was announced at a meeting of the church council later that day. The next day it was made public to the entire church membership. Ervil appeared to acknowledge the decision gracefully and was thanked for his years of service by Joel and the others. Verlan was appointed to the presidency of the church, but Joel continued to hold down the office of the First Presidency and, with the patriarchal office being vacant, he absorbed that position also.

Ervil was never one to accept defeat gracefully. Throughout 1970, he stepped up his denunciations of Joel and tried to win supporters to his point of view. Aided by Dan Jordan, Ervil would preach his version of the doctrine to anyone who would listen. Some inflammatory statements were made by both Dan and Ervil. This was the scenario as the conference of February 1971 convened and there was much tension in the air. The battle lines were being drawn.

Ervil contended that Joel didn't have the authority to arbitrarily remove him from his patriarchal office and that, according to scripture, if the patriarch fell from grace he would have the right to appoint his own successor. He continued to insist that Joel was a fallen prophet who had also failed the community financially, alluding to some land deals on which Joel had been swindled. He insisted that he was still the patriarch and would occasionally assert his claim to being "The One Mighty and Strong," a designation Joel insisted belonged to him alone.

The schism was now inevitable. Everyone would be forced to choose for themselves whose doctrine made the most sense — Ervil's or Joel's. Most of the people continued to blindly follow Joel, thinking they could ride his coattails into some important office in the government Jesus would establish on earth, but the Chynoweths were not among them.

Like everyone else, we had to choose. We ended up on Ervil's side, but it didn't start out that way. We tossed it around and agonized over it for a long time. Mom and Dad and Mark got together and pored over the scriptures morning, afternoon, and evening trying to prove that Ervil was wrong and Joel did, indeed, have the right to remove him from the patriarchal office. But the more they studied, and the more they read, the more convinced they became that Ervil was right and Joel was wrong. So many of the claims Joel made were simply not backed up by scriptural evidence. For example, his claims of infallibility were circumspect. Nowhere in the scriptures did it say anything about the Melchizedek Priesthood being an infallible office.

Finally, Mom decided to ask Joel point blank if he considered himself infallible. Joel answered her question with another question: "Was Joseph Smith infallible?" Mom said no, and then Joel asked, "Was Jesus Christ?" When Mom said yes, Joel replied, "Well, so am I." Since he couldn't substantiate his claims with scriptural evidence, that was one more strike against Joel as far as we were concerned. Ervil, on the other hand, had never made any such claims. Everything he said or preached could be backed up by scripture.

On other occasions, Joel came to the house for meetings with us and Mom bluntly asked him why he was collecting tithes himself, rather than allowing the bishop (Dad) to do it. Joel got nasty and threatened Mom with her church membership, saying he had the power to cut her off. Statements like these did nothing to endear Joel to us at a critical time when we were trying to decide who to follow.

On still another occasion, while Joel was addressing the congregation, he made a statement that was in direct reference to the deepening rift between he and Ervil. "Do you want to wander for forty years in the wilderness or do you want to follow me and go straight into the Celestial Kingdom?" he asked. That was fairly typical of what Joel believed about himself. He walked around acting holy and saintly, as if expecting everyone to kiss his ring. He dispensed his blessings among the people, many of whom didn't deserve them, without doing anything to address or correct the problems they were facing. He was encouraging them to blindly follow a personality cult that was all style and no substance.

Mom and Dad and Mark even consulted other LeBaron brothers about their dilemma. They went to Alma and he had nothing concrete to offer. He was not a scriptorian. Neither was Verlan. When my parents and Mark tried to discuss it with Verlan, he merely laughed and dismissed Ervil's position lightly, as though they were talking about a naughty child who would sooner or later rejoin the fold. It frustrated my family that they couldn't get answers from those who should have been in the best positions to give them.

Finally, it reached the point where there could no longer be any doubt that the Chynoweths supported Ervil. It was a hard realization for us, but we were determined to do what we felt was God's will. This is what all our prayers and scriptural research concluded. Having convinced ourselves of this, we then set about trying to convince others.

Shortly before he was killed, many years later, Mark told me that he ran into some very stubborn obstacles in trying to convince the people that Ervil was right. Most of them hadn't taken the time to examine the scriptures like he had and, when backed into a corner with logic and scriptural evidence, they simply came out saying, "Well, I'm going to follow Joel anyway." This is what we were up against — people who weren't going to think for themselves but were going to allow themselves to be blindly led.

As the summer of 1971 approached, things really began to heat up. Many people, myself included, have come to the conclusion that much of Ervil's change in behavior and modus operandi could be attributed to the influence exerted on him by Dan Jordan. Dan, who had been one of the original Quorum of Twelve Apostles, was a forceful, outspoken man and he had, over a period of time, worked his way into Ervil's inner circle. In time, he became Ervil's closest confidante and had Ervil's ear anytime he wanted it. It was Dan, primarily, who formulated the quasimilitary philosophy that Ervil advocated in insisting on his right to enforce civil law on the people.

In May 1971, Dan and Ervil's public remarks and actions

prompted Joel to call for a conference to resolve the conflict that had arisen. Joel and Verlan were in San Diego at the time and the conference was scheduled to be held at Colonia LeBaron. As Joel and Verlan approached El Paso, they saw Ervil and Dan in a car heading in the opposite direction. On arriving at Colonia LeBaron, Joel was told that Ervil and Dan had been in the colony for several days, saying inflammatory things and trying to line up supporters. To one of the apostles, Ervil reportedly said he was prepared to kill anyone who opposed him. Then Joel learned that Ervil had left the colony saying he didn't have time to attend the conference.

The conference was held anyway. Joel ordered Dan released from the Quorum, and also said he was disassociating himself from all further responsibility for Ervil and his actions. He assigned Verlan to deliver the order to Dan personally in San Diego and added a message of his own: "Tell them for me that they are a couple of forked-tongued bastards."

From that point on, Joel began to get even uglier. He had taken a tolerant, forgiving approach toward Ervil for many years, but now that he had seen his leadership questioned and undermined by his younger brother, he started fighting back. It was sometime in June 1971 that I witnessed an incident between the two that was indicative of what was going on.

We were still living in Los Molinos and I was walking home one afternoon. I had to go through the gate to get into our yard, and Ervil and Joel were standing in front of it. I had to walk around and behind them to get into the yard. Joel had his back to me and I couldn't hear much of what was being said, but I could tell the conversation was hostile. Joel's fists were clenched as he spoke, and a few times he jabbed a finger toward Ervil's face. Then I heard him say, very menacingly, "And if you don't stop this, I'll kill you!"

I could see Ervil's face clearly and he seemed the calmer of the two. He had sort of a half-smile on his lips and he hadn't said a word in response to Joel's threat. For a split second I could see Joel's face also, and it was flushed red. His eyes were flashing with anger. I hurried into the house and didn't overhear any more of what was said, nor did I want to. It was heavy stuff for a thirteen-year-old to be exposed to. Mom had been standing by the window at the time, and she also heard Joel's threat.

This may have been just an empty threat on Joel's part, made in the heat of the moment without much thought given to its implication. Nonetheless, it ran contrary to all the accounts that have been written about Joel being a passive, forgiving, saint-like personality. It showed that he, too, could become explosive and violent-tempered when pushed hard enough.

Although Ervil didn't get angry or respond in kind with a threat of his own, he undoubtedly filed it away in his mind, ready to use against Joel later on. After we began following Ervil, he would constantly preach to us that the Firstborners were out to kill us and we had to get them first. Threats such as the one Joel made against him were obviously used to reinforce this paranoid belief he always held.

According to Verlan, it was also around this time that Ervil had taken aside a man named Fernando Castro (one of the Twelve Apostles) and laid a full scenario out before him. It was in Los Molinos and Ervil was obviously confident he could win the support of Fernando, an influential Lamanite. He told him that because of Joel and Verlan's actions in releasing Dan from the Quorum, they were to die. Then he reportedly took Fernando up the hill overlooking Los Molinos and unveiled his grand plans to turn the village into a seaside resort, complete with luxury hotels, marinas, and other amenities to snare the "Gentiles'" money. Inticing him with promises of millions of *pesos* for his cooperation and support, Ervil tried to win Fernando over to his side.

Fernando had been converted by Ervil many years earlier and Ervil had also conferred the priesthood on him. He loved and respected Ervil, but he remained loyal to Joel and Verlan and promptly reported the incident to them. In accordance with church law, Ervil and Dan were summoned to a hearing before the High Council regarding their membership. Verlan delivered the message to Dan and Ervil, who were in San Diego at the time, and they said they would not honor it. Their refusal to appear before the High Council resulted in their excommunication from the Church of the Firstborn.

This was the last weapon Joel could have used against Ervil, and it was rendered ineffective. At that point, Ervil didn't care what his brother did to him. In fact, it might have had the opposite effect Joel hoped it would. If he had been hoping it would make Ervil come crawling back to the church, penitent and pleading to be reinstated and promising to cease his attacks on him, Joel had greatly miscalculated. All it did was liberate Ervil from whatever remaining restraints bound him. Now he could talk and preach his version of the doctrine freely. And he did just that. He would come down to Los Molinos and hold court with anyone who would listen to him. He now began claiming that the patriarchal office he continued to hold was the highest office in the church, and all earthly and celestial authority next to that of Jesus Himself belonged to him. Even though Joel officially anointed Verlan as patriarch in August 1971, Ervil maintained that the office still belonged to him.

Meanwhile, tension was mounting about the ownership of the land in and around Los Molinos, as well as some land Ervil had sold in Chihuahua that belonged to his mother. Titles to the land were, indeed, in doubt since much of it was unregistered with the proper authorities and it was often difficult to determine whose money had paid for what. It is known that Ervil had to bail Joel out of some bad real estate deals on occasions with his own money, but to what extent Ervil, rather than the church itself, owned the land was always open to interpretation.

Because of this situation, it was Joel's position that he didn't have the right to keep Ervil out of the community or from preaching his version of the doctrine. Consequently, the use of the church buildings on Sunday was divided between the followers of each. Joel's people would have the building for an hour and Ervil's would have it for an hour. Ervil accepted this arrangement, and his meetings were usually held after Joel's. However, a serious problem arose on Sunday, November 7, 1971, when Joel's group held the church for more than their normally allotted time.

It had become customary for Joel's group to hold a Sunday school service on the first Sunday of the month and follow it with a sacramental meeting. This was done for the convenience of those who worked in San Diego and spent their weekends in the colony so they could attend both services. We felt that this was an infringement on our rights to use the church. So, while some of Joel's people were taking a break between meetings, Mom and I walked in at 11:00 with a few members of our group and began our Sunday school service.

I sat down at the piano to play hymns and Mom led the singing. Dan came in, laid some books down by the pulpit, and opened with prayer. The Firstborners present in the church, mainly the wives of the other LeBaron brothers, were shocked that we would just walk in and take over like that, but we felt justified. It was our time they were taking up. They tried to continue their meeting, but we drowned them out and they soon left.

An angry crowd gathered in the street outside the church. Tensions were evident. As Dan conducted the service, we were distracted by the sounds of shouting and arguing outside. Ervil was defending our right to begin our service when we did, saying that Joel and his people had not respected their end of the arrangement. Ervil also told the people it was his land the church had been on, and he made some other claims about who the church's lands in Baja California belonged to. For a while it seemed as if a violent confrontation was in the works, but order was maintained. Soon the truth about what happened came out.

Three months earlier, Dad had asked Verlan and Alma to release him as bishop and stake president. Joel Castro had been appointed bishop and, though Ervil discussed the church-sharing arrangement with him, Joel had not conveyed it to his newly appointed counselors, José Leon Perez and Eulalio Perez. Consequently, José, Eulalio, and Cuthberto Zarate were at the center of the argument with Ervil and they threatened to go to the police. The dispute lasted for about an hour and a half, which was as long as our service went on. As we left we drew all kinds of dirty looks from the people in the street.

A day or two later, some of the Joelites went to the authorities in Colonia Vicente Guerrero and lodged a formal complaint against us. Among the things they said was that one of us (they wouldn't say who) was armed. The authorities sent for Cuthberto and told him that no one was to use the building until the rightful ownership of it could be documented with legal papers. The Joelites continued using the church anyway, saying that the order had no force of law since it wasn't made in writing. Joel LeBaron wasn't in the colony at the time of the incident, but when he returned, a few days later, he was told their side of the story. He said, "Well, if they can prove that this land is his [Ervil's], with a title, we'll just move off. Besides, it's no great loss."

Things were to get worse — much worse — in the year that lay ahead.

CHAPTER 7

On July 5, 1971, I began keeping a diary. It wasn't anything fancy; certainly not one of those expensive gold-leaf, hardcover books with a lock and key like so many other girls my age were keeping in the States. All it consisted of was some roughly trimmed, ordinary lined paper, bound together by string. Later on, when the lined paper ran out, I used the blank back pages of computer print-outs. It was all I could scavenge up, but it suited my purposes just fine. In all, there were seven of these "bound volumes," covering the period between July 1971 and June 1977, and two more spiral notebooks from the late 1980s.

The earliest entries in my diary were in pencil. Much of the writing has almost faded after nearly twenty years. But those crude entries, with all their misspellings and grammatical inconsistencies, have nonetheless enabled me to reconstruct much of this story. They provide the recorded evidence of so much of what was going on around us and what was going on within me, personally, during those often-turbulent years. Without them, many of my memories would have been irretrievably lost. I can look through those pages now and recall details about Ervil: his courtship of me, the little

71

trysts we had when we were alone before we were married, and other details about our relationship. I can look back on many things, such as the other suitors I had, my experiences in school, and other facets of our religious and social life. And even though I didn't write every day (sometimes weeks or months would go by between entries), I kept my diary faithfully for the next six years until Ervil ordered me to stop writing. I would later resume writing sporadically, and to this day I still make occasional entries when something of importance comes up that I feel needs recording, or if I need to "talk" to someone. These writings are priceless in having preserved such a vital segment of my life.

At first I wasn't quite sure what I wanted to say. Many of my earliest entries seem relatively trivial. But many of them were important, for they spoke of the turmoil and conflict going on around us as the church began to divide. And they served a useful purpose: I needed someone (or something) to talk to. I was going through some very serious changes in my life. I needed to release my feelings and emotional conflicts somehow, somewhere, and a diary served that purpose ideally.

A month and a half after beginning my diary, I chose the name "Pat" as my imaginary confidante. I can't explain why I selected this particular name; I just did. It sounded more real than just writing "Dear Diary" and, in time, Pat became almost like a real person. I would write to her as if she really existed and tell her the kinds of things I wouldn't have felt comfortable telling a living person. After all, I was only thirteen years old when I began keeping a diary. I was going through some mental and biological changes that I either found embarrassing or otherwise difficult to talk about. It was my therapy, and I'm glad I had this outlet for expressing my innermost thoughts.

It surprises most people to hear that, despite being members of what many would call a religious cult, we lived rather normal lives. We were not fanatical ourselves, even though our leader was. Every other word out of our mouths was not scripture, like many so-called "born-again Christians." We read other books besides the Bible and kept relatively open minds about the world at large. And, unlike those cults such as the "Moonies," whose members are kept on a leash or otherwise confined to a given location in which they are constantly bombarded and indoctrinated with the beliefs of the leaders, we were more or less free to come and go. We lived somewhat secluded from the rest of the world, but within our own world, our own society, we weren't that much different from other people. We socialized, held dances, traveled back and forth, mingled with outsiders, and had the same desires and thoughts as others.

My diary provides ample evidence that I was a more or less "typical teenager." I thought and wrote a lot about boys, clothes, and school, and asked questions that nearly all teenagers ask themselves. I played a lot of sports, especially basketball, and took part in other activities with the kids around my age. Without television, we had to be creative in finding ways to amuse ourselves. When I had thoughts on my mind I couldn't express any other way, I wrote poems or the lyrics to rock or folk songs that had particular meaning to me. And, despite the tensions that surrounded us in our church, I did not let them interfere with my personal life, which was a whirlwind of social activity.

On July 6, I wrote:

> Some people would probably consider me immodest or just a bragster if I told them that there are a nice little handful of men and boys that are after me. That's why I try to keep it my own private affair, or else I'll tell my Mom but there are times and things that you just can't tell your Mom everything. So I guess the best thing to do is to tell someone so to get it off your mind.
>
> Here I am, barely 13 years old, and I've got something like 6 or 7 guys after me, and most, if not all of them, know I'm only 13 too! Sounds ridiculous but it's true.

It wasn't conceit that compelled me to write this and other entries in a similar vein: I was merely stating the reality. As I said earlier, there was intense competition for the females in the colony, and both married men and single young boys were competing with each other. I had long, light brown hair parted down the middle, and I had always looked older and more mature than I was. And, because I was the bishop's daughter and my family was influential in the church, I was considered a "good catch." Marriages were consummated for "political" reasons as often as they were for love.

Among my suitors at that time, besides Ervil, were Verlan's son, Verlan M., and Andres Zarate. Verlan M. was six years older than me, and he was probably the most persistent. I liked him as a person and he and I often danced together, but I was still too young to get really serious about him or anyone else. I would put him down and he would tell me I was a cruel person, but it was merely my way of saying, "Hey, back off! Keep your distance!" I just didn't want to get seriously involved with anyone until I got older.

Andres was the son of an important Lamanite in our community. He was about five years older than me. The Zarates and the Chynoweths, in time, would become almost one family, and the seeds for that were sown even back then. Dad was married to Noemi Zarate and would soon afterward marry her younger sister, Chela. Later, after Noemi's death, Mom would adopt and raise her five children, two of whom were Dad's and who are still living with us today.

In 1971 the Chynoweths and Zarates were so close I often regarded Andres as a brother (he was, in actuality, a brother-in-law to Dad, making him an "uncle" to me). It didn't matter to Andres, though, and he told me as often as he could that he loved me. He wrote me the sweetest, most flowery letters in Spanish, some of which I copied verbatim in my diary. I loved him, too, but I had to give him the same treatment I was giving Verlan M. I had to keep him at a distance. He kissed me a few times and told me how much he loved me, and he even held my hand against his chest so I could feel his heart beating. He was sweet to me and I told him I loved him like a brother, but he wanted me to love him in a way that went deeper than that.

And, of course, there was Ervil. He was much older than me (forty-six at the time), so I couldn't use the same techniques on him that I used on the younger boys. He was a little too experienced with women to be put off by my coquetry. He had staked his claim to me at least a year earlier and possibly even earlier than that, and he never hesitated to remind me that one day I would be "sealed" to him for time and eternity. On August 26 I ended my diary entry for the day this way:

Mom caught Ervil and me, and she really told him off. She told him he'd have to wait two years because I was too young. Boy, I've never seen him look so guilty! Serves him right! (He was only hugging me. Nothing more serious.)

I suspect Dan was after me as well, at least for a while, anyway. Thinking back to the first time I met him, it certainly seemed like the case. I was about twelve years old, and many people were at the house who were in town for a conference. I had been helping Mom in the kitchen, trying to feed the thundering herd that had descended on us. Mom told me to knock on the bathroom door and ask Brother Jordan how he wanted his egg prepared. I did that and out popped a face that looked like Bob Hope, covered with shaving cream. He had a merry, mischievous twinkle in his eye and asked me to repeat my question. When I did, he said, "How about with a couple more?" I thought that was hilarious, and it proved to be fairly typical of the sense of humor he displayed in those early days of his association with us. After that encounter, he came by the house fairly often and was quite attentive to me.

On Sunday, October 10, 1971, instead of going to church, we had the service and readings in someone's home. There were about ten or eleven of us. Dan gave the talk, confirming many of our beliefs with scriptural evidence. I was sitting next to him, looking on admiringly, I guess, because I was impressed with his knowledge and confidence. But my looks must have been interpreted another way — by one of the girls there as well as by Dan himself.

At a little party afterward, a girl named Malinda kept giving me dirty looks. As the get-together ended, Dan asked if he could "chaperone" me back to my house, and I asked him why he thought I needed a chaperone. I had always come and gone freely, day or night, and never needed anyone to escort me before. So Dan said, "Oh, you've probably been doing scandalous things since you were ten or eleven."

"Boy," I replied indignantly, "I'm sure getting a good reputation around here! Malinda's been giving me the dirtiest looks tonight."

Dan merely blew it off and I went, all upset, to Mom and told her. Mom, as always, was comforting, but it hurt me to think that the minds of people who were supposed to be God's chosen could be filled with such crude thoughts.

Anyway, Dan didn't appear to be pursuing me much longer after that. I suspect that Ervil had warned him off, saying I was spoken for. Dan and Ervil traveled almost continuously together, and he had been promised one or more of Ervil's daughters and stepdaughters for his own wives by then.

In late September 1971, Ervil and Dan came by with Arthur (Arturo), Ervil's oldest son who was fourteen at the time. Ervil asked Mom if Arthur could stay with us and Mom thought it over. Dad and Mark were up in Nevada gathering pine nuts, an annual project some of our church members took on to make money. My brother Duane, who had quit school after sixth grade, was working with Vic back in Utah so, except for Noemi and her kids, it was just Mom and me at the house. We agreed to let Arthur stay with us and he did — for quite a while.

Like the Zarates and others, Arthur became one of our "family." I had trouble getting along with him at first because there were things about him that were different from the rest of us. He had lived most of his life in Chihuahua and conditions were different there. He had trouble adapting to our way of life in Los Molinos, and I was terribly impatient with him. In time, he and I would get along better. But it was rough going at first. Arthur would, in later years, play an important role in the church during Ervil's final incarceration and death, and would die a violent death himself.

One prophetic entry in my diary is worth recounting. On October 12, 1971, I wrote the following:

> You know what, I definitely think someone with a lot of talent for writing should write down all of Ervil and Dan's life and adventures. It's really fascinating! Dan was talking to us last night. I had no idea Ervil had done so much and had so many experiences before, and neither did Mom.
>
> I didn't know Ervil had ever been so hard off as to beg for 25 cents to catch a bus with.
>
> Oh well, I guess someday somebody will do it. Who knows? I might do it myself.

Eighteen years later, I find myself doing just that.

As 1971 drew to a close, we found ourselves increasingly alienated from the rest of the community. Because we had chosen to side with Ervil, the Chynoweths, the Zarates, the Rios family, and a few others were blackballed and shunned by most of the other villagers. Though there were no acts of violence or threats made against us, we still sensed the hostility in the air and knew it was directed at us. Life became pretty unbearable, and it was becoming more and more apparent we would have to leave the colony. There was nothing left for us there and no reason to go on staying. But we hung on for another six months, keeping pretty much within our own circle of family and other followers of Ervil.

January 1972 was a hectic month for us. On the fifteenth, Deanna Tracy, daughter of one of the church officials, and Sammy LeBaron, Alma's son, were married by Alma. We had a wonderful dance that night and I danced with nearly every LeBaron boy who was even close to my age. Mom and Dad, who had gone up to Utah a few weeks earlier, surprised us by returning that night. They brought me a belated Christmas present — a new accordion my Aunt Jenny had brought back from France.

On January 20, around 8:00 P.M., Noemi went into labor with the first of two children she had with Dad. He raced her to San Quintin and an hour and a half later he came home shouting it was a boy. They named him Harvey after Dad's father. Nine days later, Lorna and Ervil had their fifth child, a girl they named Andrea Monique. Ervil came by the next day and he and I had a few good chats together.

On February 18, Dad, Mark, and I went up to Ensenada to a house Ervil and Raul Rios were renting. Along the way we stopped to see the Zarates, and Andres and I had a few minutes alone together. It was obvious he was still after me, but I made it clear to him that there could never be anything more than good friendship between us. I asked him who he was going to marry and he sort of shrugged his shoulders and nonchalantly replied, "Somebody." I wanted to know who, so I said I would tell him who I would be marrying if he told me, and he agreed. I told him I would marry my brother-in-law, Ervil, and he told me he would marry Yolanda Rios (who, ironically, later became Ervil's twelfth wife, just before me).

We arrived at Ervil's house late. I just went into an empty room, unrolled my sleeping bag, and curled up for the night. The next morning, Dad and Mark went on to San Diego and I stayed behind to clean up the house. I swept, dusted, puttied around the windows, and even helped Raul with the painting. I thought Dad was going to come back the next day and pick me up, but he didn't get by until a few days later. When he did, Ervil talked him into letting me stay and Dad left without me. Ervil and I went shopping for furniture, towels, and sheets. He bought me a pair of pants, which I desperately needed. I had been wearing the same pair for three days, and they were covered with dirt, putty, and paint.

We went back to the house and I was just putting up the towels when Mom walked in with Dad. She was furious with him for leaving me alone with Ervil and she insisted I come back home with them. It was obvious that she didn't trust me (or perhaps didn't trust Ervil) and I guess now I couldn't blame her. During those few days, Ervil had assured me that it was perfectly all right to "explore" my body. After all, he now said we were engaged. This exploration — actually a molestation of a thirteen-year-old girl — is something I would completely block out of memory until I was grown.

There was no ring involved in our engagement, nor would there be one when we got married. It was more or less a pledge we made to each other that we would get married when I got older — a reaffirmation of the intentions he had made known to me at least two years earlier.

In my diary I noted, "I am very much in love with him, and him with me. And I know that it is God's will and someday we'll ·get married." A few days later there was a church conference in Los Molinos and Ervil came by. He stayed only for a few minutes. I got to wish him a happy birthday a day late (he had just turned forty-seven) and we shared a kiss and a few words. That was it.

In the years before I married him, my feelings for Ervil were very ambivalent, to put it mildly. I was never really physically attracted to him. He had been handsome as a young man and, even in middle age, he still retained some of that handsomeness. But he just didn't do anything for me. He was the prophet whose doctrine we had chosen to accept, and marrying him would be fulfilling God's will. That took precedence over my own wishes or desires. Though marrying someone of my own choice would have made me happier, I felt that I had a higher role to fulfill. My personal happiness, like everything else, would simply have to be sacrificed for what I was led to believe would be right in God's eyes. I wasn't being offered a choice. Looking back on it all now, I can see that I was trying my hardest to convince myself that I did love him because, if our getting married was inevitable, I would just have to make the most of it. If I could condition myself to love him the way a wife should love her husband, our marriage would be all the more bearable.

Less than a month later, Mom and Dad found out about Ervil and I being engaged. Of course, they didn't approve. About the same time, I decided I was too young. "So I'm going to break up with Ervil," I wrote in my diary on March 15. We continued to see each other after that, anyway. Whenever he was in town, or if I was in San Diego while he was there, we would get together. He never stopped reminding me that one day we would be married. I had already come to accept that as inevitable.

In my diary on May 6, I wrote:

> By the way, I haven't told you anything about Ervil since I said I was going to break up with him. I didn't break up with him but I got a bad spirit and a negative attitude towards him but I got over it. The devil was really after me hard. My Mom was on to me and against Ervil, and there was a big thing but now I love him all the more and I get this warm feeling inside me everytime I think of him. But I don't dare show anything around Mom 'cause she'd have a cow.

About five days later, after a dance, Andres Zarate and I found ourselves alone, walking the streets of the village. He was the one "living person" I could really talk to. Though it hurt him knowing I couldn't be his, he seemed to accept gracefully that I belonged to our leader and deserved to be happy with him.

On that particular night Andres noticed that I had been looking sad and he commented on it. I told him that I felt "locked up" and couldn't do anything about it. He pressed me to elaborate, so I told him about Mom and how she couldn't seem to accept the fact that I was growing up; that I was becoming a woman with my own feelings and sentiments. By this time, Andres and I were holding hands and I felt even sadder — for him as well as myself.

"Mom can't seem to believe that I could be capable of loving someone the way I love Ervil. And I will marry him someday," I said.

"When?" Andres wanted to know.

"When God tells me to."

"Why don't you marry him now? Or tomorrow, or the next day — whenever you feel like it?"

"I'll marry him when God tells me to," I insisted. "But Andres, I'm afraid. I'm afraid that someday they'll kill him and I'll be alone with twenty thousand kids."

I started to cry and put my head on his shoulder. He spoke to me gently and reassuringly.

"Don't cry, Rena. Nothing will happen to him."

"No, Andres; they're going to kill him," I persisted. "It's written in the scriptures, and I don't want them to."

"Rena, you marry Ervil," Andres said, getting me under control. "I know things will be hard but, whatever happens, I'll be there. I know it's written in the scriptures, so you just have to be strong. Very strong."

He continued to grip me by the shoulders and comfort me. "Now, you're going to marry Ervil," he went on, "and just don't worry about that obscure future. Just live now and when the time comes, I'll always be there."

I started crying again and I clung desperately to him. He held me close and I could feel the warmth of his feelings coming through. He still loved me, yet he was telling me to marry another man.

I felt so guilty and selfish pouring out my feelings for another man to someone who loved me, but he made me promise to be strong and to marry Ervil when the time was right for both of us. Never have I known a man more gallant than he was. I began to fear for him as well, thinking that when the time did come, Andres *wouldn't* be there like he promised. He was the type of person who would die defending Ervil.

When I closed out my diary entry for that night, after faithfully recording the conversation above, I wrote:

> But I guess I shouldn't think such negative thoughts and be thankful for what I have, knowing that when the time comes, God will prepare the way for me.

There were other occasions in the weeks and months after that when Andres and I found ourselves alone together. We would kiss and hug, despite the fact we both knew I was pledged to Ervil. It was as if we were stealing moments from our youth that we knew we wouldn't have much longer, and were determined to make the most of them. God, how I loved him. I knew that, if circumstances were different, we could have made each other very happy. Those were very memorable moments for me.

But, as if my life weren't complicated enough with men, another incident came up during that time that really scared me. The town's grade school teacher, Rosa Perez, had a brother named Antonio. He came up from Acapulco to visit her. Antonio was at our house working on our piano while Mom was up in San Diego, trying to help Lorna and the kids get settled into their new home there. While she was doing that, there was a phone call telling Mom that her dad, Grandpa Ray, had died, so she stayed a little longer. Dad wasn't home the day Antonio came over to work on the piano. Antonio saw what he thought was an opportunity, and he started coming on to me.

It began harmlessly enough with the usual flattery which, of course, I ignored. I had been through it with dozens of men and boys already, but Antonio took it further. We both had putty knives in our hands and were scraping the varnish from the piano with them. He caught me off-guard and reached over to try to kiss me. I reacted defensively, in a fraction of a second, and stabbed him in the eye with my putty knife. That got him away in a hurry. I laughed and dared him to try it again as he raced off to get some paper towels for his bleeding eye. My mockery of him only made him madder. He began threatening me, telling me he would do worse than what he had tried to do already.

I left the room to go make beds, and he finally seemed to calm down. He called me back into the room and I felt he had learned his lesson and would leave me alone after that. But he started in again, even more menacingly than before. He said he had the power to take me away from my parents, from my boyfriend, and that he could prevent me from getting married. He really scared me and, when he left for Acapulco that same afternoon, I felt relieved.

By spring, we'd already begun taking the first steps toward moving to San Diego. As I mentioned earlier, the majority of the people in the colony were hostile and cold to us because of our loyalty to Ervil. After Mom moved Lorna and her kids into a small place in San Diego, she began looking for a place for herself, Mark, and me. I wanted to finish school in the U.S., which was another reason for us making the move. In June she found a cute little two-bedroom apartment and took a job managing the apartment complex.

Dad stayed behind in the colony with Noemi and the kids and her sister, Araceli ("Chela"), whom he would also marry on January 23, 1973. Since he stepped down as bishop, progress in the colony virtually came to a standstill without his leadership and money. All he had left in the world was a little plot of land to make as productive as soil and weather conditions permitted.

On June 23, 1972, I made the move to San Diego. It was the beginning of a new chapter in my life, and certainly one of the most eventful.

CHAPTER 8

During the summer of 1972, just as we were getting settled into San Diego, the seeds were being sown for Ervil's establishment of the Church of the Lamb of God. Ervil, Dan Jordan, and Ervil's cousin, Conway LeBaron, were working day and night, writing pamphlets expounding Ervil's doctrine.

When I saw him during this time he looked about ten years older. He had more wrinkles in his face than I'd ever seen before, and he didn't look too well, physically. He was obsessed with his mission and so he didn't shave, he hardly ever bathed, and sustained himself on continuous cups of coffee. When he sweated, that was all you could smell coming out of his pores — coffee.

While the men were writing and rewriting their pamphlets, some of the women were taking turns typing them. Among them were Ervil's daughter Lillian and his wives, Anna Mae Marston, Linda Johnson, and Rosemary Barlow. The three men wrote a five-page letter to Alma LeBaron and a thirty-page letter to Verlan, denouncing the doctrine being preached by the Church of the First-born.

In July some new members joined us, a family from Indiana

with the last name of Sullivan. Lloyd was the father and with him he brought his wife, Bonnie, and his son, twenty-year-old Don. Later his nephew, John, would also join us. They, too, would later play an important role in our church and our lives. I described Don in my diary as "a very nice boy" who was also "smart and open-minded."

Early in August I took Andrew, Lorna's oldest child, on a trip back to Los Molinos. I had missed graduation and needed to get my report card so I could enroll in public school in San Diego. But I wasn't able to get my report card. The director of the school had gone to Oaxaca for the summer. The boy who told me this said he remembered that I used to live there and play basketball. He talked me into staying until at least the next day so I could help field a team to play a girls' team that was coming down from Ensenada. I rounded up a few of the girls I knew and we practiced that day. Later we went swimming in Verlan's pool and I found out there was a dance that night. Naturally, I was asked if I could play for it.

After washing up and getting dressed, I went to the dance and had a good time but my back started hurting me. I'd had a fall a few weeks earlier and it had been bothering me on and off. Sammy LeBaron took me home and asked if I wanted him to rub it. I said yes, and only later realized my mistake. I laid down on my stomach in what had been Mom's room and he began rubbing my back. After a few minutes I felt his hands trembling and could hear his breathing becoming irregular. He was no longer rubbing me but, rather, exploring. Horrified, I rolled over and saw a strange expression on his face. His eyes had this sort of pleading look in them and he whispered, "Rena, I love you."

I put my hands over my face and he gently took them away, holding them and talking softly to me about his feelings. I got up and walked away, figuring I'd better get out of the bedroom. I stood with my back to him in the hallway, and he approached and put his arms around me. I pulled away and tried to figure out how to extricate myself from this uncomfortable situation. I reminded Sammy of our religious differences and he said, "Oh, we can work that out. We can talk together and see who is right."

Having failed to discourage him with that, I told him I was too young. But he came right back and said he would wait for me if I would promise him I would wait for him. Of course, I couldn't promise him that. He insisted, and finally I told him, "Sammy, I will marry the man God tells me to."

He smiled and replied, "I like that. But we can get to know each other and I could come over to your house to visit or something."

That was my way out. I agreed to that idea, thinking that it would be a good way to get him free of the others in the colony and talk the gospel to him. Maybe we could make a convert out of him and I would be helping get God's work done. Sammy was a member of the Quorum of Twelve Apostles in the CFB; converting him would have been a major victory for us.

He put his arm around me as I walked him to the door, said good night, and left. I slept badly that night thinking about him and the way I had treated Andres. They were both really sweet, but I just wasn't ready to get serious about them or anyone else except Ervil. And even that wouldn't come to pass until I got older.

When I returned to San Diego, Dad, Mom, and I left immediately for Utah to attend the Chynoweth family reunion. My oldest brother Glen was going into the army, and we wanted to see him before he left. It was the first time I had seen his and Kathy's twins, Sandy and Cindy, and they were already two years old. We had brought Tarsa, Lorna's oldest girl, with us, and the three of them played great together. Overall, we had a good time and it was nice to see all the relatives again. When we returned to San Diego a few days later, the storm that had been threatening to break for so many years finally did.

A CFB conference was scheduled to be held in Colonia LeBaron on August 26 and 27. Mark left on the night of the eighteenth with Lloyd and Don Sullivan, allowing themselves ample time to get there and settle in. Two days later, on the afternoon of Sunday, August 20, 1972, Joel LeBaron was shot to death in Ensenada.

I don't remember exactly how we found out about it. Everything about those few days was a blur. It was a phone call, but neither Mom nor I can recall who it was from. Gradually, a little at a time, we began to piece the story together.

Joel had been on his way from Los Molinos to the conference in Chihuahua. He had stopped at the home of Benjamin Zarate, Andres' father, to pick up one of his cars that was left there to be worked on. With Joel were two of his wives, Jeannine and Kathy, and his fourteen-year-old son, Ivan. When Joel arrived, Andres was there along with Gamaliel Rios, one of Ervil's staunchest followers. Andres told Joel his father had moved and his brother, Cuthberto, had the keys somewhere on the other side of town. The two wives drove him in Joel's pickup truck to find the keys while Joel and Ivan stayed behind to try to get the car running.

Gamaliel talked Joel into coming into the vacant house so they could talk about the gospel. Soon after that, Dan Jordan arrived. Ivan later told police he heard the sounds of a fight going on inside and a window breaking. Two shots were fired. Then Ivan claimed to have seen Gamaliel jump out a side window and Dan hustle out the front door. The two of them sped off in the same car. Ivan went inside and found his father lying on the floor in a pool of blood. A crowd gathered quickly, and the police arrived shortly afterward. Joel's wives returned without Andres and were hit with the news.

We were as shocked as everyone else over Joel's violent death. We knew Ervil had been saying Joel would have to die for his "apostasy," but we never believed it would actually happen the way it did. The first question in everyone's mind was, "Where is Ervil?" No one seemed to know. None of us saw or heard from him for quite awhile afterward. He was, however, the prime suspect, even though no one at the scene of the murder actually saw him there.

The murder really turned the CFB against the rest of us. Mark, Don, and Lloyd, who had gone to Colonia LeBaron for the conference, were subjected to violent threats from the people there. Alma D. LeBaron III, Alma's son and the colony's chief law enforcement officer, threatened to kill them if they ever came back, and Floren LeBaron escorted them out of town.

Mark and Don returned to San Diego, shaken by their harrowing experience in Colonia LeBaron, but the worst was yet to come. Mark was told by the lead singer he'd been working with not to come near her house. She was a member of the CFB, and she feared someone was going to try and bump him off.

Then, a short time later, Don was driving alone and one of his hubcaps fell off. As he stopped to pick it up, he claimed that someone fired a shot at him. He was unhurt, but it scared the hell out of him. No one knows who fired the shot. It could have been any one of the millions of crazies driving around California with guns, firing randomly at people just for the hell of it. Or Don could have been making it up just to scare us. In retrospect, knowing now what we do about Don, it seems possible. But, at the time, the rest of us were convinced it was someone from the CFB and they were out to get us. We started locking our door at night and leaving the porch lights on. Don went to a K-Mart and bought himself a gun.

On Saturday, September 2, Mark and Don drove to Los Molinos to get some money from Dad. After they left, we went out and bought a paper and there was a story quoting Siegfried Widmar. A $24,000 reward was being offered for information leading to the arrest and conviction of the seven people he claimed were responsible for Joel's murder. The seven were named as Daniel B. Jordan, Ervil M. LeBaron, Conway LeBaron, Raul Rios Mendez, Gamaliel Rios Mendez, Andres Zarate, and Mark Chynoweth.

Later that same day, while Mom and I were at Lorna's, a poster was plastered to our door by Dale Leaney, son of one of the CFB Apostles. The poster had pictures of all of them except Mark. It said the Mexican police and FBI were looking for them, and Mark was believed to be living and hiding out in San Diego. We thought this was getting a little ridiculous, since we had never made any secret about where we lived. Everyone in the church knew, and Mark's phone number could be obtained simply by calling Information.

Mark and Don were supposed to return immediately after getting the money from Dad, but neither of them came back that night. Instead, Dad came up and told us that as soon as Mark and Don arrived in Los Molinos, they were surrounded by police and arrested. The gun that Don had bought recently, for his own protection, was found in the car and cited as "proof" they had a hand in Joel's murder. The two of them were hauled off to jail in Ensenada.

The next day, Mom, Lillian, and I drove to Ensenada to see what we could do about getting Mark released. When we arrived, we went immediately to the police station and had to wait an hour before Mom could get in to see someone. Lillian and I, standing in the next room, overheard a man named Rene talking to someone on the phone. He was talking about Ervil and Dan. They had been seen in Tucson, then in Utah, then in several other places. Obviously, a big manhunt was under way.

After the police finished questioning Mom, I was ushered in and they asked me a lot of questions, probably hoping to establish Mark's connection with the murder. They asked me if I had given Mark a list of things to be picked up at Pauline's, one of Conway's wives, but I had no idea what they were talking about. They finally let me in to see Mark and as they did they began calling him a liar, saying I told them I hadn't given him any list. "Not her," Mark shouted indignantly, "my other sister, Lorna."

Then they took Lillian in for questioning and began interrogating her. They accused her of knowing where her father (Ervil) was, even though none of us did. They really frightened her. Finally, they let her go and we went out to buy some tacos for the guys. They hadn't eaten much in the last few days. We weren't allowed to see them again that day, but we did get to talk to the police quite a while and we told them our side of the story. We could sense that their attitudes toward us were beginning to change. We spent the night at Lillian's mother's (Delfina's) house and went back to the police station early the next day.

We waited about an hour for Rene to come. While we were waiting, Alma, his son Abel, and Raul Perez came in with Ossmen Jones, another staunch Joelite. They didn't say a word to us as they marched into the chief of police's office. After a long time they left, again brushing past us without a word, except for Abel, one of my former admirers. He stopped to shake hands with us. I had always liked Abel and had danced with him many times during our happier days back in the colony. I felt sorry for him, having to live around so much hatred for us.

Finally, we got in to see Rene and we began explaining our way of life to him. He couldn't believe that Lillian was proud of her father and that he had seven wives and many children. We explained that our men, unlike many others in society, really do love their wives and do all they can to support them and their children. It seemed as if he and the others were beginning to respect our ideas and what we believed in.

Our side of the story really needed to be aired because all the police had heard about us previously were lies. Ossmen Jones, Siegfried, Verlan, Alma, Floren, and others had been parading everyone they could into that police station, trying to link our men with Joel's murder. They brought in "testimonies" from anyone they could convince to do so. They spread the word around the colonies and asked anyone who had ever heard our men utter anything even remotely violent to come forward and give a testimony. They accused us of being "fanaticized" and said we would do whatever our leader told us to do. Some of them claimed to have heard Mark say he'd be doing the world a favor if he killed Joel. One of these testimonies even came from our dear cousin, Susan Ray, who was living in Los Molinos. That hurt the most because Susan had always been close to us, especially to Mark.

Mom took Lillian and me home then went back down to keep trying to get Mark released. Finally, after almost a week in jail, Mark was freed when the police concluded they didn't have enough evidence to file charges. Don was released around the same time. The Firstborners obviously weren't happy about it, but there was nothing they could do. They had failed to establish a connection between Mark and the murder, despite their scores of testimonies.

Mark later told me about what happened when he and Don were first taken to the jail. He and Don were stood against a wall and told to put their arms up. When they did, several police officers slugged them hard in the stomach, trying to make them "confess." When that failed, they were thrown into a ten-by fifteen-foot room he called "the dungeon." With fifteen people in it, there was barely room to stand up, let alone lie down on the floor. There were inch-long cockroaches and spiders crawling all around and a little hole in the wall in one corner of the room where they could go to the bathroom. When we arrived they were being treated a little better and had been placed in better cells, but they had seen firsthand how the Mexican jails lived up to their ghastly reputations.

As for Ervil, it was quite awhile before he surfaced. He and Dan were known to be out on the road somewhere, but we later learned that they were in Utah most of the time, writing pamphlets and open letters to the leaders of the Firstborn Church. These pamphlets, which expounded on Ervil's doctrine on the true priesthood, gave great insights into what was going on within his mind. He had, through his statements and previous pamphlets, laid the groundwork for the rationalization of Joel's murder, and now he had to justify his actions.

Throughout the fall of 1972, Ervil and his staunchest followers churned out still more pamphlets and flooded the two Mexican colonies with them, making certain everyone knew where he stood in relation to the true priesthood issue. He wanted everyone to know he was "The One Mighty and Strong," not Verlan, who had assumed Joel's mantle of leadership. Many of Ervil's writings around this time attacked Verlan directly and by name, making it clear that Verlan might be next in line to die a violent death. Verlan began taking precautions to protect himself and continued doing so for the remainder of his life.

At the time Joel was murdered, and for five years afterward, I didn't know for an absolute fact that Ervil did, indeed, order the murder. Until it became a pattern with him, years later, we initially believed that he was incapable of ordering such a foul deed — especially against a brother to which he was once so close. Of course, everyone suspected him of masterminding it. He was even jailed for more than a year on suspicion and convicted by a lower court, but a higher court ruled the evidence inconclusive and overturned the conviction. It seemed obvious to everyone else, including the media, that Ervil definitely had a role in what happened. But it was never firmly established beyond the shadow of a doubt in court. It wasn't until 1977, after Ervil and I had been married for two years, that he finally told me Joel had to be "eliminated." His reasoning was that Joel planned to bestow celestial blessings on twenty men who were unworthy of receiving such blessings at the upcoming conference. He had to be killed before he could do this, so Dan Jordan was sent to carry out the fatal mandate.

While all this tension and turmoil was going on around me, I was experiencing another shock: school. I had been living outside the United States for six years. I had attended schools where Spanish was the mother tongue and lived in villages where Latin customs prevailed. The world I had known was slower-paced and primitive by comparison. People looked, dressed, and lived differently in the U.S.

I had been eight years old and in third grade when we left Utah. In the fall of 1972 I was fourteen and ready for high school. I had to lie and tell the school officials I was sixteen. That was the only way I could be placed at the level I felt I should be, eleventh grade. In the Mexican schools I had nine classes a day, as opposed to six in the American school, and I had acquired enough credits to place me at the level of a junior. I felt confident I could handle the workload and was sure I was as smart as the best of them. But I had no idea how the American system operated or what was required for graduation. I was totally baffled. I had to rely on a guidance counselor to help me plan a schedule.

My first day of school was a culture shock. I was taken aback seeing how many couples there were. Boys had their girlfriends backed up against a wall or a locker, necking with them, and I remember thinking to myself how "corrupt" they seemed to me. It was a big social game to these American kids, and I didn't get the impression they were in school to get an education. The girls wore provocatively short, short skirts and platform shoes and both boys and girls wore torn, faded bell-bottom jeans that dragged on the ground. The "sloppy" look was in; it was still the era of the sixties, even though it was 1972.

In the bathrooms, the girls smoked and took turns keeping a watch for teachers. Many of the girls wore tons of makeup and talked about boys, using expressions that were completely foreign to me. I listened unsympathetically to them bad-mouthing certain teachers, their parents, and school in general. I felt like an alien from another planet. I had come back to the United States and felt fortunate for the opportunity to get a good education. I couldn't understand why these people, who had the same opportunity, didn't appreciate it the same way I did.

I got used to the routine, but continued to feel different from the other kids in school — superior on one hand, inferior on the other. I was convinced that, religion-wise, I had it all over them. I belonged to a church whose head was God's chosen representative on earth and was practically on speaking terms with Him. Yet, I felt inferior when I looked around and saw kids with fancy clothes, their own cars, and other trappings of middle-class affluence. We were poor and were raised in an environment where poverty was the norm, yet we had more than most of the others around us in Mexico. I had been one of the most popular and sought-after girls in school. Here in the U.S., I was an insignificant nobody, completely ignorant of the rules of the social game.

I did manage to make a few friends quickly. They were all clean-living and religious people, though they belonged to different churches. April Johnston, my first friend, was a "Jesus freak." Every other word out of her mouth was "Praise the Lord," or whenever something happened, bad or good, it was always "God's will." That part kind of got to me, but I liked her anyway.

Then there was Keith Cox, who was in my poetry class. He belonged to the Church of Christ. One day he came over to the house to meet Mom, Duane, and Mark, and he and Mark talked about religion for hours. Soon after that I went to a meeting at Keith's church with him and April, just to see what it was like. Though I had my beliefs in my own church and felt very strong and comfortable with them, I never closed my mind to other faiths. It often helped me reaffirm my own feelings toward Ervil's church when I saw what others believed about the gospel, the scriptures, and the nature of the priesthood.

The best and longest-lasting friendship I made was with Betty. She had come from a small Catholic school and I guess the attraction was that she was a "goody two-shoes" like me. She lived a sheltered life and was anti-drugs, anti-smoking, and anti-premarital sex, and she held to conservative, old-fashioned views. The vast differences in our religions didn't matter. Despite her conservative approach to life and the things around her, Betty still knew the ropes. She knew her way around the jungle I found myself thrust into and helped me out of many scrapes my naivete got me into.

One incident in particular comes to mind. Unbeknownst to our parents, we were hitchhiking back from Los Molinos. It was a foolish thing for two girls to be doing, but I didn't think so at the time. Two nice Mexican guys picked us up. One of them asked — in Spanish, of course — if we would like to go see a beautiful lake they said was nearby and I, innocently enough, said, "Sure." They turned off the main road and Betty, who didn't understand Spanish, demanded to know what was going on. When I explained to her about the lake, she said, "You tell them to turn around right now!" I didn't understand what all the fuss was about and it didn't hit home until she teased me about it years later. I was so naive!

For months I had been writing poems in my diary and keeping them to myself. I didn't think they were particularly good, but that didn't matter. They were meaningful to me and a good way of getting my feelings out in the open. So I was more than a little surprised when my poetry teacher, Mr. Martin, said he liked one of my poems very much. He told me that, with just a little work, it was good enough to be published.

When my first set of grades came in, I got an A in swimming, a C in U.S. history, and B's in everything else. Not bad for somone just coming into the system from another country.

Elsewhere around us, life in San Diego also took some getting used to. In Mexico we had dances and youth gatherings, but very little else in the way of social activity. In the U.S., there was a park, a swimming pool, a donut shop, and an ice cream parlor all close by our apartment. Supermarkets were a mind-boggling experience. In Mexico, all we had were small stores and no frivolous places like ice cream and donut shops. There we'd had very little meat, fresh milk, and other staples; here in the U.S. they were commonplace and taken for granted. Virtually everything around us was new and different.

Outside of school and our personal lives, there was still the nagging question: "Where is Ervil?" Police and investigators in countless cities and states in two countries were asking themselves the same question, yet not coming up with any answers. That question was finally answered on December 13, 1972. Accompanied by his attorneys, Ervil calmly walked into the police station in Ensenada and surrendered.

When he made this surprising move, Ervil's attorneys had asked that the murder charges pending against him be dropped. Ervil confidently predicted that he would be free in seventy-two hours. Under Mexican law, that was the amount of time those seeking to have charges pressed must file them. The Joelites moved quickly, and within a day or two the judge declared there was enough evidence to hold Ervil beyond that time. He would go to trial after all.

CHAPTER 9

As 1973 began, Ervil was sitting in jail in Ensenada. He seemed to be in good spirits and he continued writing pamphlets which he gave to his followers to type up and disperse to the colonists in Los Molinos. One in particular I remember was his answer to the accusations against him over Joel's violent death. He remained confident that he would be found innocent and released. We felt the Lord would protect him and righteousness would prevail in the end.

I didn't go down to visit him that much. I was caught up in my new life in the U.S. and was very busy. When we did visit him, Mom and Lillian and I usually went together. Only once during that time do I recall being alone with him. He told me he still loved me and reminded me that he and I were going to be married one day. He held my hand but didn't try anything else. I would have resisted if he did. By this time, the thought of marrying him had become repulsive to me.

It was around this time that I met Michael Barnes. He and several other sailors were staying in some of the apartments Mom managed while they attended medical corps school for the navy.

Michael and I began to spend a lot of time together, and I could imagine spending the rest of my life with him.

Michael was from Oregon and his parents were quite wealthy, but he and his father did not get along too well. He was quiet and reserved but could get very defensive if criticized. He could be very hard-headed and hated to be told what to do. I suspect one of the reasons he joined the navy was simply to get out of his parents' house.

Michael was nineteen. His birthday was the day before mine. As I've explained, I had come to hate my birthday, but in 1973 it was something special. I made Michael a birthday cake and the next day, on my birthday, two of my girlfriends surprised me with an impromptu party in the hallway at school. They gave me two record albums — one by Carly Simon, the other by Don McLean. I took the albums over to Michael's apartment to play them on his stereo and he greeted me with an orchid corsage and a really beautiful card. I couldn't get over it. No one had ever treated me that special on my birthday before.

After going out together for a few months, Michael and I talked about getting married. Since there were obvious religious differences between us, neither Mom nor I felt I should marry him before we brought him over to our faith. Mom and I would talk to him about the Ten Commandments which were the backbone of our church. These were the "minimum requirements" for the Law of God that Ervil taught, as the way of attaining God's Kingdom. It made sense to us and it was up to us to convince others that this was the key to attaining the highest blessings. We also explained to him our beliefs on the true nature of the priesthood, and though he never actually converted, he made an honest effort to understand. He didn't scoff at our beliefs or our lifestyle or get self-righteous about his own faith as many others would have done. I had to respect him for that.

Other things were happening around us that spring. On April 28, Mark and Lillian got married. It was a simple, yet beautiful wedding. We held it in our apartment and it was the first time in about seven or eight years we had the whole family together. Glen and Kathy came down from Utah with their kids, and Vic and his wife Nancy were there too. Lillian looked absolutely gorgeous with her long dark hair halfway down her back and a pretty white and pink dress.

We, of course, didn't know it at the time, but it was a marriage that would last for life. It was a true love relationship. Mark, like all the other men in our church, had ample opportunities to take multiple wives but he never did. Lillian remained his only wife until his death fifteen years later.

Ervil, still in jail in Ensenada, was obviously unable to attend, but Mark and Lillian had his blessing. By this time Mark had been ordained a high priest by Ervil, and Lillian was his favorite daughter. Other than Conway LeBaron, whom he had tried to marry Lillian to previously, there were few others he would have considered more worthy of her than Mark.

On the night of the wedding, Michael's brother, who was also stationed in San Diego, called him aside. He told Michael that their father had been diagnosed as having terminal cancer and only had a few months to live. Despite being constantly at odds with his father, Michael still felt terrible over the news. He began cursing and blaming God and locked himself up in his apartment to sulk. I felt bad for him, of course, but I couldn't understand his behavior and his disrespect for God. I tried explaining to him that death wasn't the end of everything, that it was the beginning of a beautiful afterlife, but he wasn't in the mood to listen. I left him and for the first time in my life got drunk, trying to forget him and the way he was acting. I promptly regretted it once I got sick to my stomach.

The next day he seemed all right again and apologized for the way he acted. We went out to look for some boxes to pack his possessions in because he would be graduating corps school on May 10 and was being transferred to a naval hospital in Portsmouth, Virginia. I couldn't stand the thought of him leaving and knew I was going to miss him tremendously, but I didn't think he was going to be gone that long. When he returned, I would be waiting for him — or so we thought.

For his remaining few days in San Diego, Mom let Michael move into our apartment to save him some money. Mark had moved out after he and Lillian got married, so there was an extra room. Mom loved Michael very much and treated him like one of her own sons. It was no secret to her how we felt about each other. He had her stamp of approval, despite our religious differences. She and I were both confident we could eventually bring him into the fold. Michael was the type of person you could have a lot of confidence in and I was sure one day he would be rich. He just seemed to project success and what it took to achieve it. We had talked about getting married and even began making plans. He was certain he would be stationed overseas and, when that came to pass, I would be going with him — as his wife.

Shortly before he left for Virginia, we went out for a lobster dinner one night. While we were waiting to be served, Michael said to me, "Rena, don't ever change." I wasn't sure how he meant that, so I asked him to elaborate.

"Don't ever change your beliefs," he said. "Because what you believe in right now is what's going to change the world."

This kind of surprised me, since he had never before come that close to accepting our beliefs. Then he continued, "God has been very good to me. If it hadn't been for him I never would have met you." He also said God had helped him pass his corps tests, since he hadn't really studied for them, and he went on and on about how much God had done for him. It made me so happy to hear him say all these things after the way he had reviled God after learning of his father's illness.

Then he told me the reason he had taken me out was to put a ring on my finger but that would have to wait until the next day. He told me, though, that we should start considering ourselves engaged. I felt really happy that evening and I was looking forward to our life together. The next night, true to his word, he gave me a ring — fourteen-karat white gold with nine diamonds.

He handed me the little box, and as soon as I opened it he said good night and went to bed. I sat there for a few minutes in a daze, staring at this beautiful diamond ring, and I finally tried it on. It fit perfectly. I went to his room to thank him, but he was acting kind of strange. I couldn't tell if he was scared or mad. I was excited when I went into the bedroom Mom and I shared and Mom wanted to know why. I turned out the lights before she could see the ring, deciding to wait before telling her. Or maybe I would just wait until she noticed it.

She did. The next night, in fact. I was playing the piano and she grabbed my hand, looking surprised when she asked where I got it. I told her and she called Mike over.

"Do you really mean this?" she asked him, holding up my hand with the ring on it.

"Yes," he weakly replied. Mom reached over and hugged me and congratulated us both.

Later on, when she and I were alone, Mom asked if I knew what I was getting into. She emphasized that Michael had not fully accepted our religion and wasn't a celestial person yet. For me to marry someone not under a celestial covenant as we were would have been a criminal act, she explained. I knew that and acknowledged it and gave her assurances that there would be no wedding until he proved himself worthy of God's highest blessings. That's what would determine whether or not I married him. He had to accept God in the same way we had and be willing to learn to serve Him faithfully.

That same night and the next day, Mom sat me down and began telling me about some of the hardships of her early married life. These were things she had never told me before, and it meant a lot to me to hear it. She was finally acknowledging that I was no longer the little baby girl she had to shelter and protect from the world. I was becoming a young woman, and she had come to grips with that fact. She explained that God came first and foremost, and desires of the flesh were not anywhere near as important as serving the Lord and doing His will.

On May 15, I broke the news to Dad when he came up from Mexico and asked if he would give Michael permission to court me. He flatly refused at first, but I explained to him what my terms for marrying him were. Dad agreed to go along with that. The only problem was, it wouldn't be the kind of courtship we were used to. Michael would be going far away soon. Our courtship would have to be conducted by mail and an occasional phone call.

Michael graduated corps school on the seventeenth and almost immediately left for Oregon to see his parents. He was gone about ten days, then left again to go to Virginia. But, before he did, we had a little time together and we got into some very heavy necking. I thought I let him go further with me than anyone had ever gone. Of course, I was blocking out the incident with Ervil years before. My emotions, of course, were very confused. On the one hand I wanted to show how much I loved him, but I also knew not to do these kinds of things before getting married. We didn't go all the way, but it was enough to shake me up emotionally. When I got home that night I wrote it all down in my diary and got it off my mind.

After Michael left for Virginia, my heart grew very lonely. I kept myself busy with school, housework, and even a few outside jobs, but my mind was on him constantly. I wrote him long, often-mushy letters, telling him how much I missed him. I even wrote to his mother and his grandmother. I wanted them to know how much we loved each other, and I wanted them to approve of me.

On June 12 I got my first letter from Michael and he called the same day. He didn't say much, except that he was too busy to write or call sooner. It didn't matter to me; the fact was, I'd finally heard from him and I was so happy when he told me he loved me. That made the long wait worthwhile.

Later that month he called me and was very depressed. He was working in the naval hospital and a couple of his patients died. He blamed it on himself and was really down about it. We came to an agreement in that conversation: if I would study about his government, he would study about our religion. I agreed and began reading all the books I could about the Constitution and the U.S. government.

That spring, Noemi had another little boy with Dad. They named him Paul. When I wrote about it in my diary, I expressed disappointment because I had been counting on a girl, but Dad was certainly happy about it.

Also late in June I got a postcard from Andres Zarate. It was the first time I'd heard from him in more than a year. He didn't say anything about Joel's murder or whether or not he had played any part in it, but he did say he was married. I was glad for him, hoping that it would take his mind off me. Then later I heard through the grapevine that he told several people he was coming to the U.S. to marry me also. I felt bad that I might have to tell him about Michael, but it never came to that.

On June 24 Mom and I went to Ensenada again to see Ervil. When we got there, his son Arthur and Teresa Rios, another one of his wives, were also visiting him. Arthur told us he had been in Utah working with Ed Marston and Don and Lloyd Sullivan getting Ervil's pamphlets into circulation. Mom and I and Arthur talked to Ervil about how we should go about circulating his latest pamphlet, then Ervil asked to talk to me alone. Mom and Arthur left.

Ervil noticed the ring Michael had given me and asked about it. I told him about Michael, and he said it bothered him to think I could love someone other than him. He told me he still loved me very much and that I should have married him a year ago. I told him I was glad I hadn't because I wouldn't have been very happy that way, especially with him in jail. "A person is *always* happy when they're doing the will of God," he said.

"Well, I don't think it's the will of God yet," I answered.

My stubbornness finally won out, and he agreed that it was best for my mind to be on one man than a whole bunch of them. He mentioned that it was a crime for someone under celestial covenant to marry someone who wasn't, and I explained to him that I wouldn't marry Michael until he agreed to become one of us — even if it took three or four or five years. Ervil said I probably wouldn't go straight to hell for that. I felt very uneasy talking about this subject with him, and I was glad when it came time to leave.

School was out for the summer. I tried to busy myself as much as I could. I wrote to Michael often and also wrote to Andres and Elsa, Ervil's daughter whom I'd been close to in Mexico. I went to my first rock concert, which featured Chicago and the Doobie Brothers. I traveled back and forth to Ensenada and Los Molinos a few times, socializing with Dad and his wives and kids, and other kids my age.

I have described incidents of my youth that have little to do with our religion and what we believed. But they're important to mention because they show how "normal" our lives were in every way but our beliefs. We mingled freely in society, we interacted with people who didn't believe as we did, and we attended functions and events — such as movies and concerts — that some other religions would have labeled frivolous or corrupt. We did not sequester ourselves from the rest of the world.

Most people have a preconceived notion of a cult as being a bunch of fanatical people running around preaching doom and gloom and keeping to themselves when they're not out proselytizing. We certainly did our share of preaching to explain our faith to anyone who would listen, but we never tried to force it down anyone's throats. We passed out pamphlets, usually door-to-door, but we didn't ring doorbells and try to lure the people into doctrinal clashes. Anyone reading our literature was free to make up his or her own mind. We didn't physically accost passersby on the streets, trying to convert them, or verbally abuse them with threats that they were going to perdition if they didn't follow Ervil. The hellfire and brimstone was all there, in Ervil's pamphlets, and anyone reading them could take his words for what they were worth. If they wanted to join us and become a part of what we were all about, we were more than happy to welcome them. We would explain the scriptures to them, without resorting to indoctrination or coercion. If they thought we were full of crap, they were entitled to their own opinions and we respected their rights to their beliefs.

My relationship to Michael, although nothing particularly out of the ordinary, serves to further exemplify how typical a teenager I really was. Except for the passages about my religious feelings and my relationship to God, my diary probably reads no differently than one any other girl my age might have kept. Until Ervil and I got married, I was just one of millions of other teenagers out there worrying about my weight, my complexion, my hair, my clothes, my boyfriends, and my grades in school. I was no wild-eyed fanatic, even though the media later portrayed us that way, and I was a far cry from being "brainwashed" like the reporters would have everyone believe. There was very little difference between me and anyone else my age.

For the rest of the summer and into the early fall, I wrote to Michael often. He didn't write nearly as often as I did and his calls became less frequent, but when we did talk he would assure me he loved me. I finally saw him again in early October. I knew he was coming, but I wasn't sure exactly when. I was riding my ten-speed bike home from school one day and heard someone call my name from across the street. It was Michael. We ran to meet each other in the middle of the street and hugged, stopping traffic in both directions. I started crying and shaking like a leaf. It was the first time I'd seen him in more than four months.

Michael had Ed Marston with him, so he drove me back to the house while Ed rode my bike over. Ed had been staying in the apartment with us. Now we were faced with an uncomfortable situation. Mom said Ed had been acting strange and depressed since Michael showed up that morning, and we both guessed why. Earlier that summer, I had gone to a weekend-long Independence Day celebration in Ensenada to hear Mark and his band play. Ed and I danced together much of the time. I suspected that he was beginning to like me, and it became more obvious as time went on. Since Michael would be staying with us, Mom didn't want Ed in the house at the same time. My friend Betty came by and drove Ed to the bus so that he could stay with Linda Johnson, one of Ervil's wives.

Ed didn't seem too happy with this arrangement, but he had to go along with it. It was fairly typical of the way he had been treated all his life. He always felt like a stepchild, which, unfortunately, he and the other three Marston children were. He was the son of Anna Mae Marston, one of Ervil's wives, and she always regarded the children she had by Ervil to have a higher calling than her children by her first husband, Nephi. Ed had a very low level of self-esteem and therefore kept a low profile. I was only vaguely aware of his existence and didn't pay much attention to him. Years later, he told me he had been in love with me since I was fourteen, but he couldn't bring himself to say anything about it at the time. Our lives did draw closer together, as it turned out.

The first weekend after Michael's arrival, Mom, Arthur, Lillian, Ramona Marston, Annalee Barlow, and I took him to Mexico with us. He had always had a bad impression of that country, having seen only the border towns like Tijuana, and we wanted him to see where and how we used to live. We showed him around Ensenada and Los Molinos, introduced him to friends and family, and he got a guided tour of the A-frame Dad and Mark built. And, he got to meet Ervil.

Mom dropped Michael and I off at the jail, knowing the two of us had to talk to Ervil alone. In order for us to get married, we had to have Ervil's blessing, and it was very important to my family that Michael should meet him. Ervil started out asking questions about the navy and other things about Michael before launching into the gospel. We were in there with Ervil for about two or three hours. Ervil did most of the talking, describing the principles of civil law and the nature of the true priesthood. Ervil explained that he was there because of the conspiracy against him by Joel's followers. Annalee and Arthur came in next, and before we left Ervil asked Michael to come back next visiting day, a Thursday, so they could talk further.

After we left, I had the feeling Michael was very impressed. It seemed like the first step had been taken toward winning him over to our church. As we were walking out of the jail, Michael said, "I know what I'm going to ask him next Thursday. I'm going to ask him whether I should marry you or wait."

"I can tell you what his answer will be right now," I said.

"What?"

"He'll say wait until you know more about what we're trying to do here."

Michael agreed. As it was, he never did visit Ervil again. But I was still impressed that he would even consider asking Ervil for his blessing. Michael was the type of person who never asked anyone's opinion on anything. I really felt then that he would join us in faith and we could, indeed, get married when the time was right.

I had never told Michael anything about Ervil's intent to marry me himself. All Michael knew about Ervil was that he was the patriarch of our church — nothing more.

Michael went back to Virginia soon afterward, and my letter-writing barrage continued. I was lonely and miserable without him around. Meanwhile, in November, Ervil was sentenced to twelve years in prison for Joel's murder.

Several months earlier, the Firstborners had paraded dozens of "witnesses" into the courtroom, testifying that at one time or another they had heard Ervil make death threats against Joel or other persons. Among those testifying in Ervil's defense were Duane, Dad, and Vonda White, another of Ervil's wives. Vonda told the court that Dan Jordan had been at her house earlier on the day Joel was murdered but he was feeling ill and was going back to San Diego to recover.

Finally, Ervil testified in his own behalf. Witnesses to the trial described him as calm and collected, and he remained that way throughout, never showing any violent emotions. He presented himself to the court as a farmer, a merchant, a religious leader, and a devoted husband and father. He didn't smoke, drink, swear, or use drugs. His attorneys portrayed him as an upstanding citizen who had no part in Joel's murder. On the stand, Ervil admitted he'd had disagreements with Joel about church doctrine and land ownership. However, these were not sufficient grounds to have Joel murdered, he said. On September 11 the case was closed and the judge retired to deliberate.

It took the judge two months to render a verdict. He found Ervil guilty of homicide. Since Ervil had already served eleven months in jail since turning himself in, the judge applied it to his twelve-year sentence. He would only have to serve eleven years and one month. However, the Baja California State Supreme Court in Mexicali overturned the verdict on December 14, a year and a day after Ervil surrendered. They ruled that the lower court did not have sufficient evidence to find Ervil guilty, especially since those actually accused of doing the shooting, Dan and Gamaliel, were not in court to testify.

Despite this, however, it still took another two months to get Ervil released. Finally, on Valentine's Day, 1974, he walked out of jail a free man again.

The Firstborners and the reporters who covered the story have always maintained that a sizable bribe to the Mexican officials is what really got Ervil sprung from prison. The amount has always varied, though most reports say about $40,000 was involved. I seriously doubt that ever happened. Ervil was always hard up for money, and the rest of us were no better off. How could he suddenly come up with $40,000, sitting there in prison? The story went around that we'd sold an eighty-acre parcel of land in Utah to get the money, but that wasn't true either. We *still* own the land and it's nearly worthless. "Buying justice" in Mexico is not uncommon, but now the question arises as to who, if anyone, was doing the buying.

In my diary around this time I wrote that Ervil's conviction was overturned because the Joelites couldn't bribe the higher court judges. It was possible they could have paid off the lower court judge to have Ervil convicted. They had a lot more money and assets than we did and more people they could collect from. I never heard from Ervil what truly happened, and I never would ask him. No one has ever come forward with the truth, so the issue remains open to speculation. Perhaps there was never any bribe to begin with — from either side.

Whatever the reason, Ervil was free. And that was all we cared about.

CHAPTER 10

Ervil's murder conviction was overturned on December 14, 1973, but I didn't find out about it right away. Something more important to me happened the same day. Michael called.

I hadn't heard from him in a month and a half and was worrying myself sick over it. The first thing he said to me was, "I love you." My first words to him were, "What happened to you? Where have you been?"

It turned out he had been shot while trying to play "supercop," as he put it. He was in the hospital but was doing okay. He had been walking to work one evening when he saw a man he had turned in for pushing drugs. The man fired a shot at him and fled. The bullet hit Michael in the left arm, near his shoulder, and he admitted himself to the hospital. Fortunately, it wasn't a serious injury.

During the conversation he also told me that in five months he would be going overseas for two years — probably to Okinawa. He asked me if I would go along with him. I told him, "I'm not ready. No way am I going to be ready to get married. Besides, I'm going to college. Just no way will it work."

He told me that in February he would be going up to see his folks in Oregon and asked me if I would come up and join him. I told him I would think about it and left it at that. We said our "I love yous" and hung up.

A few days later I wrote him a letter, explaining the mixed feelings I was beginning to have toward him. I loved him very much, but the distance between us was putting a heavy strain on our relationship. I wanted him close by so we could convert him and get married under a celestial covenant. The thought of him going overseas for two years was just too much for a fifteen-year-old girl to take.

A few days later I got a very flowery letter from him, unlike any he had ever sent before. He spoke about the first time we met, the first time we went out, the first time we kissed, and brought up other memories of the times we had together. He said the thought of losing me was more than he could handle, and he was determined to fight the navy's plans to send him overseas, even if he had to go A.W.O.L. He then promised to be back with me in seven months or less.

I never did go up to Oregon with him, despite his offers to pay my plane fare. There were a lot of developments going on in my life at the time, and my family was in flux. Mark and Lillian moved to Ensenada, and Lillian was expecting their first child in April. Vic and Nancy were talking of moving down from Utah, and Nancy was due with a child in September. And I had quit school.

My life was in such turmoil that I couldn't concentrate on my studies. I was only a few credits short of what I needed to graduate high school, but trying to make it through until June was just unbearable. I signed up for night school but I didn't enjoy that either and quit. I took a live-in job with a family in the San Diego area so I could be earning my own money. I was under a lot of stress for a girl my age and in danger of having a nervous breakdown.

During the first three or four months of 1974, the relationship between Michael and me had deteriorated badly. The distance between us was a strain to begin with, but the problems we had with our individual beliefs were even greater. We seemed to live in two different worlds, with neither of us wanting to change and become at one with the other. And, as if things weren't bad enough, Ervil was out of jail and was after me again.

Sometime earlier, Lorna had moved to San Bernardino, California, and I was called to go up there. Ervil was there too. It was the first time I'd seen him since his release. I asked Ervil what he thought about Michael, and there was nothing conciliatory about the words he chose. He said Michael was no good, he didn't have a "noble spirit," and the only thing he wanted was my body. I asked him what I should do and his answer was, "Marry *me*."

I didn't give Ervil a chance to finish. I stormed out, slamming the door behind me, and sat in the car crying. I got out my pad and pen and began writing a "Dear John" letter to Michael. I told him he "didn't give a damn about God and His work," and called him "immature," among other things. But I still loved him, despite everything. The letter was my way of pleading to him to change his ways and come over to our faith. I wanted to marry *him*, not Ervil, but that could never happen until we were at one with God. I closed the letter by saying:

> Michael, I know you love me and I hope you know I love you too. But love won't get us anywhere — absolutely nowhere. There's much more to life and happiness than love. If we find the other things that are necessary, then maybe we can still make it work.
>
> Until then,
Love Rena

I sent him another letter in a similar vein a few days later. The letters I got from him were of a pleading nature at first, then the tone began to get more resigned to the fact that he had lost me and would regret it for the rest of his life. I felt like both of us were trying desperately to hang onto something we had once had but lost and we were fighting a losing battle. How much different things had been only a year earlier.

I spent a good part of the spring and summer of that year shuttling back and forth between San Diego and Ensenada and Los Molinos. Despite the hostility we faced from the other people there when we finally moved, Los Molinos still held a special place in my heart. It was the place where I'd had so many beautiful memories and good times. Whenever I would go down there to visit Dad and Noemi and Chela and the kids, I would be reminded of those beautiful days and nights when the happy young girl that was me played the accordion and the piano and danced at the dances with more boys than I could count. I thought, especially, of Andres and the very special moments we shared. God, how things had changed in just a few years. Now I was sixteen years old, but feeling much older.

On June 17, while staying with Mark and Lillian in Ensenada, Ervil came down. That night I wrote in my diary, "That damn bastard just won't leave me alone. I can hardly stand to be near him and when I *am* around him I act like an ass."

As if my troubles weren't bad enough, I was involved in an accident. I had been driving around Tijuana with Mom looking for a place for Vic's wife, Nancy, to rent. She was due in September and wanted the baby to be born in Mexico. All of a sudden a kid ran out in front of the car and I couldn't stop. I hit him, though not seriously. He had a cut on his forehead and we stopped, took him to the doctor, and paid the bill. Of course, there was a police report to be made out and Mom said she was driving (I didn't have my license at that time). We spent nearly that whole day in the police station, and I was not in a very good mood by the time our ordeal was over. I wanted to get out and relax.

Mark and his band were playing in Ensenada. I wanted to go see him, but he wouldn't let me go and drove off without me. I was determined, though, and set out on foot. A guy I didn't know pulled up and offered me a ride and I accepted. He told me he had to make a stop first and I believed him. He drove off the main road heading out of town and then stopped the car out in the middle of nowhere. When I saw what his intent was, I pulled out a knife I carried in my purse and held him off for a while, but he wrestled it away from me.

At that point I began telling him that my virginity was the most important thing in the world to me. That didn't stop him. He finally grabbed me, threw me on the ground, and started tearing my clothes off. Somehow I managed to break free of him and I took off running toward the highway. Racing blindly in the darkness with him right behind me, I tripped and fell. He tripped over me and fell too. I was scraped up and bleeding and moaning in pain. He gave up trying to rape me and drove me back into town. Even though I was hurting, I made him drop me off a few blocks from the house so he wouldn't know where I lived. I made it the rest of the way home on foot — painfully, but with my virginity miraculously intact.

To further complicate matters, still another man came into my life at this time. Dean Grover Vest was a giant of a man at seven feet two inches. He was about forty and had a well-trimmed beard he literally *had* to grow because he couldn't shave. A war injury in Vietnam had blown part of his face away and he contracted "jungle rot." If he cut himself while shaving, serious infection could set in.

Dean had a hard life and went through some horrifying experiences. In addition to the war injury, which left him with a steel plate in his head, he also did a long stretch in prison. He killed an army officer in a fit of rage and spent between ten and fifteen years behind bars. Much of that time was spent in solitary confinement and, with nothing else to do, he read extensively and educated himself. Later, while still in prison, he took some kind of correspondence course and eventually got his teaching certification diploma. As a result of all that reading, he was one of the smartest people I had ever known.

When I first met him, Dean was living in San Diego. His wife had just split from him and she left their two children behind. I was living in Ensenada with Vonda White and her kids and she was also caring for his two children, three-year-old Margaret and one-and-a-half-year-old Eric. Dean would come down on weekends to see his kids.

By this time, Michael and I were pretty well washed up and I felt drawn toward Dean for a number of reasons. First of all, he was one of us, so there wouldn't be the conversion problem I'd encountered with Michael. Here, at last, was an option, I thought. I might not have to marry Ervil after all. Then there were the children. Seeing him trying to raise two kids without his wife really touched a tender nerve in my heart. I helped Vonda out with the kids and began feeling very maternal about them. I almost began regarding them as my own, and they grew attached to me also.

Dean was a jovial, kind-hearted, big old teddy bear of a man, despite all the hardships he'd been through. He was a little cynical, but he laughed at life with a biting sense of humor. It wasn't long before I found myself falling in love with him and trying to picture us being married. But, as always, there was Ervil to contend with.

On September 3, 1974, I made the following entry in my diary:

> ... Oh, I just want to make sure that I'm really worthy of Dean — that way there's a better chance for us both. Will I make a good mother to his two children? I hope so and I *want* to. I love those kids, but it's still a lot of responsibility. I'm only 16 years old! So young, stupid, careless, daring, and *impulsive*. But I want and need to be needed. But maybe Lynn [Rodenkirk, the girl he was supposed to be courting] has first chance. Maybe I won't get any of this. Anyway, I've decided if God *wants* me to marry Ervil He couldn't possibly want me unhappy so, whoever He decides on I've made up my mind to be happy with ...
>
> ... There is so much I can learn from him, and I love to listen to him talk. And those eyes ... big, dark-blue eyes — as sharp as an eagle — kind of like Michael's but bigger. They sort of — well, when he looks at you your eyes meet and stay there. He has a sort of hypnotic power that's rather frightening ...
>
> ... I'd be so *happy*. I just *know* I would adore him so much it makes me *mad*! I try to tell myself, "He's probably not as neat as you think." He's probably hard to please, grouchy, gone all the time, impotent, and everything else. But I don't think anything could really matter that much. I love him just the same. I just hope I don't have to do it from a distance forever.
>
> Love,
> Selfish Rena

Four days later, Dean took me, Duane, and Duane's fianceé, Laura (Chaparra) Amador to the movies. There, while some French flick was playing, he sort of proposed to me. He didn't ask: he simply told me that he was going to marry me and I was going to have his children. That really scared me because, despite my feelings for Dean, I was afraid Ervil would say, "No way," and there I would be, alone again.

The night after that, Dean and I were alone at Mark and Lillian's house where he was staying for the night. One thing could definitely be said about Dean: he wasn't subtle. He could be very blunt when he wanted to be and very often was. He said to me, "You know, you could be an easy lay if we weren't abiding by the rules."

I wasn't sure how to take that statement. I looked at him in bewilderment for a few seconds, then asked, "Is that an insult or a compliment?"

"It's a compliment, of course," he said, with his merry eyes twinkling.

He did tell me again that night he loved me and asked if I thought I could love him. Before I could answer, Mark and Lillian came home and I had to beat a hasty retreat. But, though I didn't answer him, I wrote the answer into my diary

> I love him — but if Ervil came right now and said "Forget it" I know I'd do it because God's always right and I've been wrong so far — probably because I wanted things my way. I only hope this is God's will because I want to marry him very much.

Of all of Ervil's other wives, the one I was closest to was Vonda White. Vonda was like a big sister to me, something Lorna never was, and I could often confide in her. I told her about my feelings for Dean and she understood and sympathized with my plight. She knew that Ervil was after me and, like the other wives, she wouldn't have minded sharing him with me. But Vonda wanted me to be happy with someone of my own choosing. She had a long talk with Dean and then a long one with me. I always respected her advice. She emphasized that doing God's will was more important than letting your emotions take over and govern your life. If it was God's will that I marry Ervil, then I should do it. "It's better to do God's will in the first place. There'll be less regrets later," she said.

But she also told me, "Wait until you're twenty-five if that's how long it takes. Just make sure you're ready to. Don't do it just because everyone says it's right. You have a right to know for yourself what's the right thing to do. It takes a lot of doing to learn to love another person but it's possible. After all, I did it."

My love for Dean was bound to cause problems between me and my parents. They accused me of using him to avoid having to marry Ervil and said I really wasn't in love with Dean at all. It has always amazed me how other people, especially your parents, always seem to know what's best for you when it comes to matters of the heart. To get me away from him and give me time to think things over, they talked about sending me to Utah to help Nancy with the baby that was due. She had decided against having the baby in Mexico and stayed in Ogden instead. I welcomed the chance to get away from everyone who was interfering in my life, even though it meant I would be separated from Dean and his two little ones.

But I didn't go to Utah. Mom sent me to Los Molinos instead, telling me I was acting like a spoiled child, and I should stay there until I grew up. While I was there, Linda Johnson, Ervil's eighth wife, came down from San Diego and said Michael was looking for me. It made me very happy that he still cared for me, but it also confused my feelings for Dean even further. My love life was turning into a real complicated morass.

We had been waiting in Mexico for several weeks for Ervil to come down and give us instructions on what we were supposed to do next. He finally arrived on October 3, bringing Lorna down with him. Vonda went out to call Dean and leave word for him to come down also.

In my diary for that day, I wrote, "Ervil sees the change in me and he thinks I'm open season and keeps making passes at me." He was looking through my photo album and found my senior portrait, which he removed and stuck in his pocket. I got mad and argued with him and tried to get it away from him. I told him he didn't need a picture of me and called Vonda to assist me, but she wasn't much help. She, like most of the other wives, was afraid of him. Finally, I called him a "dirty old man" and stomped out of the room, minus one portrait.

I locked myself in the bathroom and five minutes later I heard what sounded like Dean's voice. I opened the door and peeked out just in time to see Dean dive into Vonda's bedroom. I started shaking all over. Ervil hadn't heard anything about Dean and me at that point.

114

A few hours later, the verdict was in. Ervil said, "No." Dean "wasn't good enough for me," and I was his. How I cried when I thought of Dean and the things about him I would be missing — especially his two beautiful children I had come to feel were my own. In my diary that night I wrote:

> God, please give him [Dean] a good woman and help him forget me and help me forget him. I was a fool to think that I couldn't make the same mistake two times in a row. I was so sure it would be right — it seems so perfect to me. I'd have responsibility, a family, certain independence, lots of love and an excellent teacher to educate me and a strong man to keep me in my place. But — no — I'm supposed to marry *Ervil* — God — *Why?* Why, why, why?
>
> I'll never have independence. I'll have to go back to school, train for a career or job or else I can sit around and leech off of my parents or go on welfare when I'm 18.
>
> Is that what's expected of me? Is that how you earn Celestial Glory?

October was a busy month for all of us. Duane and Laura got married on the twelfth in Salt Lake City. Then, right after Glen and his family left, Dad got married to Annalee Barlow. Glen and his family were still practicing Mormons, and we felt that it would upset him to see his father take a fourth wife. Annalee was the daughter from a previous marriage of Rosemary Barlow, Ervil's seventh wife. It seemed like our whole flock was moving back to Utah. Vic never left and Duane had been up there working with him for a while. Now Mark and Lillian were moving up, then Mom, then Dad and Annalee. Then me.

Dad and Annalee took an apartment in Salt Lake City and I moved in with them. The building was owned by Merlin Kingston and his family. Kingston headed a fundamentalist polygamous group like ours, but it was much larger and wealthier. They had a few thousand followers in Utah and Idaho and were very affluent. They owned mines, timber lands, industries, stores, and other real estate. Dad and Annalee took jobs in one of their factories and I went to work in one of their fabric stores. So did Ervil's daughter, Becky, who later became Vic's second wife.

Ervil had long cast covetous eyes on the Kingstons and their prosperous financial empire. He periodically made a number of attempts to get them to tithe to him. He tried threatening them, but that was as far as it went. To protect their interests, the Kingstons employed armed guards with high-powered rifles. For Ervil to try anything against them would have resulted in some serious bloodshed. Apparently, Ervil must have thought better of it and left them alone.

Ever since his falling out with Joel in the late 1960s, Ervil had preached to us constantly about how the Firstborners were out to kill us. His paranoia seemed to increase after Joel's murder. Even when Verlan tried to extend an olive branch to Ervil, he would reject it. In a steady barrage of pamphlets and other public and private statements, Ervil continued his attacks on Joel and Verlan and the Church of the Firstborn, calling them "false prophets," "apostates," and other choice words. But, along with his doctrine, he also preached fear into us. We would never be safe as long as they were around to pose a threat to us, he would say. "We had to get them before they got us," was his message.

Of course, we believed him and took appropriate precautions as much as possible. The incident in which shots were allegedly fired at Don Sullivan was still fresh in our minds. Then an incident occurred in July 1974 that seemed to confirm Ervil's worst fears.

Sometime earlier that month, a shipment of arms was stolen in California. Among the stolen weapons were machine guns, rifles, and grenades. No one knew who did it but, on July 15, border patrol agents at the San Diego-Tijuana crossing stopped a pickup truck belonging to Verlan LeBaron. On the truck were some of the stolen weapons.

The FBI tried to keep the incident hushed up until they recovered the rest of the armaments, but somehow we found out about it anyway. If ever Ervil needed justification for the paranoid statements he had been making against the Joelites, this incident played right into his hands. It was all the evidence he needed to justify his next actions — and it set the stage for a major tragedy that was to follow.

CHAPTER 11

Sometime in late 1974, Ervil decided it was time to make a strike against his adversaries in the Church of the Firstborn. The failure of his former church to acknowledge him as its head after Joel's death, and their subsequent anointing of Verlan, rankled him immensely. He had made several attempts to win church members over to the Lambs of God and get them to tithe to him but, at that point, he had all the converts he was ever going to get from them. They continued to follow the teachings of Joel, with Verlan wearing the mantle of leadership.

Late that year Ervil called us all together in San Diego. The time had come, he said, to carry out the will of God against our enemies. "The Lord wants this done," he said. He went on to say that we *had* to get rid of Verlan, that he was going to ruin the people and lead them astray. To him it was the most important thing in the world to eliminate this person, his own youngest brother.

At first I didn't know why we were there. No plan had been revealed to me, but we were told, in effect, to remain on standby until he gave the word. It was all very mysterious and clandestine. We were like a military team, "soldiers of the Lord," to use a common expression. We rented a house and were there for about a week. We made up aliases for ourselves and practiced calling each other by our code names. I'm sure most of the guys knew what it was all about, but I certainly didn't at that point.

For a few days we had nothing to do. Ervil hadn't given us any instructions yet. One night we were so bored we went over to a pizza place and played pool, just to give us something to do. We played a few games and went back to the house. Ervil came over and I suggested going back and playing a few more games of pool. Ervil chastised us for engaging in such an "evil vice." He said we were going to get hooked on it and it was going to "control" us. I thought he was being a little ridiculous, thinking we could get hooked on playing pool, but that's the way he was. On other occasions he had accused me of getting "hooked" on TV or other pastimes he considered vices. It may have bothered him to think that something other than himself could "control" us.

Finally, the day after Christmas, December 26, 1974, we made our move. I drove south from San Diego in my little Fiat with George (Jorge), Paul, and Isaac LeBaron — three of Ervil's sons. Mark, Duane, Ed Marston, and Don Sullivan drove down later that day in a stolen Ford pickup truck. Ervil told us to head for Los Molinos.

We were told to "get Verlan" and in order to do so we had to create a diversion that would bring him into the open. Dean Vest, with his military experience, had taught them about high-powered weapons and how to make firebombs (Molotov cocktails) when they were back in the States. Dean was not along on the mission, but it was his know-how that provided the backdrop for the damage caused to lives and property in the colony.

I arrived in Los Molinos earlier that day with Ervil's three sons and went over to our A-frame house. Duane, Mark, Ed, and Don arrived in the area later and we met at the beach around 5:00 P.M. Then, after 9:00 P.M., and with Duane driving the pickup, the guys snuck into town and hit the tallest house in the village with a firebomb. The three-story "tower house," as it was called, burst into flames. Ervil said God's game plan was that Verlan would show up to help put the fire out and he would be killed. If other vil-

lagers got in the way, whether they were women or children, it
didn't matter. They were all "traitors who deserved to be eliminated."

After setting the tower house ablaze, the guys drove a short
distance away to see who would show up. Many of the townspeople
came rushing over — some trying to extinguish the flames, others
trying to help the people inside escape — but no Verlan. That's
when the shooting started. The guys began firing on the crowd
gathered around the tower house fire. Then moving down the
street in their stolen truck, they headed toward Verlan's house. The
guys fired more shots and tossed Molotov cocktails at other houses
along the way. After spraying Verlan's house with shots and toss-
ing a few firebombs at it, they sped out of town.

It turned out that Verlan wasn't in Los Molinos or even in
Mexico that night, although some of his wives and children were.
His wife Charlotte took most of the children and fled in the darkness behind their house when they heard and saw what was coming
and their lives were spared. Many of the other villagers also fled for
their lives in the cold, dark night, while others — mostly the young
men — stayed around to perform whatever heroics they could.
Some of them went from house to house, from roof to roof, disposing of the Molotov cocktails before the houses caught fire, or helping put out fires that had already started. Others helped tend to the
wounded and drag them to safety.

I don't know who did most of the shooting or damage that
night. With Duane driving, he obviously couldn't do too much else.
Mark was given a gun that didn't fire too well because it was
thought he didn't have the heart or the stomach for the gruesome
work that was to be carried out. Don and Ed were the gung-ho followers of Ervil who probably did the most shooting. Later, in my
presence, they even argued over which one of them shot the most
people.

When the firebombing and shooting actually started, Ervil's
sons and I were at Dad's house. We stood outside and watched the
tower house burning, about half a mile away. The land was very
flat, so it was easy to see a long way. That's when we heard the
shots. Then we saw the truck speed up as it drove along the road

leading to Verlan's house. More firebombs were tossed and we saw some other houses and buildings go up in flames. That's when Ervil's sons and I left, driving out a back route leading away from town. The guys and my group did not travel home together.

In all, the commando raid was over in less than half an hour. Our objective — to get Verlan — was not accomplished.

To this day, I'm still not sure why Ervil wanted me there. All I did was drive his three young sons down, then stood off in the distance where we could see the fires burning. I'm not even sure why he wanted his sons to be there. They didn't do anything either, except George, who may have thrown a firebomb or two at a few houses that were under construction and not even lived in yet. Perhaps Ervil felt he had to find *something* for me to do, and I think I was supposed to do some "scouting" for the guys, but no one ever gave me any instructions.

As for his sons, since one or more of them would succeed him someday, he may have wanted them to get a firsthand look at how to carry out "the Lord's work." I really don't know what Ervil's thinking was and I was not privy to the planning that went into the raid. All I can do is speculate. But, as far as our role and our reasons for being there, that is still a mystery. We were nothing more than bystanders. The whole raid didn't make any sense to me. However, Ervil said it was the Lord's will and we didn't dare question him because we'd be questioning God.

That night the boys and I stayed in Ensenada in a house Ervil's wives — Vonda, Anna Mae, and Linda — and their kids were sharing. We were all crammed in the small place, huddling around the one gas stove that was supposed to heat the whole house. I spent a few days there, in hiding.

Only later did I learn that two young Mexican men, Manases (Moroni) Mendez and Edmundo Aguilar, were killed in the raid on Los Molinos; thirteen others were wounded. I don't remember feeling any remorse on hearing this news, but if I didn't it was only because Ervil had us convinced that it was the Lord's work being done. Today, of course, I look back and see how senseless and brutal it all was. It was a horrible tragedy that should never have happened.

After staying in Ensenada for a few days, I got up enough courage to head back to San Diego alone. At the border checkpoint in Tijuana I got stopped and they ran a check on my license plate number. Then the questioning started. My car had been reported in Los Molinos on the day of the raid and a detective asked me about it. I told him I was standing a good distance away and didn't venture any closer because there were plenty of people there already. I thought I would only be in the way. Then, when I heard the gunshots and saw the firebombs being thrown from the speeding truck, I did what any sensible person would have done: I got the hell out of there.

At that point they probably would have let me go. They didn't appear to have any reason to hold me until I opened my big mouth. "Well, what do you do when a person's underage?" I blurted out. They were standing there holding my driver's license and I thought they had noticed my age, but it was a stupid thing for me to say anyway. It gave them a reason to take me into custody. They hadn't realized I was underage until I opened my mouth.

After unsuccessful attempts to contact my parents, I got thrown into the "juvie" (juvenile) hall for the night and spent the next two days there. I was scared, being in there with girls who were in for prostitution, drugs, theft, and murder. Here I was, a frightened girl locked up with hardened criminals. I didn't breathe easy until Mom came down from Las Vegas (where she was staying) to pick me up. Apparently, none of my captors suspected me of anything further in the Los Molinos raid and they released me into Mom's custody. Shortly thereafter we received word that our A-frame and shop had been burned to the ground.

Soon after the incident, I went up to Utah, but I don't recall staying there too long. At this time, January 1975, I was bouncing around from one place to another. I hadn't seen Ervil after the raid, and I had no idea where he was. Never at any time in my life previously had I felt more rootless. I didn't know what I was doing or where I was going. I didn't have a home and I didn't belong anywhere. I was very lonely and unhappy. For short periods I stayed with some of Ervil's wives in Ensenada, then I spent a little time with Lorna and the kids in San Bernardino. Like Ervil and most of his followers, I was scattered to the four winds. I felt as if I were on the run and, in a sense, I was.

In February, still lost and lonely and so confused, I went on a trip with Mark, Lillian, and their baby boy, Mark Brandon. All I knew was that we were going to meet with Ervil in Yuma, Arizona. Nothing else was said about the purpose of our trip.

When we arrived in Yuma, Ervil was there with Dan Jordan. Don Sullivan, who had an appliance business in Phoenix, came a little later on with someone else (I think it was his cousin, John Sullivan). It was the first time I'd seen Ervil since the raid on Los Molinos. He talked to us about things I cannot remember today. Nothing, that I recall, was said about the raid itself, but it was some kind of a "military strategy" meeting. They were talking about someone else who had to be bumped off and it might have been Verlan to which they were referring. All the talk about violence and blood to be shed made me very uneasy.

Every time Ervil would see me he would still ask, "When are you going to marry me?" or "Don't you think it's about time?" or at other times he would flatly tell me, "I think it's time now." I would get mad and have a few choice words for him and stomp off. This was our little routine, and it had gone on for four years. Somehow I knew that one day I *would* have to marry him, and in one-half of my mind I had almost resigned myself to that eventuality. In the other half of my mind, though, I was fighting it, resisting, and holding out as long as I could. Perhaps I was clinging to a vain hope that someone, some gallant knight on a white horse, would come along and rescue me — someone I could love and who would also be acceptable to Ervil. Only something like that would finally get Ervil off my back.

In my diary on December 1, 1974, I had made notes on a conversation I'd had the night before with Annalee Barlow, Dad's fourth wife. It read as follows:

Dear Pat,
   Lee and I had a discussion last night of how I'd be happy. She can see that I'm going down and, in a sense, I'm dragging her down with me. I asked her for a solution. Then I told her when she said that I had to make a choice that I didn't *have* much

of a choice. The way it's been put to me is I either marry Ervil or go to hell. Now that's some choice! That's why I'm just playing for time. I don't know how much longer I have . . .

While the group of us were gathered in the motel at Yuma, on February 3, 1975, Ervil called Dan into the back bedroom of the motel for a closed-door conference. A few minutes later Dan came out and told me he wanted to see me outside. He took me out to his station wagon parked in front of the motel, sat me down, and stared coldly at me. During this trip, Dan had hardly spoken a word to me. But now he had plenty to say, and what he said had a profound impact on my life.

"You need to marry Ervil," he said bluntly.

I was stunned. So that's what they were in the back bedroom discussing. That's why I was brought here to Yuma. Ervil hadn't been successful in roping me in himself, so he sent his head honcho out to do his dirty work.

Naturally, on hearing Dan's words, I balked and protested.

"Look, you're going through this rebellion stage and it's time to grow up and quit acting like a child. You *must* marry Ervil," Dan repeated.

"Like hell, I will!" I protested indignantly.

Dan's eyes grew colder, more penetrating. Determination punctuated his next words.

"You will either marry Ervil *today* or this is your last chance. You will go to hell," he said in a commanding voice, continuing to stare coldly at me.

His words sent a chill up and down my spine. I had been told this before, but I was still not prepared for this ultimatum that was coming from Dan. The half of my mind that had been fighting Ervil all those years was prevailing at the moment. I was not going to meekly accept my fate as all of his other wives had done, regardless of whether or not it was God's will.

"No! No! No!" I screamed at Dan in protest. "I don't care! I'd rather go to hell!" I began crying and jumped out of the car.

My nose was running and my face was soaked from crying so much. I walked over to the motel pool and splashed some cold water on my face. I sat down on a chair nearby and started praying, "Please, Lord, don't let this happen to me." I cried and prayed, alone, for about two hours before I calmed myself down. Finally, I decided that God must want me to marry Ervil and it was foolish to fight it any longer. I got up and walked back into the room where Ervil and Mark were talking strategy. Lillian was sitting there, holding Brandon. I went up to Ervil and asked him, "Will you marry me?"

His face just kind of crumpled, as I recall, and he was speechless. He hugged me and I cried some more.

I must say that I was a far sight from being a "blushing bride" on my wedding day. My hair was long and stringy, parted straight down the middle, and my eyes were puffy from crying so much. My "wedding dress" consisted of exactly what I was wearing at the moment: a red, white, and blue T-shirt that looked like an American flag and ragged bell-bottom jeans, the kind that were "in" during the 1970s. The cuffs on my jeans were so long they dragged on the ground and holes were worn in them by the heels of my shoes. My jeans were held up by a red, white, and blue macrame belt with a red, white, and blue Pepsi-Cola belt buckle. I must have looked very "patriotic" that day, if nothing else. I certainly didn't look like the virginal bride I actually was.

Ervil and Dan held a hasty conclave in the back bedroom for a few minutes, trying to come up with the appropriate words to "seal" Ervil and me in marriage. They seemed a little confused as to what the words should be, and Dan had to write some things down on a piece of paper. They emerged from the room and Ervil stood by my side while Dan planted himself in front of us. Mark and Lillian, the only witnesses, stood off to the side.

The words Dan used were not much different from those used in any other type of wedding ceremony, civil or religious, except that Ervil and I were being sealed for "time and eternity." It wasn't "'til death do you part." That's what we always meant when we talked about having a celestial covenant between us and between us and God. Marriage was both in this world *and* the next. As Dan was saying the words, all of which took maybe five minutes at the most, Ervil and I were holding hands a certain, sort of secret way, that only God's chosen people knew of. And that's all there was. No rings were exchanged, no paperwork was signed. What we were doing was not legal under the laws of the U.S. or any state, but it was legal in the eyes of God. That was our position. That was all that mattered to us, and the laws of men were trivial and invalid.

By the time I married Ervil, I had reached the conclusion that it must have been what God wanted because it surely wasn't what *I* wanted. As I noted earlier, my life was an emotional mess at that time. I thought that, perhaps, by marrying him, I would achieve a sense of stability and "belonging," in addition to doing what almost everyone else felt was right in God's eyes. I was incredibly lonely and depressed, separated from the two men I had loved the most — Michael and Dean — and had given up all hope of a white knight coming to my rescue. I had resigned myself to being the thirteenth Mrs. Ervil LeBaron, and I was going to make the best of it.

Our "wedding dinner" consisted of onion rings at Jack-in-the-Box. We drove up and placed our order with a mechanical clown. That's all I recall eating that night. No wedding cake for us. Mark and Lillian and the baby left a short time later, and I was left alone there with Ervil and Dan. The two of them had separate bedrooms in what was sort of a suite, and when it was time to go to bed, Ervil and I had our privacy. Dan had gone to sleep by this time. Ervil and I closed the door, took our clothes off, and climbed into bed. I was a bride in the context of what we believed, and this was our wedding night.

For many years — through scores of men and boys who had been after me, through a rape attempt, and nearly stabbing a man's eye out — somehow I had miraculously managed to hang onto my virginity until my wedding night. I continued to hang onto it through my wedding night and for a while after that. Ervil LeBaron, the "notorious womanizer," as the media called him, husband of thirteen women and father of more than fifty kids, wasn't up to snuff when it came to consummating his four-year quest to seduce the elusive Rena Chynoweth. To put it bluntly, he couldn't get it up that night.

Oh, but he tried, though. He tried and tried but just couldn't get it going. Nothing happened. I was a complete novice in sexual matters and so I wasn't much help. I just lay there, waiting for him to get it over with, but his efforts just fizzled out. He apologized but that was no help, either. I felt hurt and rejected and thought maybe something was wrong with me. Maybe I wasn't attractive to him. Being as young and inexperienced as I was, I had no way of knowing that these things sometimes happen to the best and most virile of men. I was an emotional basket case at the time anyway, and this only added to my frustration and anguish. We could do little more than roll over and go to sleep, which was probably the best thing for both of us at that moment. It had been a long, emotionally drawn-out day for me.

The next morning Mom surprised me by showing up. I don't know how she knew I was there. Ervil or Dan or maybe Mark might have called her. She stormed in and really laced into Ervil. She accused him of having "ruined" one of her daughters' health already by neglecting Lorna and the kids, and she wasn't about to let him ruin her only other daughter. Ervil calmed her down at some point and won her over with the smooth logic that always rolled so naturally off his tongue. When they were done, Mom took me out and treated me to breakfast. By that time she seemed resigned to the fact that she had given up both of her daughters to the same man.

She and I went to the Pancake House and I had the most delicious strawberry crepes I'd ever had in my life. Mom gave me the usual motherly advice about what marriage was all about and told me to go ahead and try to make the most of it. God's will and His work were the most important things that had to be done in life and, if this was what God wanted, it was pointless for us mortals to question that.

At this time Mom and I hadn't been getting along too well and I had been sort of indifferent to her. I was going through a rebellious stage and I resented her efforts to control me and my life. But that morning I felt she was my mother again, and I began to appreciate a little better what she had been trying to do for me. I knew that, despite what I preceived as her constant meddling in my life, she really loved me and only wanted what was best for me. That's the note we left it on when she departed later that morning.

On December 1 of the previous year, when I wrote in my diary about my conversation with Annalee, I had asked her to write down all the reasons I should marry Ervil and I would write down all the reasons *not* to. While she did give me a few good reasons why I should go through with it, I came up with fourteen good reasons why I shouldn't. They were:

1. I'd never have a man around to depend on or to help me with the family problems.
2. I sort of need a man to put me in [my] place when I'm messed up.
3. I'd have to either go to work or go on welfare in order to support myself.
4. If I went to work I'd have to leave my children.
5. I'd be so busy with my job my children would be neglected and not taught the right things.
6. If I stayed at home with [the] kids they'd be well taught but I wouldn't have the money to take care of them. Money isn't everything but it sure helps.
7. I'm a social person in some ways. If I wanted to have fun there wouldn't be anyone to do it with.
8. I'm afraid I'd get lonely and search for other ways or persons to have fun with.
9. He takes too long to say things, no matter what he's trying to say.
10. When he says intimate things, I know it's a bunch of shit. Like: "You're the most beautiful . . ." or "Don't you know that I'm madly in love with you" or "You're my most favorite wife."
11. I know he must say that to every one of them and I think it's rotten, repulsive, disgusting — thoroughly disgusting — and blasphemous. If he has to say all that shit to his wife then . . . never mind!
12. In a way I'm a loner. I'd enjoy my privacy living alone, living my own life style without other wives or whatever bothering me.
13. He's too insensitive in some ways.
14. He gives me the *creeps*!!!

But, despite all these good reasons — especially the last one — and others which I probably didn't think to list at the time, I married him anyway. I was now Mrs. Rena Lei Chynoweth LeBaron. The young girl I had been was now married to the head man of our church. As I had told myself and had been told so many times before, if it was God's will then I would have to make the most of it.

CHAPTER 12

After our wedding, Ervil and I stayed in Yuma for another day or two before heading west toward San Bernardino. One of the first things he did when we got there was make a call to a man named Bob Mackie, a member of the Church of the Firstborn. He asked Bob to meet us at a nearby Denny's Restaurant so they could talk. First, however, we drove around to make sure we weren't being followed or set up. Ervil had to satisfy his paranoia before we could go inside to meet with Bob.

Ervil spent hours trying to convert Bob to the Church of the Lamb of God, telling him to leave his job and follow him into the missionary field, but to no avail. Bob was a good listener and gave Ervil a chance to spell it all out for him, but I could tell he wasn't interested. Ervil apparently couldn't, though. He was so wrapped up in what he had to say, he wasn't looking to see if he had the other man's interest. Bob left, saying he would think about it, but we never heard from him again.

From there, Ervil and I went on to Las Vegas, where Dad had taken a job managing some apartments and was living with Annalee. That's when he found out that Ervil and I had gotten married.

Dad was and still is a very sentimental individual and, in keeping with his nature, he had tears in his eyes. He congratulated us but I don't remember much else about our visit. We didn't stay there long.

Dad had moved to Vegas from Salt Lake a short time earlier because Ervil said that was the place we were all to gather and make money. But, of all the ways there are to make money in a place like Vegas, Ervil said he had a vision from God to go into the mushroom business there. The mushroom business! Of all the billions of dollars flowing through Las Vegas every year, of all the kinds of businesses you can go into there and make money, he wanted us to grow mushrooms? That's the way he was. He and Lloyd Sullivan were always coming up with these hair-brained schemes for making money. Another time he said God told him to go into the hardware and grain feed business. And when these businesses failed to pan out, it was always because the rest of us weren't trying hard enough. He never would admit that he was wrong and his ideas were asinine to begin with.

Ervil and I spent a few nights in Vegas and slept together but, again, nothing happened between us. I had begun my period right around the same time. We drove on to a little place called Mountain Green, right outside of Ogden, and rented an unfurnished three-bedroom house. Dan came up and joined us, and he and Ervil began work on a pamphlet they said was "going to change the world."

Just about this time, the Church of the Firstborn issued its olive branch response to Ervil's actions in the killing of Joel and the raid on Los Molinos. In a one-page flyer, drafted on CFB stationery, the missive was entitled, "The Church of the Firstborn of the Fulness of Times Raises a Standard of Peace to Its Attackers." It read, in its entirety, as follows:

> Having been twice attacked on our lives and properties, the first attack resulting in the murder of our beloved Joel F. Le-Baron, the second attack resulting in the murders of Edmundo Aguilar and Manases Mendez, and the wounding of 13 other men and women and the burning and damaging of homes in Los Molinos in the Ejido Zarahemla, Baja California; we the members

and officers of the Church of the Firstborn of the Fulness of Times make this offering of peace to the people under the leadership of Ervil M. LeBaron and to himself. We ask them to restrain themselves from any further acts of violence against our people, to respect our godgiven rights to life, property and the free exercise of conscience and no more proceed criminally against us in treading down our inalianable *(sic)* civil rights.

This we do according to the word of the Lord God of Israel (D&C 98) and with the world as a witness, following the order and law of God in these matters and to justify our restraint in the eyes of all honorable men in not retaliating against the offenders.

Verlan LeBaron
Patriarch over the Church

From the tone of Verlan's letter there should have been no mistaking its conciliatory intent. At least that's the way anyone else would have seen it. All they were telling us was simply, "Please leave us alone." However, Ervil didn't see it that way. He didn't *want* to see it that way. He was so consumed with hatred for his younger brother and so obsessed with gaining control of the Firstborn Church that he twisted Verlan's words 180 degrees. As a result, a one-page letter generated an eighteen-page pamphlet.

Ervil called this pamphlet, "Response to An Act of War From the Church of the Lamb of God to Its Attackers." As if to symbolize its intent, the pamphlet's front cover was done in blood-red against a white background when it reached its printed form.

The typing that went into this pamphlet was an absolutely grueling ordeal. Ervil had his daughters Elsa and Becky, along with stepdaughter Ramona Marston and me, taking turns on the two typewriters we had (Elsa and Ramona were both married to Dan, and Ramona was pregnant with their first child). Anna Mae also helped us out for a while. I wasn't very good or very fast. I had taken a year of typing in high school but only got C's in it. The other girls were so much better than me, especially Becky. I couldn't figure out where or how she learned to type so fast, since she had gone to school in Mexico where typewriters are luxury items few people there can afford.

We had to triple-space each line and, when we finished a page,

Ervil would write in the margins and completely fill up every available inch of blank space. Then he'd go onto the back of the page and continue writing there. He'd draw little arrows in every direction, all over the place, and it was hell trying to decipher his handwritten notes. Once we managed to figure out what he wanted to say and where it was supposed to go, we'd have to go back and retype the whole page and more. Then we would give the page to Dan and he'd edit out all the new stuff Ervil put in and we would have to type it again. Then, when we gave the page to Ervil to look at, he would reinsert all the copy Dan had taken out.

For those of us doing the typing it was frustrating and maddening. We had to keep whiting out spots on the pages and retyping over them and handwriting words in that we'd missed. It seemed to go on like this forever. The two of them just couldn't make up their minds what they wanted to say. Then, when we finally got the pages to read exactly as they wanted them, we had to run them off on a justifier to get the margins even on both sides. We had to count the spaces in each line in order to do this. It was tedious work. I absolutely hated it. They wrote and rewrote night and day and were determined to get this work into circulation as quickly as possible.

Ervil, especially, was obsessed with his writing. He would go into marathon sessions where he would lock himself in the bedroom he and I shared and shut everyone and everything else out. He would go for days without shaving or bathing, putting in twenty hours a day, and he drank strong, black coffee continuously to keep himself going. Nothing else mattered. The world around him ceased to exist except for the great work he had to do in the name of God.

When the pamphlet was finally done, Ervil and Dan took it to a local print shop and had a few thousand copies run off. It was vintage Ervil LeBaron: unforgivingly venomous, hostile, paranoid, and defiant. Verlan had offered a "Standard of Peace" and Ervil responded with "An Act of War." He accused Joel and Verlan of apostasy and perpetrating "criminal acts" against God and against the people. He also said they unlawfully attempted to deprive him of his patriarchal office. In talking about Joel, he said the following, in part:

> ... After two years of fraudulent function in his spurious, self-devised and self-instituted patriarchal office, following the time in which he was formally removed from the office of President of the Church (by Ervil in 1969), this willful deceiver and betrayer of the laws and revelations of God appointed Verlan M. LeBaron to succeed him in this spurious capacity. Just prior to this time, however, Joel F. LeBaron proceeded to personally usurp political power over the people and to set up his secret military organization to exercise tyrannical control over them, thus putting forth his hand to steady the ark of God's covenant of liberty. It was through the establishment of a reign of organized crime in this manner, then, that false christs, or falsely anointed heads of the priesthood, and false prophets arose in the church in great numbers with power to deceive all, even the very elect, inasmuch as this was possible ...

Later on in the pamphlet, he said:

> ... At the height of the vicious agitation over land instigated by Joel F. LeBaron after the great and final division of the people had begun, he went to the extremity of openly and violently threatening the leaders of our church, who were his principal doctrinal opponents, with death to their faces. He did this in the presence of a group of our church members, whom he also attempted to intimidate by threatening them in the same manner. He said that if they should continue to oppose him in his private claims to the right of ownership of half the land acquired by the members of our church prior to their formal withdrawl *(sic)* from the church organization that he had so fully corrupted, he would cause them to be sentenced to death and executed by his fanatical followers ...

In a previous chapter, I related the incident that took place four years earlier in front of our house in Los Molinos when I overheard Joel threatening to kill Ervil. Ervil, who had a memory like an elephant, filed that one away in his mind and was now using it as justification for his paranoia. His paranoia enabled him to rationalize his determination to "get them before they got us."

In the meantime, I had neglected my diary for about two months while all this craziness and confusion was going on around me. Finally, on February 23, 1975, I had a chance to make an entry:

Dear Pat,

I got married about 2 and a half weeks ago ... I won't bother you with details right now. I'm not in the mood for discussing it right now.

What I want to talk about is this strange feeling inside, like something is bottled up in there. I guess it'a not a *new* feeling — I've had it many times before and it distracts me from my happiness. Because I'm supposed to be happy — I mean — I suppose I did right to get married — but there's *still* something missing. Oh, I can't yet say that I'm in love with him because I'm not. That takes a long time to develop but it's still something else I think.

One thing I know is that I miss my privacy ... I wish he'd dump me somewhere and go away for a while.

I'll *never* be like the rest of his wives who always miss him and wish he was around more, and I long to have a place of my own, a little apartment — and a job.

Am I wrong to want these things? I don't know. All I know is that I want them very much — so much that I dream about it at night and think of it every day.

It's hard to be cooped up in a house all day, every day, typing which is something I'm glad I know how to do but it's the last thing I want to do from now on. Here I am doing something that at least three other girls around can do (and much better) and all the time I have so many other talents which I want and *need* to use.

I only regret a few things in having gotten married and I've stated most of them. Others I'll probably outgrow with time. God above, I pray to you and ask only that I may be given a job doing something I enjoy and supporting at least myself. Only to have a place of my own.

Please. Please. Please.

And I concluded my entry for that day with a poem:

> With people all around
> Why do I feel this way?

A little bit of loneliness
And a deep longing to be free

My friends don't harm me
Nor do they do me any good
I want to be what I am
Not what they think I should.

That entry and others like it pretty well summed up the changes and feelings I was going through in my life at that time. There were times I was so depressed and so miserable I felt like running away, but where would I go? I had no family I could go to because, except for my brother Glen, they were all in league with Ervil, and Glen was living too close to us all in Ogden. Ervil would have had no trouble finding me there. I was still a minor, so if I took off I would surely be preyed upon by the sleazy characters out on the streets looking for runaway girls like me. I had no choices, and that was the hardest thing for me to accept.

There were times I just wished that God would strike me with lightning and get it over with. I had never stopped thinking about Michael, and that only depressed me further. Toward the end of our relationship, my family had done an about face and began alienating me from him. They said Michael wasn't "celestial material," that he would never be one of us and consequently would never be good enough for me. Michael made an honest effort to understand what we were all about, but it was much more complex than he understood. Unlike the rest of us, he wasn't raised on the civil law as taught by Ervil and he wasn't really the blind follower type, anyway. Though I would see Michael again later on and we would resume our correspondence, there was never to be anything intimate between us.

There were times I found myself wishing polygamy worked *both* ways — for the women as well as the men. That way, if I had to be married to Ervil, at least I could have had someone else that I really did love.

Around this time, in that little house in Utah, not far from where I was born and spent the first eight years of my life, Ervil finally succeeded in taking my virginity. It wasn't at all what I expected it to be and it certainly wasn't very exciting or memorable.

Of course, I had no one else to compare him to in bed, but I was aware of what I was feeling — and it wasn't much. I remember thinking to myself, "Is that it? Is that all there is to it?" He didn't particularly arouse me or turn me on. When it was over, he rolled off me and began snoring almost immediately.

I crept out of bed, went into the bathroom, closed the door, and softly cried. But crying just made me angry at myself. I tried to stop but I couldn't, so I got in the shower and tried to scrub myself clean. I kept thinking of Michael and the tears started again and I got angry at myself again. I wasn't about to let Ervil see me crying, since he would have interpreted it as weakness on my part. I found out later that crying did not evoke sympathy or compassion in Ervil; it only made him angry. I didn't know that about him at the time, but I'm sure I would have found out if he had seen me crying. Still, I knew him well enough to know that I had to put on my rebellious, defiant front around him. That was the only way I could assert whatever independence I had.

Many times when we made love after that I had to close my eyes and pretend I was somewhere else or he was someone else. I would often turn my head away or hold my breath so I wouldn't have to smell his breath. It always reeked of something awful, usually coffee. He kissed like a fish, very stiff-lipped, in a way that really disgusted me. When he was inside of me, he would say things like how good I was, how beautiful it was, and so on, and I knew he was full of crap. I *wasn't* good at that time. I wanted to be; I wanted to learn what it was all about. But he was a lousy teacher, and I didn't say anything about it. I couldn't say, "Can we try this?" or "Could we do something a little different?" I was completely inexperienced at lovemaking, so all I could do was just lie there and let him do all the work.

And he was no help, either. He wasn't adventurous and most of the time he didn't even seem to have his mind on what he was doing. He never once asked me how it was or gave me any kind of instruction. He would just say something like "Relax," but that was very hard for me to do.

He also had some very archaic ideas about things like conception and pregnancy. He wanted very much to get me pregnant, and after we finished making love he would tell me to just lie still and not move — give the sperm a chance to travel up to the womb and do its work. Now, I may have been a real dunce when it came to the finer points of sex but not when it came to biology. I had read books on conception and birth and I knew it didn't matter what you did once the sperm was released. You could stand up, play hopscotch, run around the block a few times, or whatever. If you were going to conceive it was going to happen regardless. And I told him that. I said, "That's stupid! Where did you hear that?" He would become indignant. No one could tell him anything. No one could ever question his ideas or theories. He was an authority on everything — or so he thought. He may have read only one book on a subject, but once he did he thought he knew everything there was to know about it. Even if that book happened to have been written shortly before or after the turn of the century.

In my diary, a short time later, I tried to air my feelings about Ervil, about the place we were living, and basically how I was feeling at the time. In an undated entry, probably around February or March 1975, I wrote:

Dearest *Tio* [Spanish for uncle, one of Ervil's nicknames] doesn't understand me and he takes me for granted. I thought when I finally decided to get married, I'd be happy, but, to the contrary. I really think I've tried, but I can't be happy living way out in the middle of nowhere, going around on tip-toes and talking in whispers. And, on top of that, the only money we ever have is what we can beg off Vic and Duane. I'm not try[ing] to be too proud to ask for money and all that. It's just that they're supporting the *whole damn* son-of-a-bitchin' thing and it ain't right in my eyes. I could get a job and *that* way at least support myself! But no, like *Cunado* [Spanish for brother-in-law, another of Ervil's nicknames] says: I can't make enough to support the Kingdom. But God damn it! At least I wouldn't be a burden to it. I'm not helping anyone, and I'm unhappy. I really *try* to see it his way but he's a selfish male chauvinist pig and the reason he wants me around is just for his own convenience. Well, I've been sleeping in the living room for a while now, so if he needs someone he's gonna have to go somewhere else . . . and I've decided I have the right to at least fall in love with him first.

And that's the way it went, for a long time — in fact, throughout our whole five-year marriage — with me trying to convince myself that I loved him. Sex with him was never fulfilling for me and it never got better. I never climaxed and I never even knew what one was until later on in life. I was on an emotional roller coaster with my feelings toward him. For those first few months I had him all to myself and most of his other wives would probably have envied me for it, but I didn't feel privileged at all. I would have preferred to be in *their* shoes. I'm not a jealous person anyway, and considering the way I felt about him, I didn't mind sharing him at all. In fact, my feeling often was, "If they want him so much they can have him." I was so unsure of myself with him sexually, yet there was no one with whom I could have talked about it. Even if there was someone I could talk to, I wouldn't have known what to say or ask. Sometime later, when I did happen to mention it to one of his wives (I don't remember which one), she was amazed. Apparently it hadn't been that way for her and she couldn't understand why Ervil wasn't satisfying me in bed.

After awhile Ervil must have caught on and saw he wasn't doing anything for me. But, instead of trying to teach me himself, he tried to enlist some female help in the learning process. He wanted me to go to bed with him and Anna Mae and watch them go at it, probably figuring that I'd pick up a few pointers along the way. Maybe between the three of us we would somehow figure out a way to get Rena trained.

When he approached me with this I was absolutely horrified. "Like hell, I will!" was what I remember telling him. "No way will I go to bed with you and another woman!" Anna Mae, who was sitting right there when this discussion went on, was willing to do whatever he told her to do. She was just that type of person, but not me. I balked and squawked and got very indignant. It disgusted me that he could even think of such a thing.

I remember telling Mom about this and she got very upset about it also. We were back in California at the time. Ervil had sort of dumped me off there, at Anna Mae's house, while he went off somewhere, and Mom came by to check on me. I cried to her about it and told her how unhappy I was. When Ervil came back she confronted him about it. Needless to say, this suggestion never came up again.

I have often been asked by outsiders whether Ervil's other wives and I ever compared notes about his supposed sexual prowess. The answer is no. I understand that in conventional society, women often sit around talking about men they have slept with, and they go into explicit detail about what turns them on or off. Not so among those of us who were Ervil's wives. An outsider might think this is the case in a polygamous society, when the women have a few moments to themselves with nothing better to do than sit around and gossip, but this didn't happen with us.

First of all, there rarely was idle time for such gossip. The women were busy almost constantly — cooking, cleaning, washing clothes, taking care of the children, and doing other things that were in keeping with their accepted roles. Also, sex wasn't something we openly discussed. It wasn't public knowledge how good or bad someone was in bed. The main function of sex was to produce children to carry on in the Kingdom. The more children we produced the greater would be the blessings we would receive. That was the yardstick we were measured by, not the number of orgasms we had or produced in our partners. Nonetheless, we did expect a certain amount of gratification from sex and if it wasn't forthcoming, it was just as disappointing to us as it would have been to anyone else. We were, after all, only human — and not mere "baby machines."

In the years since my marriage to Ervil I have read other accounts that said I was his favorite wife. It always amuses me to see statements like that, especially when they're written by people who didn't know us at all and may have gotten their information from second- or third-hand sources. I was his *youngest* wife — the rebellious one he had to keep in line. That may have added some sense of adventure and intrigue to his need to "conquer" me and my free spirit. I wanted to be away from him, therefore he wanted me where he could keep an eye on me. He was extremely possessive.

But as far as being the "favorite," that simply wasn't true. He never showed me any special favors. He *never* bought me gifts or took me to the movies or out to dinner. He *never* even complimented me. He didn't do this with his other wives either, at least not during the time I was married to him. I heard he used to do fun things with some of his earlier wives like Christina, Debbie Bateman, and Anna Mae, but that was before his split with Joel. Since that time his whole personality had changed. Maybe the fact that Christina and Debbie left him triggered this personality change, I just don't know.

If Ervil had any "favorites" at all, they would have been the obedient ones who did his bidding, without question, and never gave him a hard time. He could deal with that easily enough. He was never quite sure how to deal with me. I stood up to him, told him off when I felt he deserved it (which was often), and probably gave him the hardest time of any of his wives. Of course, someone with his enormous ego couldn't handle that and it was an almost-constant battle between us. He could have my body but only when *I* felt like giving it. One thing he could *never* have was my mind, at least not as completely as he wanted to. He knew that, and it must have driven him crazy at times.

What he seemed to have trouble understanding was that I was still young, adventurous, and spirited. I may have been married, but that didn't make me an old lady. I didn't want to be tied down. I wanted to do things I enjoyed, not just what he allowed me to do. For example, I was into music, especially Gino Vannelli, who had just released his first album, *People Gotta Move*. I enjoyed listening to my albums because they gave me some relief from the misery around me. Ervil, of course, was turned off by it and didn't want my records on when he was trying to concentrate on his writing. He'd yell at me and tell me to turn it off, and I'd get mad and rebellious. Finally, I borrowed a set of headphones and continued to listen in a way that wouldn't disturb his precious thoughts.

In addition to helping out in the typing and proofreading, I also cooked and cleaned and did other household chores. But, for the most part, I felt almost useless. I had talents that weren't being used and it frustrated me. I was going crazy in that house with all those people, and I welcomed any opportunity I could to get out of there, even if it was only a short food run into Ogden. At least it gave me a few minutes or a few hours of freedom I didn't otherwise have.

Finally, I'd had about all I could take of living with Ervil in that small house with people coming in and out all the time and no privacy. Vic and Nancy let me move in with them in an eight-room house they'd just rented. It had been a Chinese Christian church that moved to a bigger building just down the street. Finally, I had a room to myself. It wasn't much, but at least I felt as if it were *mine*. I earned my keep by helping Nancy with the kids and with the housework. For a while, it worked out fine.

My brother Vic hadn't been too much a part of our lives during the years we lived in Mexico and California. He had stayed in Utah and was making a good living. He was very independent-minded and, by virtue of his monetary success, he could tell anyone he wanted to kiss off, including Ervil. Nonetheless, he was a loyal follower of Ervil's — as long as Ervil allowed him to live his life on his own terms.

In 1975, while I was living with him and Nancy, Vic was in his late twenties and he worked for Lincoln Auto, a car dealer. He and his partner had contacts with the insurance companies and they automatically got all their totaled cars, which they would then sell to body shops and others who rebuilt and resold them. It was a very profitable arrangement. Duane had gone up there earlier to help him out. The money Vic and Duane were making was the primary means of support for Ervil's church and ministry.

Vic was the only one of the Chynoweth sons to take a plural wife. In order to cement his relationship with his chief benefactor, if not in outright gratitude for it, Ervil gave Vic his daughter Rebecca in marriage. Vic accepted, and on my seventeenth birthday, April 10, 1975, Ervil married them.

It wasn't a good match for either of them but, again, it was the will of the Lord and what Ervil wanted done. Becky was only about fifteen or sixteen at the time and she didn't seem to know what she wanted. She had been in Utah with us, helping Ervil and Dan type up their pamphlet, but the rest of the time she just sat around and moped. She didn't want to marry Vic and tried several times to back out of the marriage, but Ervil's will prevailed and he had a second Chynoweth for a son-in-law.

CHAPTER 13

Early 1975 was when things really started getting vicious. Ervil had everyone, especially the men like Don and Lloyd Sullivan, Ed Marston, the Rios brothers, and Dan Jordan, worked up into a frenzy. There was much talk of violence and "hits" and some of the men were beginning to conduct themselves like a para-military unit. I wasn't the type to eavesdrop, but it was impossible *not* to hear this kind of talk going on around me. And though I never knew the full details of who they were targeting or why until later on, I knew that more blood was going to be shed before much longer. It was just one of those feelings you could sense in the air.

On January 24, while a group of the Los Molinos colonists were going to the district attorney's office in Ensenada to give statements about the raid, Raul Rios stood off to the side and fired a shot at them. The bullet hit the ground and no one was hurt. The gun jammed after that. Raul was arrested and charged in connection with Joel's murder but was released not long afterward. Even though no one was killed or wounded, it was a frightening omen of what was to come.

The first to go was Noemi Zarate, Dad's first plural wife. After the Los Molinos raid she just sort of went crazy. Dad had left her and Chela with the kids while he was living in Salt Lake and Vegas with Annalee, and Noemi began doing some irrational things. Then she reportedly began threatening to go to the authorities with what she knew about the group. Word of this must have gotten back to Ervil; he ordered her silenced.

Ervil chose Vonda White to carry out his mandate. Somehow she managed to lure Noemi away from the village and shot her to death. Noemi's body was never found and she was officially classified as a "disappearance," but we knew the truth. Don Sullivan fixed the tail light on Vonda's car which had been shattered by a bullet, one of several Vonda fired at Noemi, and he told some of the others about it. Vonda was never charged with the murder.

Rhea Kunz was slated to be the next victim, but she survived due to the ineptitude of those who were to make the hit. Mrs. Kunz was an elderly woman living in the Salt Lake area who was very active in another fundamentalist, polygamy-practicing Mormon offshoot. She was also Verlan's mother-in-law. Though Verlan had a number of wives, Rhea's daughter Charlotte was his first and only legal wife. Verlan had always been very close to his mother-in-law and that figured heavily into Ervil's game plan to eliminate him. The plan was to kill Rhea to lure Verlan out of hiding, then kill Verlan when he showed up for the funeral. Rhea had done nothing personally to offend Ervil: she was merely being used as bait.

I didn't know the full extent of what Ervil and the others were plotting. Like most of the other wives and women members of the Church of the Lamb of God, I was kept in the dark. The only time the women ever were, in fact, brought in on the planning was when they were to be a part of the "hit team" itself. I didn't know anything about Ervil's plans to kill Mrs. Kunz, except for bits and pieces of conversations I caught at random.

I remember hearing Don talking about being outside Rhea's house with Arthur one night and seeing her silhouette on the curtain. Don had a gun in his hand, but for some reason which I've never understood, he didn't fire at her. He hesitated a bit too long and the chance passed. Then, fearing they'd made too much noise and would be discovered, they took off. Needless to say, Ervil wasn't too happy about that.

A short time later Arthur and Don tried again, this time with Lloyd along, but the plan was to lure Rhea away from her house. I'm not sure how this was done, but several books written on the LeBarons said it was a phone call from an unidentified woman, wanting to know more about the polygamous church to which Rhea and her family belonged. The woman reportedly told Rhea that she and her husband would meet her outside a stable in a rural area on the southern end of Salt Lake County. Rhea got into her car and drove off but, before arriving at her destination, she reportedly had a premonition something bad was going to happen and she turned back.

In the meantime, Lloyd, Don, and Arthur were nervously lying in wait for her. Lloyd supposedly saw a few cars circling around and started getting paranoid, thinking that *they* were the ones being set up, not Mrs. Kunz. In any case, Lloyd and Arthur argued, each one calling the other a coward, and they got in their car and left. They were still arguing when they got back and reported to Ervil they failed to carry out their mission. Ervil reportedly was furious with Lloyd for "blowing the assignment."

I don't know if that's exactly what happened, but it was something very similar to that. Lloyd would get one more chance — and one chance only — to redeem himself in Ervil's good graces. That's where Robert Simons came into the picture.

I had no idea who Robert Simons was, what he did to offend Ervil, or anything else about him. I had never even heard his name mentioned around our house before. All I was ever to know about him came from what I later read, either in the newspapers or in the other books about the LeBarons. From what I have learned I will try to piece it together as best I can.

Simons was in his late forties and lived in the town of Grantsville, on the salt flats west of Salt Lake City. He was also a practicing polygamist but, unlike Ervil and many of the others, he had no following other than his two wives, Samantha McKinnon and her daughter Linda. Ervil and Dan had proselytized him a number of times under assumed names, trying to convince Simons to join the church and tithe to Ervil. However, Simons was an independent sort of person and he didn't feel any compulsion to tithe to anyone. He had his farm, his livelihood, his wives, and his own life, and he didn't need anyone telling him what to do. Ervil and Dan were not made to feel welcome there.

Some reports said Ervil had fallen in love with twenty-nine-year-old Linda, and Simons found out about it. I don't know whether this was true or not so I won't attempt to refute it. It has been documented that Simons sent a letter to Ervil accusing him of trying to take Linda from him and, from the tone of the letter, he defied Ervil to try it. That may have been what convinced Ervil that Simons had to be hit. Ervil called him a false prophet and he hoped that, by striking fear into nonfollowers, he could get them to join his flock and tithe to him.

Ervil knew that Simons felt a calling to convert the Indians to his beliefs and his way of life. Simons was an eccentric who claimed to have had visions of this sort, and Ervil used this pretext to lure him away from his home. With Lloyd acting as a decoy under an assumed name, Simons was driven to a remote desert area outside the town of Wellington, about 200 miles south of Salt Lake. He was told some Indian tribal elders had gathered there to "hear his message." When Simons stepped out of Lloyd's car on the night of April 23, 1975, Mark and Ed were waiting for him. With Mark standing by, holding a .357 magnum, Ed fired a single blast from his shotgun, killing Simons instantly.

Lloyd had stepped out of the line of fire. After Simons was hit, he came back over and the three of them carried the body to a grave Mark and Ed had dug earlier that day. Mark and Ed had been there since daylight, digging the grave and marking the little dirt road Lloyd was to use. Ervil orchestrated the whole bloody affair without even being there.

After Simons' body and some of his possessions were buried, the guys stopped for coffee and headed back to Ogden. They arrived around 3:00 in the morning and proudly reported back to Ervil. I happened to be in the room, along with Lillian, Elsa, Becky, and a few others, when Lloyd walked in, holding Simons' jacket and wallet in the air in triumph. "We did it," I can recall him saying, but at that point I had no idea what he "did" or whom he "did it" to.

Lloyd was so proud of himself. He strutted around the room, giving some of the details of the hit and assuring Ervil that no one could have recognized them or the car. Then he started rifling through the wallet, pulling out a few pictures of nude women with their heads cropped off so no one would know who they were. He smirked and passed the pictures over to Ervil, who stared at them for quite a while. Lillian and Elsa huddled around their father to look at the pictures. I remember them giggling over the pictures but I didn't see them myself, nor did I have any desire to. I felt nauseated and left the room.

I didn't know all of what had been done but I had my suspicions and I tried to shut the whole thing out. Meanwhile, having seen the proof that his mandate had been carried out, Ervil congratulated Lloyd, Ed, and Mark, then ordered Simons' jacket and wallet taken out and burned.

Next on the list was Dean Vest. Here again, my information comes from books and newspaper accounts, and I don't know how reliable they are. It needs to be noted that in the early newspaper articles written about Ervil and our church, none of us were talking with the press. Much of what was included in their news stories was based on police reports and other sources that were a matter of public record. Very little of their information, until the late 1970s, came from any of the principals themselves.

So much of what happened to me or was going on inside of me during those years I have deliberately blocked out. Other than what I recorded in my diary or can now conjure up from memory, many of the details of things that I wasn't directly involved in are fuzzy. There were plottings going on around me, but I only caught bits and pieces of them and blocked them out. It's also possible I may not have understood them and didn't feel I knew enough to make note of them.

By the time the order came down to have Dean killed, I was emotionally dead. There had been other deaths and one more wouldn't have made much of a difference to me, even though it had been someone I once loved very much. I had been squelching my emotions so much, what was it to squelch one more? Consequently, I cannot give much in the way of details on how the murder was planned or how it was carried out. I can only try to reconstruct the events leading up to the tragedy, based on what I have since learned.

I would hate to say that any of Dean's actions, after I was told to stop seeing him, had to do with me, but I've never been able to shake the feeling I was at least partially responsible for what happened to him. I had unintentionally led him on and allowed him to fall in love with me and vice versa, then abruptly cut him off when Ervil commanded us to end it. Reportedly, at the time of his death, he was trying to reconcile with his wife Cherie. She was in Seattle and he was making plans to get back together with her and the kids as a family again. In the meantime, Ervil claimed to have had a vision in which God revealed that Dean was about to defect. This was the worst of all possible sins in his eyes because that meant God was offended. The price for turning one's back on God and His anointed church could only have been death.

Dean was, in fact, in the process of defecting. But it wasn't a hostile falling out with Ervil over doctrine or anything like that. He had come to regard Ervil as a false prophet whose promises and revelations weren't coming true. He no longer believed as strongly in Ervil and he wanted out of his church. To Ervil, Dean was a traitor who, if he chose to, could go to the police and implicate those of us who took part in the Los Molinos raid. Therefore he had to die a traitor's death.

There has been much speculation that Ervil really had Dean eliminated because of me. I don't know whether or not this was true; I'll probably never know. Ervil certainly knew that we had been romantically involved, but that was over with by the time Ervil and I got married. Ervil had commanded me to keep away from him, and Dean had been told to back off from me. We both had complied. Not only did we stop seeing each other, but we even put a good bit of distance between us. Dean stayed in San Diego, while I went to Utah. There is no way he and I could have been seeing each other at that time and we weren't even writing, but Ervil might still have been jealous.

I saw Dean only once after Ervil and I were married. It was about five or six weeks after my own wedding and Ervil was hauling me around with him. We went to California, where Dean was getting married to Lynn Rodenkirk, the girl he was courting before I came into the picture. The wedding was at Lorna's house in San Bernardino and Dean and Lynn came up from San Diego. The marriage lasted only a few months, and I don't know why they split up. All I know is that by June of that year, Dean was known to be making plans to leave the group and return to Cherie and the kids in Seattle.

In any case, Ervil sent Vonda — of all people — to do his dirty work for him again. Vonda had cared for Dean's kids, advised Dean and me on our relationship, and allowed Dean to stay in her house many times. It was a cruel deed to ask someone to kill a friend, yet that didn't matter to Ervil. In fact, he probably saw the friendship between Dean and Vonda as a blessing in disguise. Who else would be better equipped to do it? Obviously, someone Dean knew and trusted and would never suspect. His guard would be down, and that's exactly what happened.

Vonda had moved back to San Diego by late spring and was sharing a house with another of Ervil's wives, Linda Johnson, and their kids. Dean was reportedly making plans to fly to Seattle the night of June 16, 1975, and went over to Vonda and Linda's house to pick up some belongings he had stored there. Vonda asked him to look at a washing machine that was broken and see if he could fix it but Dean, apparently, could not. Vonda thanked him for trying. As Dean stood at the kitchen sink washing his hands, she came up behind him with a .38 pistol Ervil had given her and shot Dean a couple of times. As he collapsed and hit the floor, she delivered the death shot to his head and threw the gun down on the floor next to him.

Vonda then called the police. She told them she had been in another part of the house and came running in when she heard the shots and found Dean lying on the floor in the kitchen. She also accused the Church of the Firstborn of murdering him. They questioned her and Linda and some of the older kids, but none of them saw anything. Despite the suspicions of the police and the flimsiness of Vonda's alibi, there were no witnesses who could contradict her statements. They held Vonda for seventy-two hours but could not gather enough evidence to warrant an indictment against her. She was set free.

I have always had a great deal of difficulty reconciling my feelings toward this tragedy. Here was a situation involving two people to whom I had been close. I had loved Dean very much, and had been very close to Vonda as well. In fact, I still am. I write to her occasionally in prison, where she was finally sent after being found guilty of Dean's murder, five years later. All I can say is, like the rest of us at the time, I must have felt as if it was God's will and His work being done. It wasn't Ervil's decree; it was God's decree, speaking through Ervil. God had commanded Ervil to bump someone off, and Ervil commanded one of his Lambs to go out and do God's work in order to be worthy of His great celestial blessings. Vonda was merely an agent of God's will, according to Ervil, and he was proud of her for carrying it out. To this day, I can't attribute the killing to Vonda, even though she actually pulled the trigger. It was Ervil's finger on that trigger, not hers. That's the way it was with all the murders he ordered.

CHAPTER 14

After Dean's murder Ervil decided it was getting too "hot" for us in Utah. Police and other investigators were breathing down our necks, following us, interrogating us, and just making life very unpleasant. They had every reason to be on us and they knew it. We knew it too. Five murders in six months, all of which could be linked to us. We felt the longer we stayed around, the closer they would get to securing the evidence they needed to arrest us.

Ervil was very paranoid. He saw the boogie man around every corner, in every closet, and under every bed. We would be in one place and, after about three days or so, he would get these "revelations" that said we had to move on. "They" were after us — "they" meaning the Church of the Firstborn. "They" were following us and were going to kill us and we had to keep moving. He made us feel as paranoid as he was.

So we moved again, this time to Denver. Lloyd and Don were already there and were selling used washers and dryers from their house. Ed was there also, as was Doug Barlow, one of Rosemary's sons from her previous marriage. Some of Ervil's children and children of his other wives were there as well. Dan was also in Denver

150

at that time with his wives Sharon, Ramona, Monce, and Elsa. Soon that city became our unofficial "headquarters."

I really didn't want to leave Ogden. I had been learning photography and Kathy's father was looking for an assistant. It would have been a paying position and there was good money in it: one wedding alone could bring in four or five hundred dollars for a few hours work. I had been planning to talk to him about the job, but Ervil told me I had to move to Denver. I had no choice but to comply. In my diary entry dated May 16, I wrote, in part, "It seems like everytime I get something going, he comes along and takes me away."

A few months after my arrival in Denver we got licenses for our appliance business and rented a storefront. One of Ervil's wives, either Vonda or Linda, suggested we name it Michael's Appliance, since Michael comes from the biblical word meaning "God." We all liked the name and it stuck.

Soon after our move I became pregnant. It was confirmed by a free clinic I went to when I started showing the symptoms. To them I was "Patty Brown," just another pregnant, unwed mother. Obviously, I had no choice since there were no documents showing me to be Mrs. Ervil M. LeBaron. When I told Ervil, he was, of course, thrilled to death. Perhaps in his mind, he felt that when I became a mother I would settle down, become less rebellious, and finally begin assuming my role as a dutiful, submissive wife and disciple of his church. Perhaps, also, his act of getting me pregnant put his stamp on me and made me more bound and beholden to him.

Although I was excited knowing I was going to be a mother, the prospect was also a little scary. It meant that I would have fewer options for living my own kind of life. And it might force me to go on welfare like so many of his other wives in the same situation.

When we got to Denver many people were living in one house with only three bedrooms, one bath, and a one-car garage. I was the oldest female in the house, so I did most of the cooking. It was a real pain in the ass trying to accommodate everybody's individual tastes when there wasn't much food or money to go around.

Lloyd, especially, was hard to please. He wanted meat and potatoes and he would give me twenty dollars to go out and shop for enough food to feed twenty people for a week. Audrey, one of Vonda's daughters, and Faye Marston, one of Anna Mae's daughters, helped me out in the kitchen. They were both around fifteen at the time. We would go to the grocery store with big purses and would stuff roasts and other packaged meat in them. I hated stealing, but I didn't see any other way. We had all these people to feed and they weren't giving me enough money with which to do it. I never told Ervil about this. But someone, I don't remember who, found out anyway and we got chewed out. It wasn't the act of stealing itself that bothered them; it was the fact that we could get caught, and that would bring the law down on all of us.

Then one day I discovered at the back of the store that they were throwing still-edible food out in the dumpster. There was cheese with a little bit of mold on it, but once you scraped it off, it was perfectly good inside. The milk and fruit and other produce wasn't too bad, either. So we started shopping there as well — "gardening," as we called it. I would back the car up to the dumpster and we would load up the trunk. Then we would bring the stuff back to the house, clean it up, and use it.

The store employees caught onto us and started pouring the milk out and slashing up the food they were throwing out. Up to that point we had been going through their garbage during the day and, if any of the employees came out, I would casually ask them, "Do you have any more?" I guess it was upsetting to them to see teenage girls foraging through their trash, but what else could we do? We didn't have enough money to buy everything we needed over the counter. The store manager got very uptight and started running us off. It got to the point where we had to sneak over there at night to do our "gardening."

Our business got started in Denver when Don and Lloyd went down to the Salvation Army, picked up a few used washers and dryers, and fixed them up. This was something they had done back home in Indiana, so they already had experience. They placed an ad in the paper to sell them, and business sort of picked up from there. Ervil came along and saw what we were doing and said he had a revelation: we needed to go into the appliance business.

Our house had a one-car garage that we worked out of at first.

The guys would get old machines, bring them over, and fix them up. We would sell them for anywhere between $45 and $75, with a guarantee. A lot of times they broke down and the guys would have to go back and fix them again. The guys picked up and delivered the machines in the trunk of our car, a big Oldsmobile. We didn't have a truck at that point. I started out answering the phone and selling machines. As the business grew, more and more of our people got involved. Ervil said it was time his boys started learning how to fix appliances and do what they could to help.

Somehow or other we managed to get a truck or two and soon after that we rented a storefront in a low-rent district. The business was going pretty good and was starting to show a profit, but then Ervil and Dan jumped in and started taking every cent on the premises. They left us no money with which to buy machines or parts or to pay bills. All of us were working for nothing, and that didn't sit too well. Ervil was always having "revelations" about some unspecified project, investment, or "deal" he needed some astronomical sum of money for by the next day. He never consulted with any of us because he probably knew we would refuse to go along with his "deals."

After he would have one of these "revelations," he would call a meeting — an "economic emergency," he called it. He would sit us down and tell us it was God's will. We had to do it for the glory of the Kingdom. It would only be temporary, he would say. All we had to do was sacrifice just a little bit longer and we would get the things we needed. That would soothe everyone's ruffled feathers for a while, but he and Dan kept doing it and it really hurt our ability to conduct business as it should have been. It was one continuous "economic emergency."

Once we were fairly well established in Denver, Ervil sent for the rest of his flock. Except for Lorna, who refused to leave California, all the other wives Ervil was still married to came up, bringing their tons of children with them. It was something we simply weren't equipped to deal with yet. We definitely were having enough problems trying to accommodate and feed those who were already there without having to absorb all these other people as well. We were left with no choice but to get another house or two.

I'm quite certain Ervil was using a lot of the money from his "economic emergencies" to get his families moved up to Denver and pay the rental on other houses. That would have been fine if he went about it gradually, but he didn't. He went about it too fast and overloaded everyone.

Our houses were scattered about throughout the city. Fortunately, none of our neighbors complained about so many people living together or conducting businesses out of their homes. We could have been in violation of zoning ordinances but, as long as no one filed a complaint, the housing code enforcement authorities left us alone. Lloyd's idea was to have us doing business from our residences so we could qualify for the lower rate for the classified ads we were placing in the newspaper. In any case, we lived under very overcrowded, miserable conditions. Ervil wouldn't give any of us a chance to get on our feet before he started moving more people in.

I was suffering with morning sickness, but I couldn't let it slow me down. I had too much work to do and all those people to take care of. I could drink a little Coke in the morning and it usually managed to settle my stomach, but I was on my feet so much of the time they really hurt. Doug Barlow was really good at giving me foot massages. But Ervil put a stop to it real quick. Doug was only a boy and there was never any other physical contact between him and me, but Ervil didn't care. He was insanely jealous. I was his wife, his chattel, and I belonged to him. No other man had any right to touch any part of me.

For entertainment, during our free time, we had to devise ways of amusing ourselves. We had no TV set. Someone brought in a deck of cards and started playing solitaire. Pretty soon others were doing it, and we would have two or three decks of cards going at once. Ervil put a stop to that too. Cards were tools of the devil, and we were going to get hooked on these evil vices. That's the way it went for us. Every time we tried to do something to relieve the monotony, he would tell us we couldn't do it. We were on this earth to do God's work only, and it wasn't proper for us to have fun.

On Sundays we would have our religious meetings at one of the houses and whoever was around would teach the class. I remember Lloyd doing most of the classes, but they always ended up more as business meetings: "We've got to make more money"; "We've got to get more literature out." Our religion had become secondary to our business.

With Ervil coming and going a lot we were pretty much on our own. Dan stayed behind and ran the shop with an iron hand. He didn't know the first thing about the business, but that didn't stop him from trying to tell the rest of us how to run it. I had really gotten a handle on the business and, for the first time in years, I felt that I was doing something useful. I answered the phone, figured out costs, sold the machines, wrote out the ads and receipts, and pretty much ran the business end of the shop. The guys bought, fixed, and delivered the machines, and everything was running smoothly.

But Dan began doing the same thing Ervil had been doing — taking all the money. The guys became irate and started refusing to make service calls until they got paid. We sold all of our machines with warranties and they were breaking down. Dan wasn't leaving us enough money to fix them, so I was stuck at the phone being threatened and screamed at by irate customers. They demanded we either fix what we sold them or give them their money back. Some even threatened to sue us.

It was very upsetting to me, since I was stuck in the middle. I went through this for a few weeks until I simply couldn't stand it any longer. I stood up to Dan and told him we were either going to get these machines fixed or I wasn't going to do this anymore. And I wasn't going to kiss up to him, either. That infuriated him. He believed women should always be submissive, and he got real nasty when I challenged his actions. That's when he threw me out of the business.

To put me "in my place," Dan relegated me to one of the houses to take care of the kids and the housework. Although I hated it, anything was preferable to being a party to ripping people off. The house had gotten miserably overcrowded by that time. We had five of Ervil's other wives — Teresa and Yolanda Rios, Anna Mae, Rosemary, and Linda — and all their kids in this three- or four-bedroom house, then Don's wife moved in with us. In all, there must have been thirty of us, all crammed together, trying to make the most of what little space we had.

The house was in a single-family residential zone, so we couldn't let the kids go outside. If any of the neighbors realized how many people were living there they would have protested for sure. So, we had to keep the kids inside and find ways to keep them amused. That, of course, drove them and everyone else crazy. When we went out, we did so in small groups so no one living around us would be suspicious. Being on the run, it was absolutely necessary to maintain a low profile and not draw attention to ourselves. We needed to be assimilated into our surroundings as best we could.

Since there was no money, we weren't able to get the necessities we needed for us and the kids — especially clothes. I had one enormous pair of men's pants I wore day after day because that was all I had. To keep them from falling off me, I had to tie a string to the front and back and wear it like suspenders. Mom later sent me a few maternity blouses she had bought in a second-hand store. In desperation we would go at night to the Goodwill or Salvation Army boxes, the big metal bins in the parking lots of shopping centers where people drop off their old clothes for charity. "Gift-boxing," we called it. We would take some of the little kids with us, lift them into the bins, and they would pass clothes out to us. We got a lot of our children's clothing that way. Of course, we were stealing, but we didn't see it as such. Those clothes were there for the needy, and we were definitely needy.

I mentioned shoplifting earlier. At first it was just meat and other food — necessities we needed to survive. But since there was no money available for other things, I had to steal in order to get them. One day my luck ran out and I got caught.

I had a little pocket camera with a flash attachment that I'd bought before I married Ervil, but I had no film to go with it. I was about six or seven months pregnant and I told myself, "My child may not have any clothes when it's born, but by God at least I'll have pictures of it."

I went into a K-Mart, walked up to the counter, and asked for a roll of 24-exposure film. They handed me the film and then I went into the clothing department and pretended to look at clothes on the racks. When I thought it was safe, I took the film out of the box, tore it out of the foil package, and stuck the roll in my purse. A man in a suit came up and asked me to follow him. He led me to his office, where there were some other security personnel present. They went through my purse and found the stolen roll of film.

Then they sat me down and grilled me: who was I, where did I live. Here I was, seventeen years old, my mom and dad were in another state, and they must have thought I was a runaway. They ended up calling Mom in Utah and telling her, "We don't appreciate you turning your delinquent daughter loose in our town."

I was frightened but I still managed to hold my head high. I told them I was single, pregnant, and broke and just wanted to have some pictures of my baby when it was born. I might have even been crying at the time. I guess they felt sorry for me because no charges were pressed. After what seemed like hours, Linda came and they released me into her custody.

The situation I was living in continued to be unbearable. I was miserable and depressed. Ervil was gone, and I was pregnant, poor, and sharing a house with all those other people. It was Mom who finally came to my rescue. She had moved up to Denver from Ogden and rented a house on the other side of town. Until her arrival, she had no idea how bad our living conditions actually were. We had very little food and no toilet paper or other essentials. I had no clothes or diapers for the baby, and my due date was getting closer. For months I had been asking Dan to allot me some money for diapers and baby clothes. All I got from him were nasty responses. Up until then, Ervil had been assuring Mom that everyone was doing well, business was booming, and Denver was "the place to be." But when she saw for herself the conditions I was living in, she was appalled.

I moved into the house with Mom and Noemi's five kids, whom she was raising. Despite the crowded conditions there, it was nowhere near as bad as what I was leaving behind. I had a room in the basement all to myself. To earn my keep I helped Mom with the housework and took care of the kids. Mom was there most of the time but I did my part, anyway, not wanting to feel like a burden despite my advanced state of pregnancy.

Backtracking a little bit, I need to explain how Mom ended up raising Noemi's kids. When Noemi Zarate was killed in early 1975, she left behind four sons and a daughter. Mom heard that these children were not being cared for properly, and she went to Mexico to check on them. There she found them in a badly neglected state. They were lying around sick and unfed in soiled clothes. Chela was there with them, but she had a baby of her own to care for and that was all she could handle. Her own child was fed, changed, and cared for, but her late sister's kids received no care. Mom quickly took the situation in hand. She stayed with the kids, fed them, and nursed them back to health. Then she put them in her station wagon and drove toward the U.S.

Just before approaching the border checkpoint between San Luis, Sonora, and San Luis, Arizona, a few miles below Yuma, Mom stopped the car and sprayed it with Vic's Vapo-Rub. She hid the youngest kids under blankets and left the older ones in plain sight to let the border guards see how "sick" they were. She told the guards they were her kids and she was bringing them into town to see a doctor. They let her across, and that's how she smuggled the five Zarate-Chynoweth kids into the country. She then took them to Utah to live with her, and later to Denver.

The two youngest children, Harvey and Paul, were Dad's sons. The oldest three, Alex, Judy, and Johnny, were the children of Noemi's first husband, but their births were never registered. When Dad and Noemi went to register them, he told the authorities they were his kids. All five of them were officially registered with the last name of Chynoweth. Harvey and Paul still live with us today.

While I was going through my battles with Dan and living with all those other people, Dad, Vic, Mark, and Duane also moved to Denver. Vic had persuaded his partner at Lincoln Auto in Ogden to open a branch office in the Denver area, so the four of them went to work for Lincoln Auto II in Littleton, a Denver suburb. Dad drove the big car haulers and wreckers, while Mark and Duane were partners with Vic. Soon afterward, Annalee, Dad's fourth wife, had a baby girl who, he said, looked like me.

On April 30, 1975, I got a letter from Michael. It was just before we left for Denver and it was quite a shock to hear from him.

He was stationed in Okinawa and he told me how much he still loved me and how much he wanted to see me when he got back to the States for a visit in August. He deeply regretted the way he had treated me and was very apologetic for not being more attentive to me. He also told me that he had been married for about six months but it just hadn't worked out.

I wrote back to him a few days later but I didn't have the heart, at that point, to tell him Ervil and I had gotten married. I was curious about his marriage and asked him to tell me about it. I also told him that I still loved him, though not in a way that could be taken any further. In my letter I expounded on the differences, primarily religious, between us and wrote:

> . . . *My* world is one where you have an unlisted phone number and you watch your rear-view mirror closely. But I wouldn't have it any other way now. There's a war going on and I was thrown into the middle of it. When some people try to take away my rights, threaten my life and accuse me of being an accomplice to a murder and of attacking their colony and burning their homes, it tends to make me think all the harder that they're a little messed up.

In my diary about a month later, I made the following entry:

> . . . I think it's some sort of a sin to be married to someone and in love with someone else but, by God, I really thought I was over him! But my heart throbs, my throat aches and my chin quivers. My hands start shaking and then I think of my husband and all I can say is, it's gonna take a long time . . .
>
> The future looks so dark. What's to become of my child — will I go on welfare like my sister-wives? Where will I be — living with T. R. [the name everyone called Mom, short for Thelma Ray, her maiden name], leeching off Mom and Dad or Vic? . . .

Why was I doing this? Why was I leading Michael on and not telling him that I was married and pregnant? What was it that made me cling to a memory of something that could now never be? I don't know. I couldn't explain it then and I can't explain it now. I felt so guilty, not telling Michael the truth and allowing him to go on telling me he loved me and thinking we still had a chance.

Maybe I was trying desperately to hold onto a happier past. Maybe I still couldn't accept the role of being a wife to a man I couldn't stand and the mother of his child.

For some reason, I started thinking of Andres again, wondering where he was, and recalling the wonderful times he and I had together in Los Molinos. I guess a lot of it was spurred by a dream I had about him in July. In the dream I was back in Los Molinos and was passing the old school building. I heard a beautiful choir singing and went inside to hear them and there, among the singers, was Andres. We stared at each other and flung ourselves into each other's arms.

The young girl in that dream was happy and carefree, not a seventeen-year-old plural wife who was about to assume the awesome responsibilities of motherhood without the benefit of a full-time father sharing the daily joys of family life.

To make my emotions even more torn, I was trying perhaps the hardest I'd ever tried to love Ervil. In my diary entry of September 28, 1975, I made some notes on a conversation I had with Lloyd, whom we were calling "Doidy" by that time. Despite his fussiness at the dinner table and other strange little quirks about him, Lloyd and I had always gotten along. He was the one older man in our group I could usually talk openly with. He told me that about a week earlier, just before Ervil left on a trip to Mexico, Ervil was pacing the floor and telling Lloyd how much he loved me and how it tore him up inside to know I didn't love him. Around the same time, however, I was beginning to feel something akin to love toward Ervil. I noted:

> . . . He [Ervil] doesn't even know I love him. I just discovered it about a week ago and I've been dying to tell him. But he's never around so I sit around and dream about what I'd say if he were here. I want to make up to him for all the time he's loved me and I've been indifferent. I'm gonna get him in bed and have him make love to me at least 10 times and tell me he loves me a hundred and tell him I love him a hundred times too.

In a letter to my friend Betty, about this time, I wrote that I was happy because, "I've finally fallen in love . . . I guess I finally realized how lucky I am to have a man who's so patient and under-

160

standing — a man who knew I didn't love him and it nearly killed him because he's been in love with me for years . . ."

But, just as I was finally beginning to feel I loved him, he started acting indifferent toward me. I wanted to tell him of my feelings for him, but I couldn't sit him down long enough to talk to me. He started spending a lot of time with Lynn Rodenkirk, who had come from San Diego to join us after Dean's death. Lynn and I had been friends for a long time, but when she got to Denver her attitude began to change toward me. I couldn't understand why Ervil seemed to prefer her to me, but perhaps he was simply trying to pacify her, even if it meant ignoring me. In an undated entry in my diary, I wrote:

Dear Pat,
    I've been trying for days to figure out what-the-hell's going on. I can't get *Cunado* to talk to me. I can't sleep at night because I'm thinking about it and wondering why he seems to ignore me and spend *all* his time with Lynn . . . doesn't he like me anymore? All I ask for is a simple explanation; do I have bad breath? Is her bed more comfortable than mine? Maybe he doesn't like pregnant ladies . . . or else Lynn is really something else . . . If it's my fault then, I wish he'd tell me so I could change — but he won't even talk to me — and hardly looks at me. Does he expect me to throw a tantrum and threaten to do something awful like most of his wives do? That's not really my bag. I don't think I should have to do something so childish as that to get a little attention.
    All I want to do is talk to him — or rather — him talk to me. After all, I'm a very understanding person — if he's sick of me I'll be glad to leave. The last thing I want is for him to have to force himself to be decent to me.
    I wonder if it's just a coincidence that once he found out I was in love with him he grew indifferent . . . He just walked in my room . . . rather indifferent, as usual. I'll try to keep you posted if anything happens.
    He asked me what I was writing about. I told him I was writing about him. He says "What for?" I said "because you're what's on my mind the most." He left and went back to Lynn's room.

So ended my first attempt to fall in love with the man I married.

Dayer LeBaron

Maud McDonald LeBaron

Birthplace of Ervil LeBaron at Colonia Juarez.

Brothers Joel (standing) and Ervil, Colonia Juarez.

Benjamin F. Johnson

Benjamin F. LeBaron

Ervil with first wife, Delfina, ca. 1949.

Ervil and some of his children by his first wife, Delfina Salido, ca. 1956. From left: Sarah, Lillian, Alicia, Arthur, and Esther.

The LeBaron brothers, in service to the Church of the Firstborn. From left: Ervil, Joel, Verlan, Alma, and Floren.

Ervil LeBaron

Joel LeBaron

Dr. Rulon C. Allred (middle of back row) with others at a conference in Ozumba, Mexico. Marvin L. Allred is in middle of front row.

Daniel Ben Jordan

Stephen Silver

Ervil as patriarch, Church of the First-born.

Joel F. LeBaron

Verlan M. LeBaron

Floren M. LeBaron

Maud, Ervil's mother.

Wesley LeBaron

Earl L. Jensen

Colonia LeBaron, 1981.

Ervil in custody after arrest for planning the Los Molinos raid.

Bud Chynoweth

Thelma Ray Chynoweth

Thelma Ray and Bud Chynoweth at Bryce Canyon, Utah, about a year before their marriage (ca. 1935).

At home in Utah, ca. 1960. Rena in foreground with her mom Thelma and brother Glen.

Mark, Rena, and Duane in Santa's lap, 1961.

Rena and Duane Chynoweth, Utah, 1959.

The Bud Chynoweth family in 1961. From left: Lorna, Duane, Bud, Rena, Thelma, Mark, Vic, Glen.

The Chynoweths in 1965. Sitting, from left: Andrew, Bud, Thelma, Wendi. Standing, from left: Mark, Lorna, Kathy, Glen, Robbi, Rena, Vic, Duane.

Rena's mom and dad and Harvey (Bud's son by Noemi Zarate) at Los Molinos, 1973. In background is the church/school building and the Chynoweths' home at the Bateman place.

CHAPTER 15

Name: Erin Loraine Chynoweth Brown
Date of Birth: February 3, 1976
Place: Denver General Hospital
Mother: Patty Brown
Father: Unknown

That's the way it had to be. I was not legally married. I couldn't use my real name. And I couldn't list the name of a husband to whom I wasn't legally married. In order to get Erin's birth certificate "legalized," Nancy agreed to vouch that she had delivered the baby at her home so I could list Erin's real name and mine. The only problem was that the birth certificate listed Ogden, Utah, as the place of birth, not Denver, Colorado. Nonetheless, her name would legally be Erin Loraine Chynoweth.

I was a little disappointed at first, since I had been expecting a boy. I quickly got over it, though, after seeing how beautiful she was. God had given me a seven-pound, one-ounce child and, regardless of what sex it was, it was mine. I was going to raise her as best I could.

Not surprisingly, Ervil was nowhere around when Erin was born. Coincidentally, she was born exactly a year after he and I had gotten married, but he was on the move constantly at this time. His paranoia had taken control of his mind. He never stayed anywhere too long and always took care to maintain a low profile wherever he was. But, on March 2, 1976, he was captured in Chihuahua City, Mexico.

According to the accounts I read, he was spotted by some CFB members driving around the capital city of the Mexican state of the same name. Andres was with him in the car. Siegfried Widmar and Alma LeBaron III reportedly alerted the police. Ervil was arrested and charged with murder and other crimes in connection with the Los Molinos raid. He was flown to Ensenada and thrown into jail there.

I was still living with Mom when Erin was born and, like most of Ervil's other wives, I too went on welfare soon after becoming a mother. Right after that, when Erin was only a few weeks old, I started helping the guys out around Lincoln Auto, doing mostly legwork. I would run to the bank and pick up car titles and little jobs like that. Vic was paying me about $50 or $60 a week out of his own pocket, obviously not enough to get by on with a child, so the welfare supplemented my meager income. One of my fringe benefits was that the guys bought me a car and arranged it so that I could pay it off quickly.

With Ervil in jail, we were once again pretty much on our own, although some of his older sons — mainly Arthur — went back and forth regularly to see him. They brought "messages" to us from him. Mom went down a few times, also, trying to do what she could to secure his release. A lot of the money we were making in both the appliance and the car businesses was going to Ervil's defense. He also used some of the money to pour out a steady barrage of letters and pamphlets. Around this time he had Anna Mae and Rosemary rent a post office box in South Pasadena, California, under the organizational name of the "Society of American Patriots." He began writing critical letters to well-known public figures such as evangelist Billy Graham, Pope Paul VI, and presidential candidate Jimmy Carter and his running mate, Walter Mondale.

An example of the type of letters he was sending out is appropriate here to illustrate his thought process. This one, written when Carter was president, indicates the complexity and confusion in his words, complete with errors:

Dear Mr. Carter:

The great stand you have taken in support of basic human rights and human dignity, should be supported by the power and influence of every religious organization on earth. The law of force, without educational and cultural help, has never long withstood all the pressures and negative influences, which array themselves against the basic rights and freedoms of mankind. The teaching of the truth that makes men free, should always be liberty's foremost battle line, as well as its surest source of protection and strength. It is extremely sad to say that this is not the case in America today, and the United States Government is being left, with a very small amount of real help, to carry the great responsibility of upholding freedom, in the face of overwhelming negative influences.

As the head of the only cultural and educational government on earth, that is founded solidly upon the universal principles and laws of freedom, I hereby swear before God, and all upright men, that this intolerable condition will be changed. I am calling upon all sensible people to help make this change. We are swiftly moving out with a cultural and educational program, which is now offering your government better help and stronger ideological support, than it has ever received from any other Christian organization . . .

All political traditions, as well as corrupt spiritual philosophies, that have been either ignorantly or mischieviously designed to abolish true freedom and smother it out, must now be energetically side-stepped, over-ridden, and junked. All over-spiritualized religious nonsense, that tends to prevent the United States of America from standing honorably and responsibly, as a nation under God, must be authoritatively revoked and put down. By true law it is obligatory to fulfill the foremost requirement for sustaining America as an indivisible nation under God, with authentic freedom and true civil justice for all. This must be done by establishing and carrying out the legal functions of an educational government, on the national level, by instilling the fundamental concepts and principles of authentic freedom as commanded by God, into the hearts and minds of the American people.

The second step of utmost importance, is to change all outdated, ill-founded laws, as well as inadiquate concepts relating to basic honor and legality, which hamper the nations progress and set it back, by preventing the universal principles and perfect laws of freedom from being legally and constitutionally put into effect. False concepts and unfounded traditions are the bottlenecks, which tend to throttle the government, to deprive it of its true dignity, and strip it of rightful prerrogatives. This naturally includes the basic provisions in the law of the creator that require all legitimate aspects, powers and types of government, to fully carry out their basic obligations, and yet stay within the bounds of their legitimate jurisdiction. On this basis, every department of government, as well as each individual, must be required to be subject to the natural, just and universal laws.

Because widespread teaching of corrupt religions, the nations freedom is being assailed from within, as well as from without. Many decisive aspects of the universal legal statutes, that provide for the establishment and maintenance of a just, equitable and powerful government, are not being properly upheld and carried out, which permits the enemies of freedom to take power. This is permitted to happen because so many men in government are manipulated by the false, over-spiritualized and perverted political concepts, which have been derived from the false spiritual doctrines that have enslaved the concience of nations and peoples since the Dark Ages.

What is still taking place, in regard to each one of the first six statutes, of God's civil code, due to Dark Age type political and religious traditions, is flooding the world with vice and corruption . . .

Governmental violence, of the type that is being sponsored and cloaked by churches, and through which the most radical crooked work, and types of barbarism, are being carried out, *is the type of deception which most effectively blinds the minds of the people and enslaves their concience.* This type of lawlessness should be avoided with the greatest care, because it enslaves both church and state, by making them a part of Satans army.

In order to get this diabolical flood of corruption stopped, the great banner of freedom that has been raised, must be per-fected, strengthened and purified by the establishment of the basic laws which the Creator has commanded government to put into effect . . .

The penalties affixed by God to the overt and wilfull viola-tion, of the first six fundamental civil statutes of His penal code, should help all people to learn more about responsible self-gov-ernment, as well as help them to understand the extent and na-ture of the criminality, for which the laws of God require strict punishment . . .

This widespread criminality is being employed to manipu-late, guide and influence political government, causing it to over-throw and suppress freedom by violence, tyranny and bloodshed. The four types of church treason, are four distinct methods of cul-turally and ideologically overturning the true concepts and prin-ciples of freedom, and of blasting them out of the hearts and minds of men. When government legalizes any one of these four types of conspiracy and treason, as is now happening, it is always corrupted by the illegal process of so doing. It thereby becomes an accomplice to the destruction of freedom by church power . . .

Through long years of experience, I have learned that the teachers of religion, who wilfully betray the irrevocable principles and laws of basic civil liberty, for personal gain and worldly honors, will readily committ any type of crime or wickedness that suits their ungodly purposes — if they beleive they can do so with impunity. The Smooth job of brainwashing the people and of im-posing blasphemy as true doctrine, on every decisive issue relat-ing to the God-given rights of men, has lead to the creating of false moral and legal standards, by which crime and lawlessness in many forms, is upheld throughout the Christian world, in the affairs of both church and State.

A brutish and ungodly campaing of religious tyranny, sa-tanic propaganda and political violence was covertly instigated by Mormon usurpers against me. Every effort has been made to incite your administration to commit acts of governmental vio-lence, designed to entangle the government in terrible criminal-ity. This is precisely what happens when petty officers are per-mitted to assail the legal Patriarch of the Church and Kingdom of God, persistently inventing wild charges, related to blasphemous, perverted, Dark Age concepts of the Ten Commandments. The

182

most vicious press campaign that has ever been satanically undertaken to suppress freedom and to uphold church dictators, was designed in vain to destroy a legitimate religious movement . . .

When the suppression of the primary cause of freedom is fraudulently undertaken, and the anointed servants of our Lord and Savior are the principle objects of the assault as is the case at issue, the violence attempted is an incomparably weightier offense than the acts of which the people of God are being belingerantly and violently accused. In this case our persecutors are guilty of violating every fundamental law in the book. They are drunk with lust for power and worldly honors. All of them are outright liars and hypocrits, while their malignant, false charges, constitute blasphemy. These men are crooks and thieves, who would rob entire nations and peoples by deceptively and satanically making open warfare against the laws and principles of freedom . . .

They have incited an avid thrist for innocent blood, where the crime of murder is the object and the suppression of the basic, universal principles of freedom, is the main issue. They unhesitatingly tread down the first five fundamental laws which prohibit the major crimes of church treason and conspiracy. Every effort is being made to instigate processes and strategy by which to manipulate the United States Government and to drive it into playing a major roll in governmental murder, comparable to the entrapment of the Roman Government, in the cases of Jesus of Nazareth and of John the Baptist.

I am assured that you are a dear friend of our Lord, Jesus Christ, and fully trust that you will stand with Him in upholding judgment founded upon the irrevocable laws and commandments of God, which stand forever as the imperishable foundation of the inherrent rights of all mankind. May God help you and enable you to bring the entire nations nearer to Him.

Truthfully Yours
Ervil M. Le Baron
PATRIARCH OF ISRAEL

Much has been made of these letters by the authorities and the media who perceived them undeniably as threats. The FBI, which already had a file on Ervil, continued adding to that file and tried to keep close tabs on him. I guess in their minds they had good reason to fear those they regarded as fanatical cult leaders, after one of Charles Manson's followers attempted to assassinate President Ford. But these so-called "threats" Ervil was making were overblown. They were empty threats made by a man who was in prison and whose followers lacked the know-how and sophistication it would have taken to break through a Secret Service security shield.

Ervil may have enjoyed a high success ratio when it came to blowing away those unable to defend themselves, but if he was dealing with people who might be armed, and if there was a chance he or his followers might get hurt or killed, he was smart enough to back off. That had been clearly demonstrated during the time he unsuccessfully tried to strong-arm the Kingstons in Utah. Once he realized these people were going to fight back with high-powered rifles, he kept his distance. Given that fact, it is not likely he would have tangled with the FBI or the Secret Service, whose agents are trained to subdue or kill if necessary.

While Ervil was in prison the second time, I made only one trip to see him. It was early in July, as I recall. Duane and his wife Laura were going down to see Laura's family in Ensenada, and Erin and I rode along with them. That's when Ervil saw Erin for the first time, when she was five months old.

Seeing Ervil during this time was a big disappointment for me. I hadn't seen him in some time and was trying to build up an image of him in my mind. As I noted earlier, I was really trying hard to learn to love him. But when I saw him, that image sort of fizzled out. Nothing happened inside of me. I felt none of the love I had been psyching myself up for. I wasn't excited or particularly happy to see him. I couldn't stand to look at his face. I had Erin in my arms and I just kept looking the other way while he stared at me with a sexual leer in his eyes.

Ervil had his own little room in the jail. Inside the compound there was a courtyard and there were little rooms all around the courtyard where you could close the door and have some privacy. Mexican jailers, though they may be cruel and inhuman in other ways, seemed to be sympathetic to their fellow males' sexual urges — whether prisoners or not. The men who had wives or girlfriends were allowed to have them come visit and they could have their privacy without being disturbed. Perhaps this small concession to human nature made the prisoners less rebellious and gave the prison authorities something they could hold over their heads if they acted up. I hear it cut down on the homosexual problem American jails are plagued with.

Ervil took me to his room, with Erin on my hip, and Anna Mae was with us. She took Erin from me and held onto her while Ervil led me to his bed, which was on the other side of a curtain that screened off that part of the room. I felt very uptight having sex with him while my daughter and one of his other wives were sitting only a few feet away. It made me feel dirty. Like all other times it had been with us, it was very ungratifying for me.

I stayed in Ensenada a few weeks and went to see him on other occasions, but it wasn't a regular routine with me. I had other things to do and other people to see. While we were there Raul Rios and Audrey, Vonda's daughter, got married. I met Leo Evoniuk, a convert Ervil made in jail. Leo, who was doing time for drug smuggling, would later become a key figure in the church just before and after Ervil's death.

I also saw Andres for the first time in three years. He had been arrested with Ervil and spent some time in jail, but they had to release him for lack of evidence. He seemed rather distant and troubled, as if he had the burden of the world balanced on his shoulders. He wasn't the same Andres I knew back in our Los Molinos days.

I went to San Diego a few times to see Betty, my girlfriend from high school to whom I had still been writing, and I took Erin with me. There was also someone else I wanted to see.

Michael had written to me several months earlier while he was still in Okinawa and said he was being transferred back to the San Diego area. He was stationed at the Balboa Naval Base. I went to the personnel office there and asked for him. The person I spoke to was standoffish and told me he had no way of tracing him. But a woman there overheard me and said she knew Michael. I was given directions to Michael's office, so off I went, pushing Erin ahead of me in the stroller. I went up to this small building and the door was open. The first thing I saw as I approached the door were two feet crossed on the desk, and I knew they were Michael's. I pushed the stroller up just inside the door and stood there staring at him. He was on the phone and he looked up at me.

"Hello, Michael," I said.

He continued to look at me, kind of puzzled and said, "Can I help you?" in a very uncertain tone of voice. I stood where I was, still staring at him, waiting for him to say something else.

"Michael, don't you recognize me?" I asked.

"Should I?"

At first I thought he was playing games with me, cutting me off from his life for getting married to someone other than him. It didn't occur to me right away that he might not have recognized me. After what we had once meant to each other, it just didn't seem possible. I felt like bursting out in tears. "Michael, do you want me to leave?" I asked.

"No, lady, who are you?" he stammered.

"Michael, it's Rena," I blurted out.

His expression changed as the recognition took hold. He quickly ended his phone conversation and came rushing over to me. He threw his arms around me and hugged me and apologized. I had cut my hair short and put on some weight since the last time he saw me and so he really *didn't* recognize me. Nonetheless, he said, "I should have recognized you by those big piercing eyes."

Michael and I had been corresponding on and off while he was stationed in Okinawa ("The Rock," as he called it) and I finally told him about my marriage to Ervil. In one of his letters he acknowledged, "I have lost you." But he went on to say, "I do not think it is to a better man but perhaps one who will fulfill your particular needs."

There was another person in the office, so he took me by the arm and led me outside where we could talk. Whatever we might have talked about is just a blur to me now. I was so excited to see him again. We were like strangers to each other at first, and it took a little while to relax.

That night, he and I went to a wedding while Betty and her mom babysat Erin. After the reception, we left and drove to a park.

We sat in his car talking for a while, then went out for a walk. We held hands as we strolled around and, the more we talked, the more I felt like I knew him again. It was still my same Michael, the man I'd loved. At one point he took me in his arms and kissed me, and I was very confused. I remember saying to him, "I don't understand. I love my husband but I love you too. How can I love you both?"

He would have taken me back right then and there. He told me he didn't care if I had six kids. If I ever needed him, he would be waiting for me even if it were twenty years down the road. If I ever got tired of my situation and wanted to leave, he would come and get me.

I had noticed a change in Michael and it seemed to be for the better. He had matured considerably. He looked pretty much the same, yet there was an older, wiser, more worldly quality about him. He was not as hotheaded and fiery as he had once been. He was more outspoken, more honest, and on top of that he had developed a wonderful sense of humor.

In my diary on July 5, 1976, I wrote:

> While I was around him, I discovered that I missed having someone to lean on. I thought that my life as it is was to my total satisfaction and I thought I enjoyed being so independent and self-reliable and self-motivating. I also discovered that still he owns a piece of my heart. I thought that I was over him but seeing him again made me realize this . . .

When I left San Diego, I was feeling so much better knowing that some options were still open to me. I had a man who loved me very much and would come and rescue me if ever I wanted to split from the group. It was a comforting thought.

I made the mistake of telling Ervil I had seen Michael and he hit the roof. He ordered me, in no uncertain terms, to break off all contact — whether in person, by phone, or by letter. It took every ounce of courage and strength I could muster to write Michael a "Dear John" letter that would put an end to our relationship. Ervil had made me realize that I couldn't divide my attention between two men. I had to choose the one I married. I told Michael I could never go back to the way I was and that we could never go back to the way things once were between us. I didn't want to be friends with him anymore because it would only keep the old wounds open.

I ended the letter by telling him, flat out, "Get out of my life." He did. I never saw or heard from him again.

After three weeks in Mexico and California, I went back to Denver with Duane, Laura, and Erin. I moved into a new house with Mom and got a job with a store that sold unpainted furniture. That job definitely had its fringe benefits, since I was desperately in need of some of my own furniture. I was allowed a twenty percent employee discount and got a new bed, complete with headboard, footboard, mattress, and box springs, all for under $350. I also got a good deal on a cedar chest that I still have to this day. It was in that cedar chest, many years later, that I found my diaries and letters, Ervil's pamphlets, and other memorabilia from those years I spent with the Church of the Firstborn and the Church of the Lamb of God.

Ervil was released around November 8 or 9. He had been in jail for about eight months and had gone to trial, but no one was able to conclusively prove he masterminded the Los Molinos raid in which the two boys were killed. Like they had done when he went on trial for Joel's murder, the Firstborners again paraded a steady barrage of "witnesses" to testify against Ervil. This time they included Robert Simons' widow, Samantha, and Ervil's own mother, eighty-four-year-old Maud LeBaron. They and the others gave testimony on statements Ervil had made to them or reportedly made to them that may have been construed as having murderous intent, but in the end it was all regarded as circumstantial. The prosecution had simply failed to establish a direct and irrefutable link between Ervil and the raid.

Again, there were reports of Ervil paying a sizable bribe to the judge for his release. I still don't know how much credence one should give those reports. I can't imagine where he would have come up with as much money as it would have taken to bribe his way out. Whatever the reasons, Ervil walked out of jail a free man.

On Thursday, November 11, Nancy and I drove down to meet him in Yuma and take him back to Denver with us. I wrote in my diary, on November 15:

It was so wonderful to see him again, though, at first I didn't know how to act. After all we're practically strangers. And I was a little frightened of him. I mean, how would you feel about making love with a stranger? But, by the next day I was a little more used to him and you know — he's not all that bad of a fella.

We got along better than I ever remember and I'm not sure if it's just me that's changed and can see more good things in him or if he really has become a more "aguantable" [Spanish slang for tolerable] person. I think we've both changed and mellowed out a little here and grown up there.

The poor man has the weight of the whole world upon his shoulders, plus everybody's piddly-assed disagreements and differences of opinion that are blown into full sized and overgrown — (listen to me, I sound like Cunado rattling on and on and on). Anyway, I'm sure as hell glad that the Lord's on our side or we'd've tubed it long ago.

With Ervil back in our midst, we began once again feeling a sense of direction and purpose. Throughout all our personal disagreements with one another, the deplorable conditions we lived under, the squabbles over the management of the business, and all the rest, it was hard to keep our eyes focused on the Kingdom of God and living according to His will without our leader there to give us guidance. We had gotten materialistic out of necessity, of course. After all, we had to survive this world before we could enjoy the next one. Ervil's return had the effect of solidifying us, once more, into the cohesive unit we needed to be. At least for a little while, anyway.

He was still as paranoid as always. One night, about a week after his return, he woke me up from a sound sleep and told me he wasn't safe there. It was another of the many "revelations" he always claimed to have when he was on the run. His first wife, Delfina, had just moved to Denver, and I had to get up and take him over there.

Our next move wasn't long in coming after that. This time it was to Dallas. By early December I knew it was coming and I welcomed the chance to get out of the bad scene Denver had become. Ervil's son Arthur, an illegal alien who had begun going by the name Brian Shutter, gave me this big sales pitch about how he was going to go down to Dallas and open another branch of Michael's Appliance. Dan wasn't going to have anything to do with it, Ervil wasn't going to have anything to do with it, and it was going to be run like a "real business." He was going to learn from the mistakes that had been made and not allow them to be made at the new store. And he wanted me to go in on it with him, since I had proven myself capable of handling the business efficiently before Dan stepped in.

I agreed and Ervil gave the project his stamp of approval. He'd always had this vision, anyway, of establishing some big financial empire with businesses and franchises in a lot of major cities throughout the country. Dallas, being the boom town it was in the mid-1970s, seemed like a logical place for expansion.

So Erin and I got in Arthur's truck with my few possessions and his and drove to Dallas. Erin was just beginning to walk by then. When we got to Dallas, Anna Mae was already there and so was Rosemary. Ervil showed up a little later, followed by most of the wives and kids who had been in Denver.

Dan had become a real tyrant while Ervil was in jail and apparently began enjoying the power he had over us. Even after Ervil's return, he showed no signs of calming down and relinquishing any of the power he acquired. He ended up turning everyone in the group off — except, perhaps, his own wives — and soon there was a mass exodus from Denver to Dallas. On top of that, Mark and Duane had a falling out with Vic at Lincoln Auto II, and they got fired. With their wives and kids, plus Alex Zarate and Isaac LeBaron, they also headed for Dallas.

Pretty soon it was the same thing all over again: the whole group of us living in cramped quarters, fighting each other for space and what little privacy we could attain. We were crowded together in a few small houses, no money for food and other necessities because Ervil was taking it all, and we had to resort to "gardening" and "gift boxing" again. So much for starting a new life.

In Dallas, we managed to find a large warehouse that was ideal for our purposes. I was more or less the office manager, in charge of keeping the books, paying the bills, directing the service calls, and such. Arthur was always a rather pompous individual whose attitude was difficult to deal with and he and I had some run-ins, but Lloyd, who had also come down from Denver, managed to keep him in line.

But Arthur was never one to stay out of harm's way. He did some stupid things toward the end of the year that could have brought the law down on all of us. In Denver we had three new converts: Lloyd's nephews, Dave and Robin Sullivan, and a friend of theirs named Jack Strothman. They'd had some kind of a falling out with Arthur about something I can't recall now, and Arthur must have insulted them. The two Sullivans and Jack got fed up and left, returning to Indiana, where they had come from. But they had with them a refrigerator they took from the house Arthur was renting. Arthur had told them to go ahead and take it, despite the fact that it belonged to the landlord and not him.

In addition to that, Arthur had skipped out without paying his rent. So the landlord notified the police and Jack, Dave, and Robin were arrested with the stolen refrigerator in Indiana. They were thrown in jail and must have started talking to the authorities about our group. The next thing we knew the police were calling Lincoln Auto and asking Vic a lot of suspicious questions. In the end, no real harm was done. But it could very easily have ended up that way. As was the case in Denver, and in Utah before that, we were trying to maintain a low profile and not attract any unnecessary attention to ourselves. Not long after that, Ervil sent Arthur and his mother, Delfina, to open a "branch office" in Jackson, Mississippi.

As 1977 began, we were getting settled into Dallas and Ervil and I were at war again. I had just gotten myself to the point where I was beginning to tolerate him, if not outright love him, but he started treating me like dirt and ruined all I had been working up to. In my diary, on January 2, I wrote:

Dear Pat,
    What a way to start the new year! Things were really bad between *Cunado* and me when he left here about two weeks ago. When he left I wished he'd never come back. Now, all I want to do is try and get our differences straightened out. He doesn't understand me as a person and, of course, he's not interested in the

things I'm interested in, but I don't expect that much of him. It sure would be nice though if we had a few things in common. I just wish that what little time we have together could at least be enjoyable but he ruins it for me by bitching about little piddly-assed things that don't matter. But, no — he has to spend all the time we have together grinding and grinding and grinding and grinding on me about unimportant, stupid things like: not having towels in the bathroom and his socks weren't in his suitcase and not taking an exit from the freeway that was marked different from what it said on the map I was reading. I mean . . . I can't even hardly talk about it without my eyes starting to sweat . . . He just grinds and grinds on me to where I just can't handle it. I start getting bitchy and start to hate him.

Since he left this time I've talked with Anna Mae — but that didn't do all that much good because she has a very weird philosophy about those kinds of things — so submissive. She says to let it go in one ear and out the other, but I can't *do* that! I get ground and ground on enough down at the office without coming home to a bunch more cheap shots . . .

. . . Sometimes I think a divorce is the best answer because I don't think he can or will change. And if I continue feeling the way I do now then it is the only answer. He's practically killed anything I might have felt for him — and unless some small miracle happens, I doubt that will change . . .

I had never been much of one for drinking, but one night, after Ervil and I had another one of our battles, I stormed out and hitch-hiked across Dallas. I made my way over to our warehouse where Mark, Ed, Arthur, Lillian, and a few other people were. They had a bunch of beer and I was determined to get drunk. It was only the second time in my life I'd ever gotten drunk, and it would be the last. I'd had just about all I could handle from Ervil and everyone else by this time, and getting drunk seemed like a nice little escape.

Not being an experienced drinker, I didn't know how to conduct myself and it must have become apparent I couldn't be left alone. I remember jamming with Mark and singing and playing the drums, and I fell off the stool in the middle of a song. Everything else was a blur after that. Ed sat up with me all night and I poured my heart out to him about the way Ervil was treating me. I told him I was too young and too horny to be living alone. Ed was always a good listener and, deep down, he was a very sensitive and caring person. He promised me he would talk to Ervil about the problems we were having. I must have said a few other choice things that I can't remember. Ed never would tell me what they were.

A few weeks later, Ervil came back from wherever he had gone at that time and we sort of made up. He said he now realized how sensitive a person I was and he would try to be less condescending toward me. I told him I would try not to be so bitchy. We sort of left it at that but, as always, he was never around long enough to put his new attitude into practice.

Things weren't going well for me at all at this time. I had been working twelve hours a day, seven days a week, and had to put up with crap from everyone — especially Arthur. I had come down from Denver with him with high hopes for a successful business, and we were making a lot of the same mistakes we'd made in Denver — or worse. Then Duane, of all people — the one family member I'd been closest to — started getting weird on me. He wanted in on the business and, naturally, I was agreeable to that. However, it wasn't long before we were feuding about God-knows-what. I think after working for Vic he had gotten this attitude that women shouldn't be in business. The end result was that he was in and Rena was out. He managed to convince Arthur and Ervil to let me go while he stayed on. To this day, I can't figure out what got into Duane at that time. I know he was going through some bad times, but so were the rest of us.

Drummed out of the business a second time, I was again sentenced to babysitting detail. At the time I was living in Anna Mae's house, and we were again packed together like sardines. In addition to Anna Mae's nine kids, there were Mark and Lillian and their kids, John and Betty Sullivan and their two kids, Delfina and one of her younger kids, and Erin and me — all in a three-bedroom house.

At other times we would have Linda and Rosemary and their kids. All these kids to take care of but, unlike the previous time, I had one of my own so I guess that made it a little more tolerable. It gave Erin and me a chance to get reacquainted. I had been working so many hours that I hardly got to see her for a long period of time. There were times when she wanted something and would go up to Anna Mae, saying, "Momma." That's how well my own child knew me during that time.

Having four or five of his wives living under the same roof made it pleasantly convenient for Ervil. Three of them, Anna Mae, Linda, and Rosemary, not only shared the same house, but the same *bedroom*. Whenever he wanted one of us he would just call us into the room and send everyone else packing. It was like an Egyptian harem: when the sultan beckoned, you submitted and put your body at his disposal. None of the other wives, at least not that I can recall, ever minded or complained about this arrangement. I did, however. More often than not, when he beckoned I told him to kiss off.

One such incident, in particular, really stays in my mind. We were all sitting in Anna Mae's living room having a meeting (one of Ervil's many "military emergencies" or "economic emergencies," I don't recall which) and the guys were jumping all over him about meddling in the business. Rather than respond to them, Ervil leered across the room at me with sex written all over his face. He stood up and sort of strutted over to me like a rooster in the barnyard, as if he wanted everyone to know what was on his mind. He grabbed my hand and said, "Good night, everybody," then he started leading me away.

Unlike his other wives in the house, I had my own bedroom and Ervil pulled me in there. I was never so embarrassed in my life — nor was I ever so indignant. There we were in the middle of a meeting that *he* had called and now he was acting crude, like an animal in heat, unable to restrain himself. Nothing subtle about it.

I turned on him with more venom than I had ever spewed out at any time in my life. "Don't you ever, *ever* act like that again!" I spat out. I was furious and offended that he would think I was so cheap as to just submit to him like some mindless concubine, especially after a public display in front of all those people, some of whom were my own brothers. I don't remember what else I might have said to him, but he was surprised that anyone, let alone one of his own wives, could stand up to him so boldly. I didn't care. I wasn't about to be treated like some cheap piece of trash.

I grabbed a pillow and a blanket and stormed out of the room. I started to curl up on the floor in the hall, right outside my own bedroom, but he came out and dragged me back in the room with him. He had embarrassed the hell out of me but he wasn't about to let me embarrass *him,* especially in front of all his followers. He didn't dare let anyone get the impression that he couldn't control me like he could his other wives. He needed to save face and at least create the impression that we were sleeping together that night, even though I didn't let him touch me. Finally, he got the message and left. So ended another day in the married life of Mr. and Mrs. Ervil M. LeBaron, the thirteenth.

And then there were the times when things actually got vicious between us and physical force came into play. I don't recall what led to it, but one night I'd had about all I could take from him. I had so much anger, hostility, and resentment building up inside of me that I just wanted to beat the hell out of him. I came charging at him, swinging away. He took a swat at me with the back of his hand and knocked me backward. I came back at him and he swatted me again on the side of my head. This happened a third time and he busted open my lip. Finally, I came to my senses and realized when to quit. I raced out of there.

The first person I thought to call was Lloyd, who was almost like Ervil's personal counselor, in the absence of Dan. Lloyd gave me a warm, supportive ear and more or less pacified me, but I don't recall him doing any more than that. Everyone knew I was miserable in my married life and they didn't need the situation explained. It was my problem and I had to deal with it the best I could.

The happiest times for me were those times when Ervil wasn't around and I didn't have to deal with him. Somehow, I had always known it would come to this.

CHAPTER 16

Between February 21 and June 30, 1977, I made only one entry in my diary and it was of little importance. There was a reason for this. I wanted to leave no written record of our activities at that time that could later incriminate us.

With no written record of this period, I have to rely solely upon my memory to piece together the details of a very complex sequence of events leading up to and following the murders we plotted and carried out in the spring of 1977. Many of those details are a blur to me today and others exist in fragments, since this is also a period I have consciously sought to block out of my mind for many years afterward. However, I do recall enough to tell this story "from the inside," as a participant, rather than as a detached reporter of the events.

The name Dr. Rulon Clark Allred meant nothing to me when I first heard it mentioned at a "military emergency meeting" Ervil held with us in Dallas on April 20, 1977. It would soon mean a great deal to me and a burden I would carry with me my entire life.

This particular meeting didn't seem, at first, any different from all of the other "military emergencies" Ervil was in the habit of calling. He felt a compulsion to keep the paranoia going, to continually spark the fear about how the Firstborners were going to get us if we didn't get them first. During these meetings there would be a lot of talk about how much money we needed for weapons and ammunition and other things necessary to fulfill Ervil's prophecies. In one of Ervil's supposed "revelations" a few years earlier he had prophesied how all false prophets and apostates would be stricken down in a given period of time, I think it was about thirty-nine months. There was something in the scriptures he used to come up with this time frame. In any case, this would have put the date at May 3, 1977, and that date was fast approaching. Ervil had to make good on his prophecy or risk losing some of his key followers.

Don and Lloyd, in particular, were always on Ervil's case about when something was going to happen. Those two were the most militant of Ervil's followers, and they had the effect of galvanizing some of the others into action. After being goaded for so long, Ervil must have finally decided the time had come to make another strike.

The year before had been a relatively quiet one, especially since Ervil spent most of it in jail. The men who liked the action they had seen between late December 1974 and mid-1975 began to get edgy and impatient for more of the same. It wouldn't be long before they would see it.

For five years, ever since Joel's murder, Ervil had been obsessed with killing Verlan. "The Snake," as Ervil called him, was not making himself an easy target as Joel had been. Verlan was constantly on the move, constantly looking over his shoulder, and, like Ervil, never stayed in one place too long. In order to get Verlan into the open where someone could get a clear shot at him, Ervil knew he needed the right bait. A funeral, much like the aborted one he had planned for Rhea Kunz, would do it. But, since Mrs. Kunz was out of the question, he needed another sacrificial lamb. That's where Dr. Rulon C. Allred came in.

This particular meeting, where the plans were hatched, was held at Mom's house. Mom had just moved to Dallas from Denver. At this meeting, besides myself, Mom, and Ervil, were Vic, Don

Sullivan and his wife Noreen, John Sullivan and his wife Betty, Lillian, Ed Marston, Isaac and Paul LeBaron, Alex Zarate, Lloyd Sullivan, Guillermo (Bill) Rios, and I think Duane and Laura and Dan Jordan. Some of the children were present as well, but I don't recall who else.

Vic spoke first, giving what we called his "North, South, East, and West" speech. In his pep talk, Vic reminded us that the police were getting onto us and we had to do everything we could to protect our leader. If any of us were questioned, we were to be as uncooperative and evasive as possible. If the police asked where Ervil went, and if one of us said north, another said south, and another said east, they might conclude that he went west. Under no circumstances were we to give them any information that could be used against us.

After Vic finished speaking, all the women were ordered out of the room so the men could meet alone. I got up to leave with the other women but, just as I did, Noreen, Lillian, and I were told to stay and everyone else was sent out. We were told that this "great mission" had to be done, this "great prophecy" had to be fulfilled, and "the Lord wants this person eliminated." It was the same thing Ervil had said about Joel and had been saying about Verlan — that this person was leading the people astray, he was a false prophet, the Lord had commanded it, and he absolutely had to be done away with. Also, this would be the ideal way to get Verlan out into the open. That's when I heard Rulon Allred's name for the first time.

Rulon Allred was a naturopathic doctor living in the Salt Lake area. At seventy-one years old, he was the patriarch of a fundamentalist polygamous sect second in size only to that of the Kingstons. His United Apostolic Brethren denomination had about two thousand followers and Allred himself had eight wives and forty-eight children. The Allreds and the LeBarons went back a long way together and, at one time, the Allred family lived in exile in Colonia LeBaron. Though he was considerably older than Ervil, Allred had known him from those times back in Mexico in the 1940s. There is no record of any animosity between them. Allred and his family were on the run, having been arrested and persecuted in Utah for his polygamous lifestyle. Later they returned to Utah and, though what he was doing was illegal, the authorities more or less left him and the others alone. There were far more serious criminals to investigate than polygamists, especially since most of them were peaceful, productive, law-abiding citizens.

Allred was not a doctor in the technical sense of having all kinds of medical degrees, internships, residencies, certification, and all the rest, but he apparently had an expertise in natural remedies for treating ailments. He dispensed no drugs nor performed surgery but treated patients with herbs, home remedies, and faith. He had quite a following among his patients, most of whom were also fundamentalists, and he took little, and sometimes no, money for his services.

For years, Ervil had cast covetous eyes on the Allred faction in much the same way he had with the Kingstons. Unlike the Kingstons, however, Allred and his people were not armed. Ervil called on Allred and his high-ranking officials a number of times and demanded that they tithe to him, and each time Allred would politely refuse. They were a peace-loving group and Ervil could offer them nothing they didn't already have. They didn't go for the fire and brimstone routine, nor did they recognize his claims to the priesthood.

Rulon Allred was also Rhea Kunz's brother, making him kin to Verlan (who was married to Allred's niece). He and Verlan had been very close, despite presiding over two different sects. Ervil correctly assumed that killing Allred would bring Verlan to the funeral where he, too, could be killed. Allred was not the main target but, according to Ervil, he was a false prophet like Verlan, and so he deserved to die as well.

Getting back to our meeting in Dallas, Lillian, Noreen, and I were there in the room with Ervil, my brothers, and the other men. Ervil said he needed two women volunteers to do the job and asked for nominations as to whom he would send. One of the books written about the LeBarons said the two women should be the prettiest in the group and it might have been that way. I don't recall the exact words spoken that night. In any case, Lillian's name was the first to come up but she was pregnant and ruled out immediately.

Noreen, I thought, was also prettier than I but her name never even came up. Ervil had his mind made up ahead of time and it was silly and pointless to even ask for nominations. He knew whom he wanted to carry out this deed for him.

I was surprised, to say the least, to hear him mention my name. Mine and Ramona Marston's. If there had been a beauty contest between Lillian, Noreen, Ramona, and me, Ramona and I would have come out third and fourth. So I think Ervil was trying to flatter us with his bullshit. Whatever the case may be, whatever his reasons, Ramona and I were to be on his next "hit squad." Our target was Dr. Rulon Allred.

Ramona was in Denver at the time of the meeting and had just given birth a week or so earlier. She was married to Dan, and Dan must have had this worked out with Ervil ahead of time. He obviously had no objection to his wife going out on a kill, along with the wife of the man to which he was second in command.

Ervil and the other men present at the meeting told me what a "great honor" it was being picked to go on this mission and I would be blessed beyond my wildest dreams. This was my ticket to the Celestial Kingdom. I was virtually guaranteed entry into it. Then we got into the particulars. Ervil spelled out what this mission would accomplish in terms of getting "The Snake" out into the open where the guys would be waiting for him with loaded weapons. Verlan was to be killed at any cost, even if it meant taking a few innocent bystanders with him.

We were then placed under "military emergency" and ordered to hurry up and get the money together we would need to carry out the mission. Don was placed in charge of the Verlan "hit squad" and given his instructions on how that end of the plan would work. Don then picked the ones he wanted to go with him and he chose his cousin John and Ed Marston. Ervil, however, threw a new twist into the plan by ordering another squad to go down to El Paso and stake out Siegfried Widmar's house, in case Verlan holed up there instead of going to Allred's funeral. John was reassigned to that mission, along with Mark and Duane. Jack Strothman was assigned to the Verlan hit team as John's replacement.

While all this was going on, I was more or less in shock. But when I realized that I was picked over everyone else in the group, I almost felt a sense of honor. Our leader had chosen *me* to do this great deed, and now I felt like I had some sort of a purpose in our group. It needs to be remembered that, for a long time, I had felt almost unwanted and nonfunctional within the organization. No one was giving me any important responsibilities, other than watching the kids, and I felt almost like a parasite. Now, at last, I was being entrusted with this sacred mission, even though it would involve killing someone. I didn't object.

Then, after our initial plan was discussed and laid out, Ervil sent us all home. The Allred killing was supposed to happen on May 3 — still a few weeks away. Before we could do that, however, another gruesome task had to be carried out.

Ervil's daughter Becky, as I mentioned earlier, was given to Vic as a plural wife. Not only was she more than a little on the flaky side, she was actually dangerous to the security of our group. She was mentally unstable and schizophrenic and couldn't be allowed to walk around unsupervised. Becky must have gotten the worst of the genes on both sides of her family. There was mental illness on Ervil's side, as witnessed through his brothers Ben and Wesley and sister Lucinda; and Becky's mother, Delfina, was also a bit schizy herself.

In any case, Becky would do stupid things like get caught shoplifting and give the police our names and addresses. She also had bizarre visions like going to Hollywood and converting Farrah Fawcett-Majors and Lee Majors, stars of two of TV's hottest shows at the time. She was regarded as a loose cannon on deck, one that could swing around the wrong way and fire the shot that would sink the whole ship. There was constant fear among us that she was going to drop the nickel to the police about our Salt Lake mission or some other hit we had pulled off. Something had to be done — and soon, according to the militants among us.

To this day, I'm not certain exactly what Becky knew. But she must have known enough to pose a real threat to expose us. She was in the room when Lloyd brought the news about the Robert Simons killing in 1975, and she probably knew some other potentially incriminating things. How much she knew about our plans to get Verlan in Salt Lake, again, I'm not certain, but it would be a safe guess she knew enough to send us to the gas chamber for at least one or more murders.

Pressure began to be exerted on Ervil to "do something about the Becky problem," and the pressure was coming primarily from Don and Lloyd. They kept hounding him, day after day, and Ervil didn't want to do it at first. After all, crazy or not, Becky was still his daughter. It's one thing to order the murder of someone you don't know well or even a brother, but one's own flesh and blood? Ervil was attempting to draw the line there but, unfortunately, his most fanatical followers wouldn't allow him to do that. Becky had to be done away with if the mission was to be a success, Ervil was repeatedly told.

I was there when the order came down. It wasn't at a meeting or any other public setting. I just happened to be in the house at the time while Ervil was in his bedroom. Don and Ed were standing around the living room door while Lloyd shuttled back and forth between them and Ervil. Lloyd would exchange a few words with Don and Ed, go into the bedroom and converse with Ervil, then come back and tell the other guys what they had discussed. It was obvious to me what — or rather, who — was being discussed. Finally, Lloyd came out of the bedroom nodding to Don and Ed. I didn't actually hear Ervil give the order but I knew Becky was doomed when I saw Lloyd nodding like that. Without a word, Ed left to take care of the business at hand.

That night, Ed managed to lure Becky into a car that was being driven by Duane. Becky was told she was being taken somewhere — no one knows quite where, since there are no surviving witnesses. She might have been told they were taking her to the airport. But, in any case, it was never their intention to take her anywhere but to her death. Ed got in the back seat with her. While Duane drove along, Ed slipped a strong rope around Becky's neck and pulled tightly. Becky must have fought back hard because, as Ed told me years later, she was very difficult to finish off. His arms and hands began hurting from the strain. "Duane, I can't do this," he said. "It's too hard. Help me out." While still driving, with one hand on the wheel, Duane reached into the back and helped Ed pull one end of the rope until Becky finally succumbed.

They pulled off the road to a secluded spot, carried Becky's body to the trunk, and drove back to show Ervil. Looking into the trunk at the lifeless body of his pregnant, eighteen-year-old daughter, Ervil was satisfied that the job was done. But he bitched about the blood on the mats in the trunk. Her nose was bleeding from the pressure the rope exerted around her neck and it had dripped onto the floor of the trunk. Fearful that the blood could incriminate them, Ervil later ordered the floor mats burned.

Becky's corpse was taken into a remote woods and Ed and Duane buried her there in an unmarked grave. Some accounts say the guys had a tent set up and, while pretending to be camping, they actually dug her grave under the tent. I don't know if this is the way it went or not. I never bothered to ask Ed for details. Just hearing him talking about pulling the rope around her neck was gory enough for me. In any case, her body was never found and she was officially classified as just another "disappearance."

Looking back now, as was the case with all the murders, I see it as totally senseless. Someone in Becky's frame of mind should have been put in a mental hospital and given some kind of help. She'd had a lot of problems heaped upon her at too early an age and she couldn't handle them well. She was only about fifteen when Ervil pushed her into the marriage with Vic, and she didn't want to go through with it. In the space of just a few months, she went from being a quiet, mousy sort of person to an obnoxious loudmouth. When she started saying and doing bizarre things, Vic and his first wife, Nancy, would criticize her. No one knew quite what to do with her, and Vic didn't handle her too well, either.

Nonetheless, neither she nor any of the others deserved to be killed, but at the time we had been convinced it was God's will. Ed told me he felt that he was "putting her out of her misery," and that she needed to be eliminated for reasons of "military necessity" and security. Those were the kinds of things we simply weren't questioning. It wasn't done out of hate or because the guys enjoyed killing; it just simply *had* to be done.

Some people might say we were "brainwashed," and perhaps, in one sense we were, but it went deeper than that. Many of us had been raised within the LeBaron churches since we were very young and we knew no other kind of life. If we objected to what Ervil was commanding us to do "in the name of the Lord" and decided we didn't want any part of it, where could we go? We knew nothing else. We had almost no choice but to stay and be a party to what was going on. And, if we tried to defect, that might have brought a death sentence down on us as well.

Despite this ever-present threat of reprisals, however, Mom had strongly stated her objections about his plans for Becky — to no avail. Then she and Duane tried desperately, on two occasions, to convince Ervil that his militaristic control was not only unscriptural but didn't work. He ordered her killed but, of course, he didn't follow through. Then he ordered Ed to kill Duane. Ed may never have disobeyed an Ervil command before that time, but this was one order he absolutely refused to carry out. He and Duane were the best of friends. Ed told Duane about it and the two of them skipped town for a few days, trying to give Ervil time to come back to his senses. When they returned, nothing more was said about it. Ervil needed every available male body he could muster up for this next assignment. He must have realized that.

As May 3 approached, the militants got even more edgy. They kept asking Ervil, "When is something going to happen?" Ervil knew we weren't going to be ready by that date. We still didn't have the money together, or there may have been some other reason. So, to keep the momentum going, he would make excuses like "the Lord still hadn't said when to strike" but he assured them it would be soon. Finally, around May 5 or 6, we set out on our mission.

Don and I drove due west to Albuquerque, New Mexico, and spent the night there in a motel — in separate beds. We went shopping around for disguises we could wear when we made the hit, but we didn't find anything there. Then we met Ervil and Anna Mae and I went north to Denver with them. When we got to Denver I went to Michael's Appliance and picked up Rosemary's station wagon, which was still registered in Dad's name with Utah plates. I also met Ramona who, by this time, had been briefed on her assignment, and we also got the gun Nancy bought — a .38 special.

We didn't stay in Denver long. Ramona and I headed for our prearranged rendezvous point, the little town of Evanston, in the southwestern corner of Wyoming. From there it was a straight, ninety-mile shot into Salt Lake City. When she and I arrived, just outside of the city, on the night of May 9, everyone else was already there, holed up in a couple of motel rooms: Ervil, Arthur, Don, Ed, and Jack. We had a meeting in which we went over the plan again and then there was a pep talk, but it was the same thing Ervil had always been telling us — that it was the Lord's work, and so on. I didn't stick around too long, as I recall. I was exhausted after my long drive and I hit the sack immediately, sleeping all the way through the night.

The next day, May 10, 1977, we awoke and got ready to set out for Salt Lake. Ervil told us he was really proud of us and God would be really proud of us. We prayed together and asked for God's help on this important mission. Ervil kissed me goodbye and we were off. Ramona and I went in the station wagon; the guys took off in the other car. Ervil stayed behind with Arthur to await word on developments.

On arriving in Salt Lake, Ramona and I checked into a motel and the guys went to another. We were all using assumed names; mine was Patty Sanders. We got together, drove to the salt flats west of the city, and test-fired the guns. Don wanted to make absolutely certain they were in working order. Then we went to a second-hand store, Deseret Industries, and bought some wigs, clothing, jackets, and other disguises to wear.

I guess the realization of what we were about to do must have begun sinking in by that point because I remember becoming absolutely terrified. I was shaking uncontrollably. The hit was to take place in Dr. Allred's office in the Salt Lake suburb of Murray, Utah, and I knew where it was. I had been shown maps and given a description of him, so I knew where we had to go and what our target looked like. There was no turning back now, and my anxiety was getting the better of me.

Don saw how nervous I was and he came up and put his arm around me, assuring me it would be all right. God was with me and it was okay to be a little nervous, he said. "You'll be all right. Don't worry," he kept reassuring me.

At some point, I don't recall exactly when, I took the station wagon over to a gas station to get it inspected. The sticker had expired and I couldn't risk getting stopped for an equipment violation. The car passed inspection with no trouble.

Later that afternoon, Ramona and I went back to our motel room to await further orders. I tried to rest but, exhausted as I was, I was still too nervous and keyed up to get any sleep. I can't remember if we had a prearranged time to meet with the guys or if we went when they called. We knew they had to go out and steal a couple of pickup trucks and get everything set up to carry out our plan. We had it worked out so that we would leave the station wagon parked a short distance from the doctor's office and Ramona and I would drive over there in one of the pickups. The other truck with the guys in it was to stay behind in the same place the wagon was parked, outside a Skaggs luncheonette.

As we arrived in the rendezvous parking lot near the doctor's office, about 4:45 that afternoon, Ramona and I were already in our disguises — jeans and T-shirts, and we both wore short, curly wigs that were different colors than our own hair. The guys handed us our guns — the .25-caliber with a clip for me and the .38 for Ramona. They gave us a few words of encouragement, and sent us on our way. By prearranged plan, they were to sit there at the rendezvous point and wait for us to finish the job, then they would take our weapons and clothes and we would all scatter in different vehicles.

After driving up to the doctor's office we parked around back and walked inside. In his reception area, there were chairs lined up along two walls. There were three other people in the waiting room, a man sitting by himself and a couple who looked like they were married. Ramona went over and sat down next to the lone man, while I walked over to the glass cubicle where the office was and peered inside. The door was open to the section of the doctor's office leading to the examining rooms in the rear. As I looked through the door, Dr. Allred was coming out of one of the examining rooms.

He was exactly as he had been described to me — tall, slender, gray-haired — a nice, pleasant-looking man. He came toward me, nodded, then turned to his right and went into a little laboratory area with a sink behind the door where I was standing. He was no more than three to five feet away from me. I knew the moment had come to do what I was sent there to do.

Reaching into the pocket of the blue parka I was wearing, I pulled out the gun and fired at him. There were seven shots in my clip and I emptied it. I heard him gasp, "Oh, my God!" once as he fell to the floor, bleeding. It all happened so quickly.

Ramona continued sitting there for a few more seconds. Allred's wife Melba, a nurse, came running in after hearing the shots. "What are you doing? What do you think you're doing?" she shouted. She grabbed for me but I shook her off as Ramona got up and walked toward the door. When we got outside, I didn't know if he was dead and I told Ramona to go back and make sure. I was out of bullets.

Ramona went back in with the .38 and a man named Richard Bunker, who was there on business, grabbed her. As they struggled, I saw what was going on and rushed over. I pointed my gun right at his head. Seeing my weapon inches from his face, Bunker's eyes grew wide with fear and he pleaded for his life, saying he had kids. He let her go, not knowing my gun was empty, but he somehow managed to get us out the door and slammed it. He held the door for a few seconds, then raced toward the back of the room and ran into the bathroom. Ramona fired two wild shots with the .38 and we prepared to get out of there. During the struggle, however, some things had fallen from Ramona's purse and, apparently, out of Bunker's pocket as well. Not wanting to leave any possible evidence behind, Ramona and I quickly gathered up everything that dropped, including a pocket calculator belonging to Bunker. Then we made a hasty exit.

Walking quickly around the side of the building to the back, we drove off to meet the guys who were waiting in the other stolen pickup truck. Ramona and I took off our wigs and the jackets we had worn with our disguises and handed them, along with the guns, to the guys. They asked how it went and we said, "Fine." I don't recall any other discussion about the incident. Ramona and I got in the station wagon and took off, heading straight for Denver, doing the speed limit all the way. We arrived between ten and eleven hours later without incident.

The guys were under orders to stay abreast of the funeral plans for Allred. Then, at the appropriate time, they were to cruise by, keep an eye out for Verlan, and hit him on first sight. If he was in a crowd, they were to spray it with bullets if necessary — whatever was necessary to make sure he was dead. If any innocent bystanders got hit, they too deserved to die, according to Ervil. If they had to go inside to get Verlan, they were required to do it.

The guys were also in charge of disposing of the clothing Ramona and I wore and other evidence, including the boxes the weapons came in, but they carelessly pitched them into a dumpster. These items were found a few days later after an investigation into the Allred murder had gotten under way. Later on, they would find their way into a courtroom — to be used as exhibits in a murder trial.

CHAPTER 17

If our primary goal that week of May 1977 had been to kill Verlan, then the mission was a failure. Verlan did, indeed, show up at Rulon Allred's funeral on Saturday, May 14, but so did thousands of other mourners. And so did the police and the media. Security around the funeral was so tight and there were so many television crews present that Don, Jack, and Ed simply lost their nerve. They cruised by the funeral site with weapons loaded and ready but, apparently, Don saw how foolhardy it would have been and called it off. By this time I was back in Dallas.

The Allred murder made national headlines. Newspapers and TV news reports speculated on all kinds of motives in the beginning. Feuds between rival polygamous sects, jealousy among the wives, and even drugs were all suspected in the early part of the investigation. But eventually the trail of blood led to Ervil LeBaron. No fewer than a dozen state, local, and national investigating units were called in on the case and the conclusion was inescapable: Ervil LeBaron had struck again. The manhunt was on.

Two days after the murder, Ervil crossed the Mexican border with Arthur behind the wheel. The rest of us who weren't living in

Denver converged on Dallas. After our long drive from Salt Lake, I dropped Ramona off in Denver and went to Vic and Nancy's house. Ervil had earlier told Nancy to move to Dallas and she had her possessions packed when I arrived. I drove straight through to Dallas with one of Nancy and Vic's kids in the car with me, taking No-Doz pills like candy to stay awake. I had gone a week without much sleep and was in a daze much of the time. Nancy followed behind me in another car with the rest of the kids. When I got to Dallas I was exhausted.

So much of what happened in those few days is fuzzy in my recollections. I had done a traumatic thing. Despite assurances from Ervil and the others that it was God's will and the right thing to do, I still couldn't shake the feeling that I had done something horrible. No longer was I just an informed bystander; now I was an active participant. I don't recall discussing the incident with Vic or Nancy or anyone else prior to my arrival in Dallas when I told John Sullivan about it.

By this time, the story was in all the papers. During our drive down from Colorado, Nancy and I stopped to get something to eat in a small town in Oklahoma and there was a story in this little country newspaper about a polygamist doctor being murdered in Utah. Two unidentified young women were being sought in connection with the crime. Even though I was too numb with shock to register any emotion, it was incredibly frightening to know I'd committed a crime that made national headlines.

I stayed in Dallas a couple of weeks to rest. To have stayed any longer would have been risky. The investigation was closing in rapidly on Ervil LeBaron and his followers. With Ervil down in Mexico, a leadership vacuum was created and Lloyd rushed in to take command. Here, again, events get blurry, but the next thing I recall was being whisked off to Jackson, Mississippi, where Mom had moved not long before. Ervil ordered her to move because of the way she spoke to him over Becky's murder. I took Erin, who was only fifteen months old, and went with Lloyd and his wife Bonnie and their little girl, who was about Erin's age. We stayed at Mom's for about a week, as best I can recall.

Lloyd suddenly decided he was a prophet and started writing.

I typed and proofread for him and we started getting to know each other more intimately. He flattered me, telling me how "wonderful" I was and things like that, and he also began confiding in me. Very few of Ervil's followers dared to question his claims to prophecy. If they did, it wasn't done openly, especially not to one of his wives. That could have proven to be a deadly mistake for anyone doing the questioning because these things had a way of getting back to Ervil quickly, whether he was around or not. But Lloyd knew I wasn't like the rest of Ervil's wives, so he started opening up to me. He said Ervil must be a false prophet, since the prophecy Ervil made hadn't gone down the way he said it would. It was obvious he was becoming disenchanted with Ervil's leadership and was in the early stages of making a break from the group.

Lloyd was also coming on to me pretty heavy. Despite his wife being there, he still made advances toward me. Lloyd and Bonnie were staying at a house not far from Mom's. He would come over to Mom's as often as possible and we'd work in the living room. He was always finding ways to ditch Bonnie and take me along with him to the store or wherever. He never made passes at me in front of Bonnie, but she still suspected something was going on. She was very jealous and ugly toward me.

Lloyd began telling me his life story, about the failure of his first marriage, and lurid details related to that. Then he would tell me how "desirable" I was and it made him sad that I was unhappy with Ervil — something he had long known because I had confided in him previously. As I mentioned earlier, he was the first one I went to for consolation after the time Ervil hit me in Dallas. Lloyd seemed to know all the right buttons to push and he preyed upon my vulnerability.

There were times Lloyd put his arms around me and tried to kiss me, but I didn't want to get involved with him or anybody. I made that clear but it took a lot more than that to deter him. Later on, he started having these bizarre "revelations" about me and he would tell me about them. During an odyssey that took us to Indiana and back, he told me that if I would go to the top of a mountain and declare to God that I was divorced and free of Ervil, we could marry ourselves in the sight of God, right there on the mountain.

Of course, I balked against that idea.

Another time, as we were driving along, he had a "revelation" in which he saw me in a long, beautiful white dress. "Of course, a wedding dress!" he cried out. "That means you're supposed to marry me!" I never did let him seduce me, but he got awfully close. By this time, I had decided I wanted out of the marriage to Ervil and I talked freely about it with Lloyd. I guess, because of that, he thought it was open season on me, and he tried to present himself as a better alternative. He would be more attentive to me and my needs than Ervil was, or so he said.

While we were still in Jackson, Lloyd placed a call to the shop in Dallas. I don't know whom he spoke to but he was advised that we should stay in hiding. The gun Nancy bought for the Allred murder had been traced to her and she was arrested. The police had come by asking for me. We decided to leave Jackson and headed north. We stayed with one of Lloyd's nieces for a few days somewhere along the way to Indiana. Later, when we moved on again, Bonnie rented a trailer in some small town, paying for it with a hot check.

While we were in Indiana, Lloyd talked to Don in Dallas and was told there was some kind of an emergency they needed me down there for. I would be told what the "emergency" was when I got there, but Don also wanted to get me away from his father. By this time, Lloyd had told Don he wanted to marry me after I divorced Ervil and Don was perhaps fearful for him — if not for both of us. Don had seen firsthand what Ervil's wrath could bring down on those who opposed or crossed him and he knew where the line should be drawn — even if Lloyd didn't. He was perceptive enough to see that Ervil might have nominated him to kill his own father and Don did not want to be put in that position. So Lloyd drove me to the airport and I flew down to Dallas where Don met me. That was the last time I ever saw Lloyd.

It has always amazed me to read someone else's interpretations of what was going on at the time. In *Prophet of Blood*, a book written about Ervil in 1981, authors Ben Bradlee, Jr. and Dale Van Atta said that Lloyd and I were having an affair. I was embarrassed and disgusted when I read that. It's true that I had seriously considered what it might be like being married to him. He had a lot of the qualities I liked in a man and, since he was one of Ervil's "chosen men," I figured (wrongly, of course) that he could be God's "second choice" for me. It was like a rerun of the same feelings I had for Dean Vest. I was looking at Lloyd as an escape from Ervil. *Anyone* was more appealing and attractive than Ervil, as far as I was concerned.

But as far as going to bed with him, I never did. I was raised on the Ten Commandments and taught that adultery is a very serious crime. If I hadn't had these teachings so firmly instilled in me, I would have taken advantage of the many opportunities that came my way over the years. While it's true I might have been in love with Lloyd — or at least *thought* I could love him — I still had to keep beating off his advances. I had no intention of sleeping with anyone while I was still married to Ervil.

In *Prophet of Blood* it was said that Bonnie acquired a tape recording I made in which I talked about Lloyd and I getting married. As I recall, I borrowed Lloyd's cassette player and a blank tape while we were staying in the rented trailer. I didn't have my diary with me and needed to air my feelings. I talked into the tape in much the same way I would have written to "Pat" in my diary. On the tape, I expressed my feelings for Lloyd and said how happy I could be if I was married to him. Apparently, it must have fallen into Bonnie's hands. But the book also said there was a second tape, one Lloyd made for me. I have no recollection of that.

When Don and I got to Dallas, he took me in hand and warned me not to get involved with his father. Don was scared over what Ervil would do if he found out. He told me that if I was unhappy and wanted to divorce Ervil I needed to go to Ervil and ask him myself to end the marriage.

The "emergency" Lloyd and I were told about was that Ervil had called and wanted to see me. I needed to leave for Mexico immediately. I don't know why he considered it so imperative I get down there. Perhaps he'd heard rumors about Lloyd and me and thought he had to keep a close eye on me. In any case, I made plans to join Ervil in Mexico but I only packed enough clothes to last me a week. I was going to demand a divorce and that was all the time

I planned to spend down there. Little did I know it was going to be a lot longer than that.

I left Erin with Mom, who had moved back to Oklahoma City, and Anna Mae drove me down to Monterrey, Mexico. I didn't expect Ervil to give me any problems over the divorce. I was certain that, for all the trouble I'd been to him, he would want it that way also. That would have been the end of it and I could get back to living my life the way I wanted to — or so I thought.

Anna Mae took me to where Ervil was staying and left us there alone. Right away, he started in about Lloyd, indicating that he suspected something was going on between us. Someone had obviously told him, perhaps Don or Anna Mae or one of the other people. He called Lloyd "worthless" and a few other choice names that I can't recall now. I didn't do anything to deter his suspicions when I told him I wanted to divorce him so I could marry Lloyd.

It must have been more than his ego could handle that I should want to leave him for one of his underlings. He started in on me with one of his sanctimonious speeches. He told me I was "in a state of apostasy" and that I needed to "straighten up." We were married for "time and eternity" and I could not get a divorce. If I didn't straighten up I would end up in hell. All my blessings would be taken from me, he said in a threatening way.

I don't remember anything else I might have said to him on hearing this but I felt defeated. I was rebellious and hateful toward him but he broke down my resistance to him. He convinced me I had no options but to stay. I cried over the prospects of being stuck with him in Mexico with no money and having to go through the same scenes I'd gone through with him so many times before. On July 9, 1977, I wrote in my diary:

Dear Pat,
    I'm in Mexico now and things are very different from what I thought they would be.
    I've found out that a celestial covenant cannot be disavowed. That God is the only one that can change that. It was a hard blow and one I didn't accept right away. And it hurt . . . I swear I'll *never* again let my emotions lead me. I just wish I could get my emotions to go where they're supposed to. It's been hard to get in

the right frame of mind and try to disentangle my emotions.

That was my last "Dear Pat," for quite awhile. It would be ten years before I wrote another. Ervil ordered me to stop keeping a diary around this time and I obeyed him. He was afraid I would say something incriminating, and he didn't want any written record of his or my activities. I was now without the imaginary confidante I'd had since I was thirteen years old.

From Monterrey we took a bus to Mexico City and then went on to a small village outside Cuernavaca where he had a place rented. He told me he needed me there to help him with his writing. The whole business with Lloyd and the fact that I had told him I wanted a divorce was forgotten. As willful and headstrong as I am, I sometimes find it hard to believe that he could have controlled me, but he did, and he was able to do it by using God as his ally. He knew he could get me in tow by threatening me with my salvation, and though that was all he had over me, it was all he needed. Salvation was *everything*.

Despite our differences, despite our frequent battles, and despite my outright hatred for him as a person at times, he was still our leader. He was still the prophet and patriarch we called upon to intercede with God for us. We had to obey him if we were to continue to enjoy God's favor in this life and the next. Those were the strings he kept us on to dance to his tune. That was the one thing he could hold over our heads. I could kick and scream all I wanted at him personally, but when he brought God into it, I was humbled. So, what had started out to be only a week in Mexico ended up being sixteen months.

Ervil had a pretty nice little house, by Mexican standards, with a small swimming pool and a few other amenities. Once I got settled in I wrote a letter to Mom. I knew at that point I was going to be in Mexico longer than expected and I gave her instructions on taking care of Erin. I wrote down for her a list of sounds Erin was making to indicate what she was trying to say — the sounds she used to ask for food, milk, diaper, etc. I also told Mom that if I was there more than another three weeks, Ervil said I could have Erin brought down. We eventually ended up doing that.

Ervil was doing a lot of writing and preaching to the natives in

and around the states of Morelos and Puebla, although I don't recall us making any significant converts among them. These were
people whose loyalties could be fickle. Ervil said he needed me to
do his typing since he didn't have anyone else who could do it. I
had never been a good typist before but, out of necessity, I got better. Ervil had me typing day and night on his pamphlets. Some of
them were both in English and Spanish and I had to translate
them. On one in particular, I spent two weeks laboriously translat-
ing while he was off somewhere on a mission. When he got back he
said, "Well, I wasn't going to use this anyway." Both versions,
English and Spanish, went in the garbage can. I was furious.

Ervil also had me type long, convoluted letters to President
Carter and Vice-president Mondale, expounding on his doctrine
and interpretations of biblical prophecies. Knowing Carter was a
born-again Christian, Ervil perhaps thought he had a receptive au-
dience in the White House. His letters were never answered by the
president.

With none of his other wives there, I had Ervil all to myself
but, as had been the case on similar occasions, I didn't *want* him all
to myself. I didn't want him *at all*. Having him alone didn't improve our relationship or my feelings for him. Every time I thought
it would improve, I was only deluding myself. He held me captive
with this "time and eternity" business, a prospect I began regarding as more and more frightening. It was bad enough I had to stay
with him in this life, let alone the next which went on infinitely.
Again I felt trapped, despairing, and resigned to accepting a fate I
never wanted.

There were times I thought about sneaking off and hitchhiking
back to the States, but I only had ten dollars to my name. And,
though I fantasized about escaping, I was frightened about what
could happen to me. My mind flashed back to the rape attempt
three years earlier and I knew it could happen again if I was out on
the road alone. Also, Ervil never left me in the house by myself.
There was always someone around when he was gone and he
wouldn't let me go into town. He was paranoid that someone would
see this "*gringo*-looking person" and our safety would be endan-
gered.

I thought a lot about Lloyd and even wrote him a "Dear John" letter (Dear "Doidy," actually) explaining my predicament and the overall situation. I began to worry that, because of his feelings for me, he was condemning himself to share the fate of Dean Vest. I don't know whether or not Ervil hatched any plans to have Lloyd eliminated, but it wouldn't have surprised me if he had. By this time, back in the States, Lloyd was publicly calling Ervil "a false prophet" and pulling himself, Don, and John out of Ervil's church. This was precisely the type of thing Ervil ordered people blown away for and I was fearful for them. Ervil still had Arthur doing his bidding, and Arthur had never liked Lloyd. He would have been only too happy to do the job for Ervil.

During the time we lived in the village, other family members came and went frequently. Arthur came down a few times, and so did Andres, and Raul and Gamaliel Rios. Ervil felt he had a great mission to perform among the Mexican peasants and apparently he was using Arthur, Andres, and the Rios brothers to help make converts. Whatever success they might have had was minimal at best. There was no great flocking to his church that I can recall.

When I met up with Ervil in Monterrey it was the first time I had seen him since leaving Wyoming on the Allred hit. During that time and afterward we never discussed the murder, even though he asked me for the details. It was a closed subject as far as I was concerned — a "top military secret." Then I found out that he was bragging and telling the Rios brothers and other followers about it.

It was a sly little comment Gamaliel made that tipped me off. He said something to the effect that I "hated doctors," and I knew at that point that he knew something. I demanded that he tell me what he knew and he said Ervil told him about the Allred murder.

"That son of a bitch," I thought to myself as I flew into Ervil's room, where he was holed up writing, and confronted him. "How dare you tell anyone!" I screamed at him. "That was a top secret mission. That's why I didn't tell you any details because you have a big mouth and can't be trusted, "You . . . you . . ."

He looked at me with a half-smile on his face and wasn't apologetic at all. He told me he was busy and to leave him alone. Then he simply turned away and continued writing. It was several days before I calmed down.

During the time we stayed in the village, I managed to keep myself very busy. In addition to typing, I was also training two secretaries, giving English classes, and doing most of the cooking, cleaning, and laundry. I was a hair stylist and beauty consultant, a swimming instructor and lifeguard, and a bunch of other things.

I remember being impressed by the sincerity of the Mexican converts Ervil did make and the fact that they weren't caught up in the materialistic traps in which we Americans so often found ourselves. They seemed so much closer to God than we were, perhaps because of their characteristic humility and the simplicity of their lives. Ervil saw it as critically important that we get the pamphlet out that we were working on because it would tell the Mexicans the rights they were entitled to and perhaps encourage them to fight for those rights. In a sense, he was encouraging them to rise up in revolt against those who were oppressing them, but with as few followers as he had, it was hard to take him seriously. A few fanatical peasants wouldn't have stood much of a chance against the Mexican army. At least that's the way the authorities must have looked at it.

Back in the States, the investigation into the Allred murder and the others was beginning to close in on Ervil's followers. Led by Dick Forbes, a special investigator with the Salt Lake County Attorney's Office, and his brother Paul Forbes, a sergeant with the Murray Police Department, the pieces of the puzzle were being fitted together and they pointed heavily in the direction of the Chynoweths. Vic, being the most visible member of the group, had a known address and a listed phone number in Denver. Dick Forbes tried pressuring him to talk. He was talking to the wrong person. Vic was not only uncooperative, he was openly hostile toward the police and encouraged the rest of us to be uncooperative as well. Nonetheless, Vic was the best lead they had. They continued to harass him and staked out his house and business.

Nancy was in Dallas, where I had helped move her right after the Allred hit. A neighbor in Denver had told police they saw her moving and they put two and two together to figure out she was in

Dallas. From the clues found in the dumpster which Don had disposed of after the Allred murder, the investigators traced the sale of Ramona's .38 special to Nancy.

Nancy was arrested in Dallas on May 22 and charged with conspiracy to commit murder. She was flown to Salt Lake, where she was interrogated and locked up. At first, investigators thought she might have been one of the women who walked into Allred's office on May 10. However, one of her kids' teachers vouched that she'd had a conference with Nancy only an hour or so before the murder took place, 500 miles away. Nancy was ruled out as a murder suspect, but the conspiracy charges stuck for a while longer. Vic bailed her out on May 26 and took her back to Denver with him.

Then the investigation centered on the younger boys. Somehow they were able to follow leads that enabled them to take Isaac and Paul LeBaron into custody in mid-July. Neither of the boys would talk at first, but eventually Isaac told what they knew about the April meeting in Dallas where the Allred/Verlan LeBaron murder was planned. Without all the details, he still ended up giving the investigators plenty to go with. They had the names of Don Sullivan, Ed Marston, and Jack Strothman to follow up on. And they had mine.

Through license plate number checks, motel registration cards, handwriting analysis, and other clues, Dick Forbes and his investigators were able to place me at the motel where Ramona and I stayed just before the Allred hit. The car was registered one digit off on the plate number, and the phony name I used on the motel registration was traced to me by a handwriting expert. All of these clues pointed toward the involvement of Rena Chynoweth LeBaron.

The next phase of the investigation centered on Jack. Dick Forbes and two of his top investigators flew to Indiana in August and were able to track him down to a gas station where he worked in Indianapolis. Jack willingly filled them in on more of the details, explaining what his role was supposed to be in the hit on Verlan. He told about the rendezvous with Ervil in Evanston and details on how Verlan was supposed to be knocked off during the Allred funeral.

However, when first questioned, Jack reportedly could not remember the name of the man they were supposed to kill. Forbes ran several names by him and when he came to the name Merlin Kingston, Jack said that's who it was. Since their first names rhymed, Jack apparently thought Kingston was the target. It took investigators awhile to determine that it was Verlan, not Kingston, whom Ervil wanted killed.

Jack also told them he and Don and Ed had taken off the clothes they wore after deciding to abort the mission and threw them, in a bag, into the same dumpster they had disposed of the other evidence. From that bag and the items in it, the police also isolated Don's and Ed's fingerprints. Jack also reportedly told Forbes that I talked to him about the Allred murder shortly after he got back to Dallas and that I said something like, "I'm glad he's dead." I have no recollection of that conversation, even though I did talk to John Sullivan about it.

By mid-September the Forbes brothers and Salt Lake County Assistant Attorney David Yocom felt they had enough evidence to secure arrest warrants from a Salt Lake County judge. The warrants were for myself, Ervil, Arthur, Vic, Nancy, Mark, Don, Lloyd, John, Ed, and Ramona. A day or so later, Vic, Lloyd, and Ramona were arrested in Denver, and Mark was taken into custody in Dallas. Conspiracy charges against Nancy had been dropped more than a month earlier, but there was reportedly a stipulation that she could be rearrested on those or other charges if the evidence pointed in her direction. On being informed in September there was a warrant out for her, Nancy worked through an attorney to arrange her surrender.

Dan was also arrested in Denver but, since he wasn't linked to the conspiracy, he was held on a minor charge. Dan had apparently dodged the draft in his native Oregon and was flown to Portland where he was jailed for a few days. Police knew he was sought in connection with Joel's murder and held him while awaiting a decision from Mexico whether or not to extradite him. The word came in that Mexico did not want to extradite him and the draft evasion charges were dropped, so Dan was released.

In early December, Lloyd, Vic, Nancy, Mark, and Ramona were taken into court for a preliminary hearing. Yocom presented testimony by Richard Bunker, the man who had been in Allred's office at the time of the shooting, and Melba Allred, the nurse who tried to grab me. Apparently, neither of them were able to describe Ramona or me accurately. Jack and Isaac also gave testimony that led the judge to bind everyone except Nancy over for trial. The prosecution's case was reported to be weak in a few key areas, but apparently the judge must have felt there was enough evidence to proceed. He did, however, set bail at a level Lloyd, Don, Mark, and Ramona could afford and they were released pending trial.

By this time, Lloyd had decided to defect from Ervil and he was communicating peace offerings to Verlan. According to what I have heard and read, he wanted to repent for what he had done while a member of the Lambs of God and hoped that Verlan would rebaptize him into the Church of the Firstborn. He was reportedly convinced that Ervil was a false prophet, an agent of the devil, and other such allegations, and he seemed anxious to unburden himself of the guilt he carried for the five years he stayed with Ervil. In February 1978 he began writing to John and Don, apologizing for having brought them in, and he asked them to defect also. Then, later that month, he arranged a meeting in Denver with Verlan. That's when everything came out.

On February 13, under heavy security, Verlan flew into Denver and met with Lloyd in the lobby of the hotel where he was staying. Lloyd treated him to dinner in the hotel's restaurant and they returned to the lobby, where Lloyd began telling about all the murders, from Joel through Allred. He also identified who the murderers were. Later that evening, after their meeting was finished, Verlan wrote extensive notes which he passed on to the investigators in Salt Lake. Among the disclosures Lloyd made to Verlan, and later to the authorities themselves, were the following:

— The raid on Los Molinos had been carried out for the purpose of flushing Verlan out and killing him. When that failed, several other plots were hatched to ambush him but these also failed.

221

— Vonda White shot Noemi Zarate to death outside of Ensenada in January 1975.

— Lloyd was among those assigned to kill Rhea Kunz to lure Verlan to the funeral, where he would also be killed.

— Lloyd had been responsible for luring Robert Simons to his death on April 23, 1975, and he named Ed and Mark as his accomplices.

— Vonda White shot Dean Vest to death in San Diego on June 16, 1975.

— Lloyd had been primarily responsible for getting Ervil's consent to have Rebecca Chynoweth done away with and that she was strangled to death by Ed Marston and Duane in April 1977.

— Lloyd had written threats on Ervil's stationery to Rulon Allred two years prior to the murder and he knew of Ervil's plans to kill members of the Allred and Kingston factions.

— The primary purpose of the Allred murder was to lure Verlan out in the open and kill him.

During his meeting with Verlan, Lloyd also reportedly gave intimate details on some of Ervil's "military strategy" meetings, most of which I and the other women were not allowed to attend. During these meetings, Ervil reportedly spoke about "the law of the .38" and used such phrases as "hot lead and cold steel" as the means of disposing of his enemies, as well as keeping his own followers in line. Giving someone a "one-way ticket to hell" was reportedly another expression Lloyd said he'd heard Ervil use. The media, which had been almost continuously reporting on the events surrounding Ervil, picked up on these phrases and had a field day with them. Somewhere along the way, the expression "blood atonement" came out, although I don't recall Ervil ever using those exact words.

Lloyd later repeated his statements to the FBI and other investigators. On March 23 he took authorities to the approximate spot outside Wellington, Utah, where Simons had been killed, but he couldn't remember exactly where the body was buried. It was located after an intensive search and then underwent forensic examination. Based on their findings and Lloyd's confession, investigators in Carbon County began building a murder case against some of our people.

Eight days later, based on Lloyd's statements, Vonda was arrested in Denver and flown to San Diego, where she was charged with Dean's murder. Don and John Sullivan had been arrested in Kansas City in the early part of March and they, like Lloyd, became willing, cooperative witnesses for the prosecution.

While all this damaging information was coming out, Lloyd, Mark, Vic, and Ramona were out on bail. Ramona decided to jump bail and she fled to Mexico. Mark also skipped out, taking a flight from Dallas to Merida, Mexico. That left only Vic as a likely candidate for standing trial because the Sullivans were now turning state's evidence and plea bargaining with the prosecution. Lloyd was flown to San Diego in late April to testify at Vonda's preliminary hearing. His testimony resulted in the judge ordering her held over for trial.

On May 25, Lloyd died of a heart attack at the age of fifty. By that time, however, the damage had been done. The authorities had all the information they needed to draw up a full indictment against us. On July 14, 1978, David Yocom went before Judge Paul Grant in the Fifth Circuit Court for Salt Lake County and had four counts of murder, attempted murder, and conspiracy to commit murder brought against Ervil, myself, Don, Ed, Ramona, Arthur, Mark, Vic, and John. This was all in connection with the murder of Allred, the attempted murder against Verlan, and conspiracy to commit murder against both of them.

I was still in Mexico with Ervil. I didn't know much about what was happening to the others; in fact much of what I've related I had to piece together from the public record and other accounts. I was blissfully ignorant and it was probably just as well. I don't know what I would have done if I knew other people were taking the heat for me. I don't even know how much Ervil knew, but he was undoubtedly kept abreast of developments. He talked to Dan frequently, usually about sending him money for his missions, and Dan must have told him what was going on. He was also calling Oklahoma City, where Mom and Duane had moved to set up a shop. He was undoubtedly aware of the big manhunt under way for him.

I tried to make the best of the situation I found myself in, being sort of confined to this small village with Ervil and the others. I believed in the mission he was carrying out among the peasants and I attempted to reaffirm my own faith in his doctrine. And I had Erin to take care of and keep me company. About a month after coming to Mexico, I had arranged to have her brought to Brownsville, Texas, and I took her across the border with me. She was a year and a half old, walking and talking a little, so she was a handful to keep tabs on. Ervil had one of his mothers-in-law, Señora Rios, living with us, along with a pre-teenage granddaughter who survived the accident that killed both of her parents, Nephi Marston and Eulalia Rios. Señora Rios and the granddaughter took over the cleaning and babysitting while I did Ervil's typing.

But the stability we enjoyed those first few months didn't last long. Ervil's paranoia took over again and he said we had to leave: "They" were closing in on us. It might have been that he didn't pay the rent. In any case, we had to hit the road — a fifty-two-year-old man, his nineteen-year-old wife, and their year-and-a-half-old daughter. Arthur and the Rios brothers also traveled with us on and off and later Ed came down to join us. As we traveled about, we would go to Evangelical Christian temples, as they were called, and Ervil would play the visiting hot-shot church leader. After he preached, the congregation would take up a collection so we could have food and a place to stay. This went on for months and we lived like nomads — fugitives, actually.

On occasion, Ervil would go off for days at a time and leave me and Erin stuck in some pastor's house. The native townspeople lived in unimaginable filth and poverty, sometimes in bamboo shacks with palm leaf roofs and dirt floors. Flies were everywhere. Sometimes whole walls would be solid black with them. These people barely had enough to feed their own families one meal a day, let alone taking on a boarder with a young child.

Fortunately, Erin was a resourceful little girl who was able to use her good looks to her advantage. She was cute and blonde and most of the people we lived among had never seen a child that fair-skinned before. I would pretend not to notice as she wandered around, going up to people's tables or houses where they were cooking, and saying, "I hungry." They would take one look at her and say how cute she was and give her some beans or tortillas or whatever else they were making. At least she was being fed.

This odyssey went on for about a year. We'd spend a few weeks here, a few months there, a few days in another place. I was expected to be the submissive handmaiden to Ervil and his brothers-in-law, Gamaliel and Raul Rios. I had to cook for them and wash their clothes on a scrub board, which I wasn't used to doing. It would take me hours to do all their clothes. My wrists hurt for years afterward (eventually I had surgery done on my right wrist). The Mexican women, who were used to it, occasionally came and helped me out. They could do this onerous chore in ten minutes or less.

I suffered a traumatic miscarriage during this time also — for which I got no sympathy or understanding from Ervil.

And so it went throughout the rest of 1977 and much of 1978. We were a church on the run. Never in one place too long, constantly on the move, disoriented, and unstable. Finally, we settled into the town of Catemaco in the state of Veracruz.

Ervil rented the two upstairs apartments of a fourplex — one for Andres and his wife and kids and the other for Vic and Nancy and their five kids. Ervil had somehow convinced Vic to leave the States, where the police and FBI were constantly harassing him. Vic sold his share of the auto partnership and they left. But for Vic, who had never lived in Mexico before, it was traumatic and disillusioning. Ervil ripped him off for all the money he could get, saying he was going to use it to buy property but using it for other things.

Finally, after about six or eight weeks, Vic became disgusted and left, taking Nancy and the kids with him. He told Ervil he never wanted anything more to do with him and they didn't tell anyone where they were going. Apparently, he felt that a better fate awaited him in the States, despite the murder and conspiracy raps he faced.

After Vic moved out of the apartment, Lorna moved in with

her flock of eight kids. I was living in a house we rented about two miles away with Señora Rios and her husband and granddaughter. Anna Mae Marston left her kids there with us, and she had about five or six kids — some of her own and some of Ervil's recently-deceased second wife, Marilu Vega. I still had Erin with me and, by this time, I was again pregnant.

The little town of Catemaco was rapidly becoming the international headquarters for the Church of the Lamb of God in Exile. Ervil called for Dan and he flew in from Denver.

It was late October 1978. My flight from justice was about to come to an end.

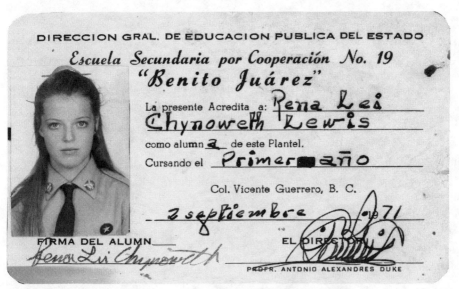

Rena's student identification card, 1971 (age thirteen).

At San Diego, ca. 1973. Back row, from left: Duane, Rena, Yolanda Rios, and Lorna. Lorna's children are (center) Mo and Tarsa; (front) Natasha and Andrew.

Rena's senior portrait, 1973 (age fifteen).

Mark's rock group, The Believers, 1967. From left: Humberto, Mark, and Seco.

Rena's brothers, Vic, Mark, and Duane, 1973.

Duane fooling around, 1974.

Michael Barnes and Rena in San Diego, 1973.

The day of Mark and Lillian's wedding. Front row from left: Lillian, Lorna, Dad, Mom. Back row: Mark, Rena, Duane, Nancy, Vic, Kathy, Glen.

Lillian and Mark on their wedding day.

Ervil and daughter Lillian, 1974.

Lillian and Mark, 1973.

The Mark Chynoweth family at home, spring 1988. In less than a year, Mark would be murdered and Lillian dead by suicide.

Mark Chynoweth on Father's Day, 1988, just before he was killed.

Mark and Lillian, spring 1988.

Duane and first wife Laura, 1974.

Duane and Lucy Chynoweth, spring 1988.

Duane and Lucy with his daughters, from left, Jenny, Cristie, Lauralee, and Angie. Both Duane and Jenny were murdered not long after this photo was made.

Duane Chynoweth, 1986.

Duane and Mom, 1988.

Jenny Chynoweth, a few weeks before she was killed.

Rena and Ed Marston, Houston, 1980.

Ed Marston, two months before he was killed, 1988.

Aaron Morel (Mo), Ervil and Lorna's second son, 1989.

Aaron (Mo) LeBaron with beard.

Monique, Ervil and Lorna's third daughter, 1989.

Patricia LeBaron, Ervil and Marilu Vega's second daughter, 1989.

Linda Johnson, Ervil's eighth wife, 1989.

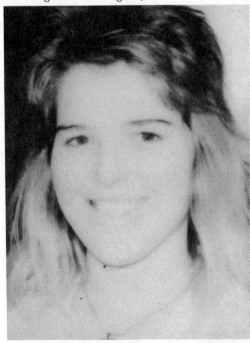

Natasha, Ervil and Lorna's second daughter, 1989.

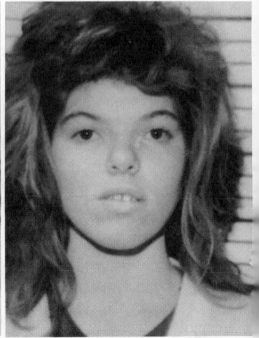

Jessica, Ervil and Lorna's fourth daughter, 1989.

Joshua, Ervil and Lorna's fourth son, 1989.

Jared, Ervil and Lorna's third son, 1989.

Norma, Ervil and Teresa Rios' second daughter, 1989.

Danny, Ervil and Yolanda Rios' son, 1989.

Rena's attorney, John O'Connell.

John O'Connell, attorney-at-law.

Mom with her adopted kids from Dad's marriage to Noemi Zarate, 1978. From left: Paul, Harvey, Judy; Johnny in back.

The day Rena's children, Erin (left) and J.R. (center), were adopted by John. His daughters Sammi and Sandy at right.

CHAPTER 18

On Halloween night, 1978, some callers came to the door. But it wasn't kids trick or treating. It was the *federales*, coming to arrest us.

I had been at Andres' apartment typing until late and I was so tired I fell asleep on a blanket on the floor of one of the bedrooms. At around one or two o'clock in the morning they came bursting in without warning, five or six of them, brandishing automatic weapons. It was one of those nightmarish scenes that freezes the blood in your veins — waking up to the crashing of a door being busted through, hearing shouts, and seeing armed men pointing machine guns at you. It was like Nazi Germany. They were wearing street clothes and they tore through both apartments, ordering us to stand up and raise our hands in the air.

I had on a pair of baggy pajamas I had borrowed from someone and I couldn't raise my arms without the bottoms falling down. It was a very uncomfortable situation. Andres' wife, America, was very hostile and defiant, telling the *federales* they had no right to be there and that they had better be careful with me because I was pregnant (about three and a half months, to be exact). They de-

242

manded to know who I was. I tried to hide my wallet with all my papers in it under a quilt, but they saw me. They opened it up and saw my driver's license and other ID and I matched the description they had on a wanted poster that also had pictures and descriptions of Ervil, Mark, Ramona, and others.

America demanded that they allow me to put some clothes on and they agreed. She held up a blanket and I got dressed behind it, then the *federales* handcuffed me with my hands behind my back and led me outside. They put me in their van, tied up my feet, and left me there all night. I don't know what they were doing all that time. There I was, locked inside a van with my hands shackled behind my back and my feet tied up for about five or six hours. I do know that they ransacked the apartments, taking anything of value they could find, even though we didn't have much. This wasn't evidence they were gathering up; they were actually stealing. They tried to steal Lorna's car but it wouldn't start. So they loaded everything up in Anna Mae's car, which I had been driving, and stole that.

They also brought Dan out, handcuffed, thinking he was Ervil. Even though the two of them didn't look anything alike, they still thought they had the notorious Ervil LeBaron in custody, and Dan didn't say anything to deny it. The *federales* had actually seen and questioned Ervil when they broke into Lorna's apartment and, amazingly, he was able to convince them he wasn't the man that they were looking for. They drove off to Mexico City with Dan and me, leaving Ervil — the mastermind of the whole works — safely behind.

The previous evening I had worked with Ervil on one of his pamphlets. It would be the last time I ever saw him.

When we got to Mexico City we were led, blindfolded, through a building. Though I couldn't see anything, I could hear the man leading me being addressed as *Comandante*, and that sounded pretty scary. Still thinking that Dan was Ervil, they put us in the same cell, a room about six feet long by four feet wide. Along one of the six-foot walls was a cement bench. Dan let me sleep there while he crashed on the floor. We spent only one night in there together. When the *federales* found out Dan's true identity and that he wasn't married to me, they moved him into an adjacent cell, a room about the same size which he was forced to share with two other male prisoners.

When I was interrogated in the *comandante*'s office, I laughed in his face, telling him, "You had him [Ervil] right in your grasp and you didn't even know it and you let him go. That just goes to prove we're right and you're wrong and God is on our side." He got very angry, knowing that they'd just been made fools, and I backed down. No telling what they might have done to me if I remained testy and defiant.

I spent a week in that cell, which was located on the rooftop of the building. For short periods of time they allowed me to walk around on the roof for exercise, and they would bring food to me. I wasn't treated badly, maybe because I was pregnant, but they did try to spy on me through a little window in the door while I bathed. Dan didn't have it quite so good. He and the prisoners he shared the cell with were kept blindfolded and handcuffed nearly the entire time. He looked absolutely horrible — unwashed, unshaven, his clothes filthy, and the little hair he had left was sticking out all over the place. He was transported to Ensenada to stand trial for Joel's murder around the same time I was being deported to the U.S.

I was blindfolded again as they led me out of the building and was driven to another building, where I was finally met by someone from the American consulate. I had been accused of being in the country illegally. I explained to the man from the consulate I *was* legal and that my passport and other papers had been taken away from me when I was arrested. The man said there wasn't anything he could do for me, but he did call Mom in Oklahoma and told her I was okay.

From there I was taken to a detention center where other illegal entries were incarcerated. I was held there for five days while the authorities tried to track down Erin so she could be brought to me. After my arrest, America had gotten on a bus and taken Erin to Lillian, who was with Mark and their kids in Merida. I had asked her to do so. The police went to Mark and Lillian's, picked up Erin, and brought her to me at the detention center.

Erin and I were put in some kind of a police car, along with a long-haired American man who was also being deported. It was a two-day drive to the border. When we got to Nuevo Laredo, I was told to get out of the car at the bridge over the Rio Grande and walk across. With Erin in my arms I began walking and, halfway across, the U.S. authorities were waiting for me.

The FBI, deputies from the Webb County Sheriff's Office, and others were on hand to make the arrest. I was informed of my rights and handcuffed. TV cameras, newspaper photographers, and reporters were all over me but I didn't have anything to say to them. Mom had come down from Oklahoma City and she took Erin from my arms. I said a few words to her, I don't remember what they were, and then I was put in a patrol car and hustled off to the Laredo jail.

My reputation as a murderess must have preceded me. When I arrived at the jail, the matrons in the women's wing were scared to death of me. I was put in a cell by myself and watched carefully from a safe distance. Little did these women jailers know that I was more scared of them than they were of me.

After getting to my cell, I was told someone wanted to talk to me. I was led to a separate room and came face to face with David Yocom. I had heard Ramona tell about how he hassled her during an interrogation, but for some reason I didn't remember that at the time I met him. He asked me if I knew who he was and I told him I'd heard the name before. At first, I thought he was one of the guys on our side. If he had played his cards right, he might have gotten me to disclose some information, but he started telling me what he knew about our group and said someone was going to go down. I knew then and there he was going to be prosecuting us, so I told him I had nothing to say and started to walk out.

"I don't care," he replied harshly. "You don't have to talk but you have to sit there and listen."

Then he proceeded to lay out the whole scenario in front of me, probably trying to scare me into doing or saying something that would save my own skin. It was obvious that Ervil was the big fish he was after, but he would still do his best to put the rest of us away also. He told me they had the Sullivans ready to testify against us and it would be in my best interest to cooperate with him.

I had not, as yet, spoken to an attorney who could advise me on my legal rights. But I knew from Ervil and Vic that you did not talk to the authorities. I kept my mouth shut and let Yocom do all the talking. When he left, he had nothing from me he could use in court other than what he might have known already.

I was arraigned the day after my arrest. Steve McCaughey, the attorney who was defending Vonda in California, met me in the courtroom. I was advised to waive extradition, which paved the way for me to be transported to Salt Lake City, where I would stand trial along with whichever of the others were in custody. Mom and Erin were in the courtroom and, just before they left for Oklahoma City, I gave Mom instructions on what Erin's needs were. I kissed them both goodbye and cried, knowing it might be some time before I would see my daughter again. It turned out to be about five months.

Ed had been captured in Mexico several months before me. Steve was his attorney, also, and I guess that's how he knew about my arrest. He would later defend Ed during the trials for the murders of Robert Simons and Rulon Allred.

I was flown to Salt Lake City by a federal marshal and his wife on November 18, 1978. I was handcuffed the whole time. Security precautions were taken, and I was isolated from the other passengers. We had to wait until everyone was off the plane before we could get off ourselves, and I was handed over to the custody of the Salt Lake police on my arrival.

When they put me in jail, I got the same reaction I got in Laredo: everyone was afraid of me. A big matron called for someone to help her search me, and two big trustys with bulldog-like faces came in but kept their distance from me. They had no idea how scared I was of them.

Within a day or two, I was forced to go through a police lineup. There were about five or six others in the lineup with me. Richard Bunker and Melba Allred, two of the people who had been in Dr. Allred's office the day of the murder, came in to try to identify me. However, they were unable to pick me out from among the others.

I was taken into the courtroom a few days later and met the attorney who would be defending me, John O'Connell. He had been appointed by the court in the absence of any available public defender. John looked like anything but an attorney on first glance. He was tall, long-legged, bearded, and looked out of place in a suit. In street clothes he would have easily passed for a hippie or a yippie. I sat there while motions were made and John was officially asked by the judge if he would represent me. He agreed and, after all the legal business was done, he came over and introduced himself. I don't remember what else might have been said at that time.

John came to see me frequently in my cell and we would go into a little visiting room for private meetings. He tried to get me to open up to him, but I was still scared and distrustful of anyone in authority. I was especially afraid to discuss our doctrine and beliefs with him because I was afraid he would be skeptical. He couldn't have been too encouraged by any of our initial meetings, but when I talked to Mom on one of my weekly phone calls, she advised me to cooperate fully and openly with him. From that point on I did.

He advised me on how to prepare for my defense and outlined what his game plan would be in defending me in court. Because of attorney-client confidentiality, I cannot elaborate on the particulars of our discussions, but I did get assurances from him that he would defend me to the best of his legal abilities. And I knew I was in good hands. John had been the attorney for mass murderer Ted Bundy, and though he lost that case — a kidnapping charge — it was the *only* capital case he ever lost.

The date of my booking into the Salt Lake City Jail was, coincidentally, the same day the news broke about the People's Temple tragedy in Guyana. A California congressman and an NBC News crew investigating the Jonestown cult had been murdered under orders of the Reverend Jim Jones. When the authorities went to Jonestown to arrest Jones, they found that over 900 people had committed mass suicide, including Jones. Right away, there were inevitable comparisons made between Jones and Ervil, and anti-religious cult feeling was at its peak. The news media was filled with stories about the Jonestown massacre, and the LeBaron cult was getting the same airplay. They attempted to lump us into the same general category, despite the fact that Jones' followers were completely held captive by their leader while we were not. There were other scriptural differences between us and the Jonestown people as well, but the media didn't appear to see it that way.

A month or so after my arrest, Mark flew back to the States and turned himself in. Ed was in jail, charged with the Simons murder, and his trial date was set for late January. Despite being an accomplice, Mark wasn't charged and he came in to testify in Ed's defense. Lillian, along with her three kids and Anna Mae's daughter, Celia, joined Mom in Oklahoma City.

With Mark's surrender, the prosecution was assured that at least four of their nine defendants would stand trial in the Allred/ Verlan case, three of whom were Chynoweths: Vic, Mark, and myself. The other defendant would be Ed. Don pleaded guilty to lesser charges and was given probation, in exchange for his testimony, and charges were dropped against John. The other three — Arthur, Ramona, and Ervil — were still hiding out in Mexico.

Although being in jail was better than being on the run in Mexico, it was still a traumatic experience. Here I was, this small, fearful, pregnant twenty-year-old, surrounded by Amazons who had committed much more violent crimes — or at least it seemed so to me. There was a big Indian woman who had slit her landlord's throat and another woman who had shot her boyfriend, a policeman, in the testicles.

During the period I was in jail in Salt Lake, from mid-November 1978 to March 20, 1979, I must have sent or received close to 100 letters, about 70 of which I still have in my possession. Hardly more than a day or two went by during those five months that I didn't get a letter from someone, usually Mom, Lillian, or Vonda, who was writing to me from prison in California. These letters, plus a little 1979 Hallmark date book in which I wrote short notes, have enabled me to reconstruct much of what was going on in my life while I awaited trial.

Since our mail was opened and read by prison authorities, obviously we couldn't communicate anything about the case, about Ervil, or anything else that would further incriminate us. Most of our letters were sort of chatty about everyday things going on around us. Mom and Lil would tell me how Erin was doing in Oklahoma City, and I would write about some of the more interesting occurrences of prison life around me. In addition to Erin and the Zarate children she had adopted, Mom was also caring for Anna Mae's daughter Celia and Lorna's daughter Tarsa.

Once in awhile we would write about scriptures, since I was getting to read them often. Vonda was also doing some heavy reading around that time, and that's what she and I usually wrote about. Occasionally there would be other letters or cards from Linda Johnson, Nancy, Laura, Teresa Rios, my niece Jody, or Vonda's daughter Audrey.

I looked forward to getting my mail every day. Not having Erin around was tearing at my heartstrings, and I insisted that Mom tell me everything she was doing — every little detail. I didn't want to miss a thing about my daughter's day-to-day activities and whatever new things she was learning to do. They would send me pictures of her whenever they could. And I would even get to hear her little voice on the phone during my once or twice a month phone calls to Mom. I missed that little girl so much, it made me cry just thinking about her.

Since most of the family was either in Oklahoma or Dallas, I didn't get too many visitors besides John O'Connell, but Glen and Kathy came down from Ogden a few times to see me. Kathy was about eight months pregnant when I saw her in December and getting ready to have her second set of twins.

In my preliminary hearing in early December, none of the charges were dropped or reduced. John and I knew we were in for a long battle with Yocom, who was out for blood. However, the judge held — in writing — that the evidence was insufficient, as a matter of law, to convict. I was still to be held over for trial because there was probable cause to believe I could be guilty. This was encouraging. Also, Yocom's star witnesses (Don Sullivan and Jack Strothman) were giving contradictory testimony and John was quick to pick up on it. It looked good for me at that point.

I had some other interesting experiences those first few weeks in jail, such as seeing Alma LeBaron being interviewed on a TV talk show. It was strange seeing Ervil's brother on the screen, talking about us and attempting to cash in on all the publicity this case was generating.

As 1978 drew to a close, the local media listed the top ten stories of the year. The LeBaron-Allred story came in ninth. The year before it had been number two. A TV news spot on Ervil was aired on Saturday, December 30. Among the people interviewed were Ben Bradlee, Jr., and Dale Van Atta, who were collaborating on a book about us. Van Atta was an investigative reporter for the Mormon-owned paper in Salt Lake City, the *Deseret News,* and he had written most of the stories about us for them. Bradlee had written a lengthy article about Ervil earlier that year for *New Times* magazine, entitled "The Mormon Manson."

Not surprisingly, on the same day, December 30, Bradlee came by the jail to see me. I wasn't overly impressed by him and I knew nothing about him, other than the fact that he was writing a book about Ervil and that my attorney had spoken to him previously. (John later said he was grateful to Bradlee for briefing him on the police version of Ervil and the Allred murder case. It helped him in preparing our own case.) I didn't even know how to spell his name correctly. I had no idea his father was some bigwig publisher with the *Washington Post* who helped break the Watergate scandal. In a letter to Mom, dated December 31, 1978, I wrote the following:

> . . . Yesterday Ben Bradley *(sic)* came to see me. Poor guy. He could tell I wasn't overly thrilled to see him. And he tried to "up" my opinion of himself. I *do* sympathize with the guy; he's trying to write a book but he can't get anyone to talk to him. I explained that he . . . was out to get a good story and I supposed he'd be as fair as possible, but that when we decided to tell our story, we'd do it ourselves and not have some outsider writing it for us . . .

Several months earlier, just before Dan and I were captured outside of Veracruz, a letter written by Bradlee to Ervil found its way into Ervil's hands. The letter was sent to Denver or some other place where our people were staying and somehow it got forwarded down to us. When I found out about it, I told Ervil, "Here's your chance to tell our side of the story." But Ervil said, "Absolutely not. When we get ready to tell our story we'll tell it ourselves." That's what I reiterated to Bradlee when he visited me in jail.

When I told him this he looked real disappointed. He said the book was going to be written whether I talked to him or not, but he said he really wanted to tell our side of the story and let people know what it was all about. He even implied that if I didn't talk they might have to make something up. To his credit, he did try to make me feel at ease in order to get me to open up, and he wasn't hostile or obnoxious or anything like that. But for me to have talked freely to him or anyone else would not only have put me in danger from Ervil and his other zealous followers, it could also have jeopardized my own case. Bradlee should have realized how foolish it would have been for me to openly discuss a pending capital case. In any event, I made it clear I had nothing to say and I stood up, indicating that our "interview" had come to an end.

In later years I did get to read Bradlee and Van Atta's book about us, *Prophet of Blood,* and I was nothing short of amazed at some of the things they had me saying at various times. Even though I never gave any information or direct quotes to either of the authors, direct quotes were attributed to me. These could only have come from second- or third-hand sources, but the author made it sound like the statements were coming directly from me. Obviously, since few — if any — of us were talking to them, certain degrees of journalistic license had to be taken.

On that New Year's Eve, I started getting very depressed. There was a lot of anxiety building up inside me about the upcoming trial, the fate of my unborn baby, and the many other things you think about when you're imprisoned and have plenty of time on your hands. I sulked for a few days and didn't want to be bothered or to talk to anyone. John called a few times and I even refused to return his calls. Finally, I told the matron to tell him I would call Tuesday, the day after New Year's Day.

But, on New Year's Eve, the matron came and told me to go into her office and wait. I thought to myself, "Oh, no . . . what have I done now?" As I walked into her office, who should be sitting there with his pipe in his mouth and his feet on the desk but

John. He took his pipe out, glared at me, and said angrily, "Close the door."

I closed the door and stared at him, not knowing what to expect.

"Now, what's this shit about 'I'll call you Tuesday'?" he said. "You think you're a real tough cookie, don't you?"

"No," I said meekly, fighting back tears.

"I don't want you to be a tough cookie," he said, adding that it wouldn't help my case. "I need to be needed."

I thought he wanted me to cry on his shoulder, but I told him I wasn't the "let-me-cry-on-your-shoulder type." I had to work out my problems on my own, I added. He seemed to accept that explanation.

I settled down and we started talking about the case, particularly a jurisdictional question that was at issue involving my right to talk to or call anyone I wanted. A problem had come up and the jail administration claimed the right to restrict my communication privileges.

The problem arose during my last conversation with my daughter. Mom had called John that morning, telling him Erin lapsed into Spanish while talking to me, and the matron listening in interrupted the call. John called the matron, who explained she had orders not to allow any conversations in a language she didn't understand. The matron also told John I had forfeited my phone privileges. John then asked to talk to me but I wouldn't come to the phone. He went skiing that day and then to the jail for what he called an "attitude adjustment and stroking session." John said he was going to work on getting these restrictions loosened.

So ended 1978, my twentieth year, a year filled with turmoil and anxiety. I had spent most of it on the run and now I was in jail. And pregnant. Whatever 1979 had in store for me, it had to be better than what I had just been through. In a few months I would know for sure.

CHAPTER 19

As 1979 began, the LeBaron story and our upcoming trials continued to make news, not only in Salt Lake City but around the country. On January 23, the *National Enquirer,* the largest-circulation newspaper in America, carried a huge headline:

"JFK ASSASSINATION
CULT LEADER IS
NO. 1 SUSPECT"

And at the bottom of the front page, where millions of people could see them, were two pictures of Ervil. They were horrible-looking mug shots taken front and profile from one of his arrests in Ensenada.

I didn't see the article when it came out but I heard about it on the news. I thought it was very funny. Ervil had been accused of a lot of things, many of them true, but this was stretching the boundaries of credibility a little too far. Glen wondered if they weren't going to pin the Lincoln assassination on him next.

The story came out shortly after the U.S. House of Representatives Select Committee on Assassinations concluded that President Kennedy was more than likely the victim of a conspiracy, rather than a lone assassin. Whether the *Enquirer* was sitting back waiting for the committee to make its findings known before dropping its "bombshell" about Ervil is anyone's guess, but the timing appeared more than coincidental. The *Enquirer*, which feeds on this sort of speculation and sensationalism, had been saying for years there was a conspiracy to kill Kennedy — and Ervil was a "hot story" when the committee findings were announced. He apparently must have struck them as a convenient little connection they could throw in there to sell newspapers.

The story went on to call Ervil "a murderous cult leader known as the 'Avenging Angel,' " another nickname I'd never heard used in reference to him. It also said he "heads a cruel killing cult that has painted the Southwest red with blood." Information for the story was based on a "secret" FBI document in which J. Edgar Hoover was reported as saying Ervil's cult "is believed to have been responsible for President Kennedy's death." The story also quoted the former Dallas police chief who was present during the Kennedy assassination as saying Ervil was his major suspect in the conspiracy.

The article also accused Ervil of masterminding the attempted murder of *Hustler* magazine publisher Larry Flynt, supposedly because Flynt was about to go public with new information on the JFK conspiracy that would link Ervil to it. Alma LeBaron was quoted as saying, "Ervil wants to take over the world and anyone who gets in his way will be eliminated."

The article, which took up two full pages in addition to the front cover, quoted FBI sources and men who might have been only marginally involved in the Church of the Firstborn in the early 1960s. Overall, it came up with some patently ridiculous hypotheses, based on speculation that defied all credibility. To this day, I find it amazing that people can think stories of this type are even remotely believable.

In the early 1960s, the CFB was only a fledgling church with Ervil and Joel working together to bring in followers. There was no talk of violence or murders back then. There were no conspiracies being hatched against high elected officials or anyone else. Ervil was too busy helping Joel bring in converts to be thinking of any elaborate murder plots against the president of the United States. His militant philosophy didn't start coming out until the late 1960s, years after JFK was killed. There is absolutely no way Ervil could have had any connection with either the JFK assassination or the shooting of Larry Flynt. Ervil was certainly no angel, and the murders that can be traced to him are indeed inexcusable, but anything beyond them is pure fiction. Nonetheless, the negative publicity this case was attracting was bound to hurt us — or so we thought.

The *Enquirer* article hit the streets around January 15 or 16. On the eighteenth, a polygamist leader named John Singer was shot to death in a struggle with police not far from Salt Lake City. The Singers and other members of their group had been home-schooling their children and the state was trying to force them to send them to public schools. Singer refused to go to court, and when the police came to arrest him, Singer fought with them and was shot. The wife who was with him at the time was arrested. The next day Singer's followers picketed the courthouse where his wife was being held, and bomb threats were received by the authorities. Coupled with the events going on around Ervil and his followers and the recent Jonestown tragedy, polygamy and cultism continued to be hot news items. I'm sure David Yocom and the other prosecutors were under a lot of pressure to convict us, in the wake of all the negative media attention focusing on polygamy and the State of Utah.

In the meantime, I was being treated almost as a celebrity by those around me in jail. They were all on my side and cheering for me. Even Judy, the matron who had been afraid of me initially, started getting friendly toward me. As far as all the horror stories you hear about women's dentention facilities, all the TV movies you see about fights going on, lesbianism, and other violence among female inmates or between inmates and guards, I didn't see any of that. At no time since my first few days did I feel as if I was in any danger from those around me. Even the food, which everyone else bitched about, wasn't all that bad to me. It was a feast of plenty compared to what I'd seen in Mexico.

However, my phone privileges remained somewhat restricted.

According to a memo I got from the jail commander on January 10, I was allowed only one call per week — to Mom in Oklahoma City. I had to give the names of anyone I talked to at that number to the matron sitting by me. I was forbidden to speak in Spanish or "in code," or in any other manner that would put my conversations "outside the ability of the matron to understand what is being talked about." The memo went on to say that John had been informed of the restrictions, they were within the law, and I could be further restricted if the authorities so desired.

Sometime during the early part of my imprisonment, Mom came up with Vic and Nancy to meet with our attorneys and they were advised that a plea bargaining option was open to me. The attorneys weren't necessarily advising us to take that option; they were merely telling us that it was there if we wanted it. We could get off with lighter sentences if we pleaded guilty to lesser charges. I could have pled guilty to voluntary manslaughter under the provision that applied to an unlawful killing where the defendant "reasonably believed that the killing was lawful." John thought it was a reasonable offer which might have gotten me only probation.

However, when it was discussed with me, I refused flat out. I wanted this case to go before a jury where I could be judged accordingly. Vic had the same attitude. A plea bargain for him would have resulted in outright dismissal of the charges, but when informed of the option he said, "They can't do that. They charged me so I have a right to trial." Our feeling was, "We did this in God's name and God better get us out of it." Mark and Ed also came up with the same conclusions. We were confident we would be acquitted.

On January 5 I went to court. John tried to get the charges quashed, but all four counts stuck. Bail was set at $50,000. John told the judge about the shabby treatment I had received in Mexico: having my papers taken away and then being deported for not having them, as well as having the authorities conveniently waiting for me at the border and Yocom coming to browbeat me before I'd even had a chance to receive legal counseling. He said it was creating a negative opinion in my mind about the American judicial system, which it certainly was.

Then John asked if I could be released into the custody of my brother Glen, who was proven to be a responsible citizen, but Yocom even fought that suggestion. Several months earlier, Glen had accompanied Duane on a trip from Oklahoma City to Mexico to deliver some motorcycles to Mark, who had jumped bail. Duane and Glen had an unpleasant run-in with the police and border patrol and, of course, Yocom knew about it. But Yocom conveniently denied having any involvement in the illegal manner in which I was arrested and deported.

Anyway, I was not allowed to be released into Glen's custody. Yocom claimed there had been bomb threats related to our case and I was considered too much of a "security risk" to be out roaming around. I can't imagine who among us would have been stupid enough to phone in bomb threats, and I'm convinced Yocom was just saying that to keep me in prison.

In the midst of all the legal issues, there were some humorous incidents at the jail. For example, when the doctor examined me to determine the condition of my pregnancy he wrote out what is probably the strangest prescription in medical history — popcorn! I happened to mention to him I had a craving for popcorn and he wrote it down on his pad and gave it to the warden. When word of this got out, the jokes started. One of the girls said to me, "We knew this doctor was a quack and this proves it."

What wasn't so funny was getting our privileges taken away for thirty days. One of the girls — "Jackie the Nut," we called her — was on a "halfway-house" program where she only had to serve nights and weekends. She used her freedom to smuggle contraband into the jail. One day she smuggled a joint in and a few of the girls were huddled around in the courtyard smoking it. I certainly had no desire to take chances and join them at that time, so I just stood nearby. One of the matrons saw us, and though they couldn't prove anything, we still went before the disciplinary board. We lost our commissary, visiting, telephone, recreation, and television privileges.

For me the television wasn't too great a loss since one of my cellmates, who was also punished, was a TV fanatic and had it on day and night. At least now, for the suspension period, anyway, I would be able to get some reading and concentrating done. But I was upset over not being able to talk to Mom and Erin. I got so angry at one point I tore out a magazine picture of three dogs eating out of the same dish and wrote above it, "Our Distinguished Disciplinary Board." I was tempted to send it to them, but I didn't.

On January 29, Ed went on trial in Price, Utah, for the murder of Robert Simons. Vic, Duane, Mark, and Lillian were on hand to testify as witnesses in Ed's defense. Steve McCaughey, who, up to that time, had managed to postpone Vonda's trial, was Ed's lawyer. John O'Connell went down also to get a feel for what might come up in our own trial. Mom stayed in Oklahoma City with the kids.

With Lloyd dead, the Carbon County prosecutor had almost nothing to build his case around. Even though Mark was present when Simons was ambushed, he was never charged with any crime and he testified in Ed's defense. Of course, he denied that he or Ed had any part of the killing. The prosecution was relying almost solely on the testimony of Don Sullivan, who said Ed had bragged to him about killing Simons right after it happened. However, Steve shot Don's testimony full of holes.

Dick Forbes was allowed to testify on what Lloyd had told him about the murder before Lloyd's death, but he was not permitted to name Ed or Mark as Lloyd's accomplices. The judge had ruled against the permissibility of "hearsay evidence" regarding statements Lloyd made to the investigators. David Yocom was there as an advisor to the prosecution but was not allowed to examine or cross-examine witnesses from either side.

When Ed took the stand, he not only denied killing Simons but also said Don bragged to him about doing it himself — a year after the murder took place. Ed told the court Don and Lloyd had done the killing, not him. Not knowing who to believe by the end of the two-day trial, the jury retired to deliberate. Only two hours after retiring, they came out with a "not guilty" verdict.

Lillian raced to a phone and called Mom, who was in the middle of writing a letter to me. "Praise the Lord," Mom wrote in the letter upon receiving the news. I had already heard about it from the TV news and we all felt that God was truly on our side. So far, anyway.

It wasn't over for Ed, though, nor for Mark. They were still facing the same charges I was being held for: murder, attempted murder, and conspiracy in the Allred/Verlan case. That would be a much tougher fight than the one in Price.

February 3 was my fourth anniversary. My husband, the man responsible for me being in jail and whose child I was carrying, was in hiding. Our anniversary didn't mean anywhere near as much to me as the fact that it was also Erin's third birthday. That meant a great deal to me; so much, in fact, that I composed a seven-page, handwritten letter to her that was a veritable outpouring of motherly love. In that letter I described, in the most tender and loving words I could summon up, just how I felt about her and I recounted many of the happy memories I had of our times together. John read the letter right after I gave it to him to mail. He said it touched his heart like nothing he had ever seen before.

Even though, obviously, my three-year-old daughter would have been much too young to read and understand what I was saying, someday she would, and I wanted to get my thoughts down for when that day came. At that point in time, my future was very uncertain. If found guilty, I could be facing a death sentence or many years — if not a lifetime — in prison. The times I would see my daughter and the child I was now carrying would be few and far between. With these and other thoughts on my mind, I composed this letter.

To my daughter

They say that remembering is living. Well, I live each day remembering and thinking of you, Erin — from that very first joyous meeting to our very last telephone conversation. Although we are separated by distance, I carry you with me in my thoughts daily. I remember little things you used to do or say. I only wish I could be with you now, watching you grow, sharing your laughter and your tears, disappointments and discoveries, your joy and your fears. But, for now I must live on memories until such time as I can be with you again. I long for that day, but until it comes, please remember, my little one, you are always on my mind. My memories of you are what help keep me going and makes our distance bearable . . .

For the next five or six pages I recounted many of the things she did during various times and stages of her young life: what she looked like when she was born, what she did to get attention, her first meeting with her father Ervil, and especially the times she lived and traveled with me in Mexico. I closed by saying:

> . . . It's been three months since I've seen you, Erin. I miss you very very much, but it's comforting to know that you are happy, you get plenty of attention from everyone, you have lots of kids to play with, and little jobs to keep you busy — and that you talk about me every day.
>
> Time goes by so fast. Why, it seems like only yesterday that I held you in my arms that very first time and already you're three years old . . .
>
> Yes Erin, these are some of the things I think about and just some of my memories of your first three years of life. I'm looking forward to being with you again, because every day that we spend apart is one less day we'll have together. I'm looking forward to the years ahead of watching my little girl grow.

Soon after that, I had John draw up custody papers awarding Erin and the child I was carrying to Mom just in case I was convicted. I didn't want to leave anything to chance, whereby my kids could become wards of the state. This wasn't John's specialty, since it had nothing to do with criminal law, but he had it done and the legal papers were filed. That took a lot off my mind.

Throughout February, the letters and visitors kept coming. Duane and Glen came to see me a few times and on the fourteenth Mom finally came up with Vic and Nancy. My most frequent visitor, though, was John. He came several times a week, once or twice bringing his law partner, Ronald Yengich, with him. John and Ron wanted to prep me for the trial and give me some idea of what type of questioning I might expect on the witness stand. Ron would play devil's advocate — the part of Yocom — and would grill me intensively, trying to gauge how my composure might hold up in court. On another occasion John brought me a dress Glen's wife, Kathy, made for me. At other times he would talk about things not even remotely related to the case, like skiing, camping, or his family. He wasn't just making idle conversation: he was trying to put me at ease and get my mind off the trial I would soon be facing. Sometimes he would smuggle treats in for me like Coca-Cola or the good kind of popcorn. The popcorn they were "prescribing" for me was usually burnt and had too much butter in it. By the time I went to trial, John had become more than just an attorney for me: he was a true friend. He remains so to this day.

Our thirty-day lockup was over after only twenty-six days. I guess they gave us time off for good behavior. On the eleventh we got to go out into the compound and were free to move about within the confines of our ward. We did whatever we could to amuse ourselves and to keep our sanity. The day after lockup ended, one of the girls, Rosemary, did a strip tease in front of the security cameras near the elevator. Knowing she was being watched, she started taking her clothes off slowly and rhythmically, like a go-go dancer. A matron rushed over to stop her but not before we all enjoyed a good laugh. Another time that month, a group of about a dozen girls from the Polynesian island of Tonga did some entertaining for us. They were in the country illegally and were being held pending deportation. They sang some native songs and did a hula-type dance. Rather than being tall, sleek, willowy young girls you see in tropical island movies, they were short and pudgy. But they were good dancers, anyway.

Soon after getting into jail I decided I wanted to get my high school equivalency diploma. I had dropped out in my senior year, only a few credits short of graduating, and I had always wanted to finish. With plenty of time on my hands in jail, I took the courses I needed to complete my educational requirements. I had a tutor who came in twice a week to help me, particularly with my math. The other courses I felt I knew well enough to pass on my own. I took the General Educational Development (GED) exam on February 23 and passed. Four days later, I received my diploma.

My pregnancy progressed without any complications. Other than ballooning up to 152 pounds and carrying a "low-rider," I didn't experience any major problems. The doctor who prescribed the popcorn for me checked me once or twice a month at the hospital. On those occasions, I had to be handcuffed and shackled with a chain around my waist while the police transported me to the hospital and back. I protested against this but it didn't do me any good.

When March arrived, my trial was less than a week away. I wasn't particularly nervous or anxious, as I recall — just restless. By March 1, I had been in jail 109 days. I wanted to get it over with. During the past five months I had run the full gamut of emotions and I was drained. Being separated from my daughter and the rest of my family, having my movements watched and restricted, and all the while carrying a child, had taken its toll on me. There was nothing left for me to do but pray, and that's what I knew how to do best. I had been counting down the days until the trial. It would be in the Lord's hands from there on.

On the second, John brought Robert Van Sciver by to see me. Bob was the attorney defending Mark and Vic. I needed to talk to him and make sure my testimony wouldn't contradict that of my brothers. Later the same day, Mom and Erin arrived in Salt Lake and John got to see my daughter for the first time. The next day, Mom brought me some nice clothes to wear during the trial, but she wasn't allowed to bring Erin into the jail with her. It would be a few more days until I was allowed to see her.

In the meantime, in Oklahoma City, Dad and Lorna arrived from Mexico to keep an eye on the kids and the business in Mom's absence and stay abreast of the trial. That earthly "day of judgment" was imminent.

CHAPTER 20

On March 6 the long-awaited trial began. Just before the proceedings opened, I got to see Erin for the first time since my arraignment in Laredo, five months earlier. I cried and hugged her tightly and told her how much I loved her. I couldn't believe how much she had grown and learned during our long period of separation. It was such a touching moment that, even now — more than ten years later — I am at a loss for words to describe it adequately.

I was ushered into the courtroom and seated with Ed, Vic, and Mark. With us were my attorney, John O'Connell, Bob Van Sciver for my brothers, and Steve McCaughey defending Ed on his second murder rap. The judge was Jay E. Banks. Of the nine people listed in the original indictment, just the four of us were there. Don Sullivan was dropped from the more serious charges in exchange for his testimony, John Sullivan had all the charges dropped against him, and Ervil, Arthur, and Ramona were hiding out in Mexico. Our fate was now in the hands of a secular legal system we had been taught by Ervil to distrust.

Prior to jury selection that day, it had already been agreed upon by David Yocom that the first-degree murder charges against

263

Mark, Ed, and me would be reduced to second-degree. This was done to reduce the number of defense challenges, and possibly because I was someone with whom the jury could sympathize. That ruled out the death penalty if we were found guilty. The murder and attempted murder charges against Vic were dropped altogether, leaving him charged only with conspiracy. These charge reductions made it possible to seat an eight-member jury, rather than the twelve normally impaneled to sit in on a capital case.

On the first day of the trial, while the prospective jurors were being interviewed, the other defendants and I simply sat there and listened. The main question I recall John asking them was if they subscribed to or had read about us in the *Deseret News*, the Mormon-owned paper that was heavily prejudiced against us. If they admitted to having read that paper, they were immediately disqualified. A pregnant woman was asked by Yocom if she might be inclined to vote for acquittal of someone who was also pregnant, meaning, of course, me. The woman just said, "Well, I imagine she got pregnant the same way I did." She was selected as an alternate.

By the end of the day, six women and two men were chosen to sit on the jury. John and the guys' attorneys were very happy with this arrangement. It was felt that a predominantly female jury would be more sympathetic toward me, especially since I was eight months pregnant.

The next day, Yocom gave a fire-breathing opening statement to the judge and jury. At the time, he was reportedly considering running for some higher office. He and everyone else knew that securing a conviction on us would have been a real feather in the cap of his election bid, whereas an acquittal would weigh heavily against him. In his statement, Yocom tried to lay out the full scenario of what happened on the day Dr. Allred was murdered, but in so doing he got a lot of his "facts" mixed up. For example, he said that during the struggle between Richard Bunker and Ramona Marston, the other girl — meaning me — pointed a .38-caliber revolver at Bunker, which would have been impossible since Ramona was the one with the .38. He also said I returned to the scene with the .38 and fired a shot at Allred's face in "an effort to destroy what we'll later find out to be what they believed to be the face of a false

264

prophet." I have no recollection of firing any additional shots. Ramona went back in and fired two wild shots with the .38, but I did not. He also got a lot of relationships confused. He had Lorna as Duane's wife, Ramona as Don's wife, and, at one point, he referred to Nancy as Mark's wife. He also said that Anna Mae was Ed and Ramona's sister. In addition, he called Mark the group's "legal advisor and financial consultant," when he was obviously describing Vic.

But he went on and on, telling the jury what had been told to him about the April 20, 1977, meeting in Dallas, our rendezvous in Evanston, the hit on Allred, the aborted hit on Verlan at Allred's funeral, and the stakeout at Siegfried Widmar's house in El Paso. He also explained how charges were reduced against Don Sullivan, dropped against John Sullivan, and never filed against Jack Strothman — all in exchange for their testimony. He went on to say that Ervil had ordered Verlan's death for reasons of "pecuniary or personal gain," meaning that Ervil planned to use Verlan's death as a means of taking over the Church of the Firstborn.

Listening to this man, I realized I had a lot of faith in John and the other attorneys to get us off. As we all sat there at this big long table, there was an invisible, unspoken support system among us. It was the first time I'd seen either Mark or Ed since before my capture in Mexico, and it was good to see everyone together again.

After Yocum finished his opening statement, John got up and gave his. He told the jury how he intended to prove that I did not kill Allred and I had not taken part in any conspiracy to kill Verlan, nor did I make any attempt to kill Verlan. John portrayed Ervil as a learned scriptorian but a weak leader who couldn't keep his followers together and, for that reason, he had no special powers to command us to do something against our own free will.

"All the people who have direct evidence and claim to have direct evidence who accuse this girl of being this cold-blooded assassin are people who themselves are involved in this killing," John said. "It will be our contention [they] were shifting the blame to others in order to escape punishment themselves. In so doing, they place primary responsibility on Ervil LeBaron who they portray as some sort of super monster with incredible power over his followers, such that he could — that Rena Chynoweth here would unquestionably commit unspeakable crimes just because he tells her to. Our evidence, and I believe the believable evidence of the State, will show that this is simply not true."

In order for John to strengthen his case for me — indeed, for all of us — it was necessary for him to put Ervil down. Ervil's administrative ability, he said, was "downright pathetic," and added, ". . . he can't seem to give simple instructions on anything." He also said that in the spring of 1977, the Church of the Lamb of God "was not the well-oiled machine that the State will try to prove to you. Rather . . . it was a group of confused and frightened people who didn't know what was going on, and were just in general confusion."

But the most important assertion he made was that Don Sullivan might have been the one who walked into Dr. Allred's office that day, disguised as a young woman, and fired the fatal shots. It was a plausible premise, since Don was clean-shaven at the time and had almost feminine-like facial features. John made it clear he was going after Don Sullivan, the State's chief witness, and he intended to show him as a violence-prone "military leader" with a fondness for automatic weapons.

John told the jury that I was in Salt Lake City on the day of the Allred murder. Also, he said that I delivered a gun to Don that Nancy bought in Denver, and Don planned to add it to an arsenal he was already accumulating there. Finally, he asked the jury to concentrate on the evidence that would be presented to them. Because of the complexities of the case and since there were multiple defendants and conspiracy charges involved, there might be a lot of confusion in their minds during the course of the trial.

Bob Van Sciver spoke next. He told the jury that his clients, Vic and Mark, were only peripherally involved in the case. "Second stringers," he called them. After giving Vic's background as a successful businessman, Bob said Ervil persuaded Vic to go to Dallas around April 20, 1977, in an effort to help the appliance business there become more efficient and profitable. During his inspection of the facilities, Vic and Don were at odds on how the business should be run, Bob said. "Don . . . was running around suggesting that the business could be best administered by the implementation

266

of military rule. If you don't follow an order it's treason," while Vic favored implementing sound business practices. The April 20 meeting, which the prosecution contended was for the purpose of hatching a murder conspiracy, was nothing more than a church and business meeting, Bob contended.

In his defense of Mark, Bob said there would be no evidence to show Mark was in Utah or Evanston during the time of the Allred murder, nor was he at the April 20 meeting in Dallas. He was in Jackson on that date and didn't return to Dallas until around his birthday, on April 29. However, Mark was ordered to El Paso by Don sometime around the middle of May and Mark went there. When he found out Don's plans for killing Verlan at Siegfried Widmar's house, Mark didn't want any part of it and returned to Dallas. Bob said this was the extent of any role Mark might have had in any of the charges he was facing.

Bob also made it clear to the jury he would be focusing his defense on Don's credibility as a witness. "I think the evidence will indicate that it's Don Sullivan who owns the guns. It's Don Sullivan who calls the military meetings. It's Don Sullivan who is the military leader. It's Don Sullivan who has the fascination with guns and dissatisfaction with the prophecies and their not coming true quick enough."

Steve chose not to make an opening statement on behalf of Ed. It was understood among the three attorneys that the State's case would be zeroing in on me, and John would have to take the lead in the defense.

While all these statements were being made, I felt sort of strange sitting there — detached, almost — hearing my name continually mentioned. There were things going on around me I didn't understand, and I felt I was on the outside looking in.

While the statements were being made and later during the trial itself, I didn't get to talk to Ed, Mark, or Vic. But during recesses I got to hug them and we exchanged a few words. Mostly we talked about family, how the kids were doing, and small talk like that. We were all sure we could win, and we kept each other's spirits up.

Despite my advanced state of pregnancy, I managed to hold

up well in the courtroom during those eight-hour-long days of sitting. I remember actually feeling good being in that courtroom because it got me out of my cell. I was at least able to move around. Anything was an improvement over being confined in jail, even being on trial for my life. I prayed a lot and felt that it was in God's hands.

Right after the opening statements and a recess, the first witnesses for the prosecution were brought in. Paul Forbes of the Murray Police Department was shown scale models and photographs of the exterior and interior of Allred's office and Yocom had him explain to the jury where the body was, in relation to the office, when he found it. He also showed where bullet holes and spent cartridges were found and gave an explanation on which caliber bullets they were — the .25 and the .38.

The next witness was Dr. Serge Michael Moore, former state medical examiner, who did the autopsy on Allred. He went into detail on the gunshot wounds found on Allred's body and said at least two of them would have been fatal. Neither of the two bullets that remained in the body were determined to be .38s.

Then two of the eyewitnesses in Allred's office the day of the murder, Melba Allred and Richard Bunker, were called to the stand that first day. Bunker described the struggle he had with Ramona and me but neither of them could positively identify me. They had failed to do so in the lineup back in November or in any of the preliminary hearings they attended. During the direct examination by Yocom and under John's cross-examination, they weren't able to give accurate, consistent descriptions that matched my features or Ramona's. They described people with different colored hair and facial features.

About two months after the murder, Bunker underwent hypnosis and from his recollections, an artist drew a composite sketch of what the murderer looked like to him. The sketch looked more like Don Sullivan than it looked like me, and John played that for all it was worth. He held up the sketch, which was entered as a defense exhibit, and told the jury it didn't look anything like his client and that it actually looked more like a man. From the start, John had made it clear that he was operating on the premise that Don was the murderer and this gave him a lot of mileage in that direction. The murderer could, indeed, have been a man disguised as a woman, John emphasized to the court.

On Thursday, March 8, Yocom continued parading his witnesses up to the stand. The most important one I remember was Phyllis Rindfleisch, the cashier at Deseret Industries the day we bought our clothes and disguises. Yocom led her in the direction of trying to identify us as the ones who had been in the second-hand store on May 10, 1977. But, of the five of us who were there, she said she saw three women and I was the only one she could remember. She said something like, "I'll never forget that face," causing our attorneys and us to wonder how, among all the hundreds or thousands of faces she must have seen, mine would be so memorable nearly two years later. She said she remembered how "happy" and "beautiful" my face appeared to her and that it kind of "shone."

It gave me an ominous feeling to see this woman, who meant nothing special to us at the time (nor did we mean anything special to her) sitting up there on a witness stand, pointing an accusing finger at me. How strange it was that I should be the only one she remembered. John and Bob later got her back on the stand and tried to discredit her testimony, but she continued to insist it was me, among the others, she recalled seeing that day.

Other witnesses included Mr. and Mrs. Alfred Tucholski, who were in Allred's waiting room at the time of the murder, and Mary Swigert, Natalie Kimball, and Boyd Hansen, who were outside the doctor's office and claimed to have seen us fleeing. The prosecution also brought up people whose vehicles might have been stolen by the guys that day, and a man named Torkelson, who described the contents of the bag he found in the dumpster that contained our clothes and other evidence. They even had a man from Pepsi testify that the serial number on a can found in the bag with Ed's fingerprints on it indicated that it was bottled at a plant in Worland, Wyoming.

On Friday, March 9, Don was called to the stand as the state's chief prosecution witness. Having been promised he wouldn't face the same charges as us, he proceeded to tell all he knew about the events preceding, during, and after the Allred murder and the aborted hit on Verlan. He talked about the April 20, 1977, meeting in Dallas where Ervil laid out the whole scenario and where Vic gave his directive on how to deal with the police. Don went on to tell about driving with me to Albuquerque and our rendezvous there with Ervil and Anna Mae. He told how he ended up in Evanston with the rest of us and finally went on to the events in Salt Lake and immediately afterward. Don said I talked freely with him about making the Allred hit, and he also said Ramona had gone in there with me.

Then our attorneys took their turns torpedoing his testimony — first Bob, then Steve, then finally John. Don was made to look like an unreliable witness by the time they were finished with him. His testimony included all kinds of inconsistencies and contradictions, and our attorneys were quick to spot and exploit them. During cross-examination, Don came across as someone covering up for himself, and the fact that he had turned state's evidence in exchange for a lighter sentence made it appear all the more so. Not only was he inconsistent on major details, he even bungled a few minor ones, such as stating his correct height.

"How tall are you?" John asked him.

Don replied that he was six foot even.

"Would you mind standing up, please?" John asked.

Don got out of the witness chair and stood up. John, who is 6'1, stood next to him and there was a big difference in their heights. Even wearing cowboy boots, which may have given him an extra inch or two, Don still fell a few inches shorter than John.

John asked him how he could claim to be 6'0 when anyone present could see how much shorter Don was than him. Then John pulled out the booking sheets from Don's arrest in which Don claimed to be 5'10. On coming to trial, Don would add an inch or two until he was a full six feet tall. John made quite a point over this issue and asked Don why he was lying about his height. Give or take a few inches and Don's propensity for lying about these things, Don could possibly have been the same height as Allred's assailant. That was John's implication.

Then John began to dwell on Don's physical features and

mannerisms. Don was a slender person who swung a little bit when he walked. He didn't have an assertive, macho way of walking like most men. His face was sort of soft and feminine-looking and, with a wig on, he could have passed for a woman, John asserted. Don was asked to try on the blue parka that had been found among the evidence in the dumpster, and it fit him perfectly. In an earlier statement to the police, Jack Strothman said that Don was wearing a blue jacket when he and Rena left to shoot Dr. Allred. The eyewitnesses said the shooter was wearing a blue jacket.

John and Bob also dwelled on the question of immunity and asked if Don was promised anything by the prosecution. Yocom promptly stood up and denied it.

Don was asked if he was a violent sort of person, and his wife, Noreen, came into the picture. Earlier, when she had been on the stand, she was asked by our attorneys if she was afraid of her husband. She said no. But in the past, Don had battered her and their child and even knocked her front teeth out during one of his rages. This wasn't brought out during the trial, but I think it was clear to the jury that Don was prone to violence and militarism and had a fondness for weapons.

Bob theorized that Noreen could have been in the Salt Lake area at the time of the murder and could, indeed, have been the second woman in Allred's office with a disguised Don. The implication was that Noreen was so afraid of Don, she would do anything he told her to, even accompany him on a military mission. Since no one had successfully identified Ramona or me, the murderers could have been *any* two women fitting the distorted descriptions the authorities had. That was the centerpiece around which the strategy hinged regarding my involvement.

Don was on the stand all day Friday as the prosecutor's friendly witness, but on Monday, March 12, he was on the defensive when he was cross-examined. By the time he was finished, his criminal past, his violent temperament, and his love of firearms had all come out in the open. His credibility as a witness was completely undermined by John, Bob, and Steve. The jury must have had serious doubts about relying on his testimony to reach the verdict Yocom was seeking.

Jack Strothman and John Sullivan also testified, but neither of them added much that could have been damaging. John was only marginally involved in anything we did, so he wasn't able to shed much light on the prosecution's case. Jack did nothing to dispel his image of being less than bright. During cross-examination, our attorneys brought out the fact that when Jack first talked to police, he told them he was afraid of Don. Don would kill anyone who talked, Jack said. By the time cross-examination ended, Jack's testimony was also shot full of holes and he was made to look even less credible than Don.

Far more potentially damaging than Jack or John's testimony was that of Isaac, Ervil's sixteen-year-old son, who was present at the April 20, 1977, meeting in Dallas. Being as young as he was, Isaac was not regarded by either side as likely to lie on the witness stand. Ervil had never assigned him to any of the hits, undoubtedly because he was too young, and so Isaac had nothing to cover up regarding his knowledge or marginal involvement. He was merely a spectator at a long-ago meeting in which two deaths were plotted. Nonetheless, he was an important witness for Yocom, and one who could certainly convict us all.

Isaac was noticeably terrified of being up on the witness stand on Wednesday, March 14, and his voice was shaking as he spoke. Yocom was trying to make him feel safe and at ease. Under gentle prodding, he got Isaac to talk about what he heard at the meeting. Isaac recounted Vic's speech about not cooperating with the police and spoke of threats Ervil made against those who might cooperate. He knew that a "false prophet" was going to be killed in Salt Lake, although he didn't know the name, and he heard that Ramona and I were named by Ervil to make the hit. He also talked about how scared he was of Ervil and some of the others who might try to kill him for testifying against them. He said he needed to escape from the group in Dallas before they could get to him.

Isaac was the best witness the State had, but our attorneys were able to turn some of what he said to our advantage. When questioned by police, Isaac told them he was afraid of Don and he painted Don as the military enforcer everyone else feared. Having him repeat this description on the witness stand strengthened the arguments our attorneys were making that Don could have been the murderer.

Delia, Ervil's ninth and youngest child by Delfina, got on the stand the same day as Isaac. She, too, was terrified of her father and the consequences of testifying against him. Only about twelve years old, she was shaking and her voice was quivering. However, nothing she said could be considered too damaging. She had been at the Dallas meeting but had no new information that would help the prosecution. By the end of that Wednesday, the prosecution rested after calling about forty-five witnesses.

On Thursday, March 15, our people got up on the stand, one by one. Mom was the first witness for our defense. She looked very dignified up there. As our attorneys questioned her about the Dallas meeting, she said it was just another one of our many regular religious meetings, followed by a discussion of business and economics. Nothing that Vic or Ervil spoke about was out of the ordinary, either, she said.

When his turn came to cross-examine, Yocom tried to shake her down hard; however, Mom held up very well. He tried to browbeat her into talking about what was really discussed that night, but she couldn't be moved from her original statements. In the end, Yocom came across almost like a bully, badgering this sweet, elderly woman. His actions couldn't have scored him any points with the jury.

Then came Nancy. She had been grilled intensively by the police and other investigators shortly after the murder, when the .38 special Ramona carried was traced to a purchase Nancy made in Denver. For two years she went through a real roller-coaster ride over that gun, being initially suspected as one of the murderers, then being suspected in the conspiracy, then having to stand by Vic when his part in the murder started coming out. Nonetheless, Nancy also held up nicely on the stand. Her explanation for buying the gun was that it had been ordered by Don, and she said I delivered it to him in Salt Lake City. Yocom tried to trap her with some earlier statements she had made when the Dallas police first arrested her, but he got nothing he could nail any of us with.

When Vic got up on the stand, he was very cool and laid back.

Despite his reputation as being testy and uncooperative with authority, he displayed none of that on the witness stand. He repeated basically what Mom had said on the stand — that the Dallas meeting was primarily about economics, and he'd come down from Denver to advise us on our business, as well as to possibly set up a Lincoln Auto III dealership in the Dallas area. His talk about police and how to respond to their inquiries, he said, was in response to the fears Ervil and Don had planted in everyone about how the Firstborners were out to get us.

When Yocom's turn came, Vic was asked how much he had contributed to Ervil's church. As he asked this, Yocom held up the tax forms Vic had filed for several years, claiming charitable deductions.

"I don't know," Vic replied. "You got the records in front of you. You tell me."

The figure was actually about $20,000. The fact that Vic was conscientious enough to report it on his taxes only enhanced his stature as a law-abiding, taxpaying citizen. Yocom's ploy to taint Vic with his involvement in Ervil's church backfired on him.

Just as he had done with all our other defense witnesses, Yocom tried to shake Vic's testimony about what was discussed at the Dallas meeting, but Vic continued to insist it was mostly business and self-defense. Like Nancy and Mom and others before him, he denied that any talk of killings occurred at that meeting.

At one point, while Yocom was asking Vic why he went to Dallas, Vic said it was to straighten out problems with the business there. When asked to describe the problem, Vic replied, "You want it in one word or two?"

"Two," Yocom said.

"Ervil LeBaron," Vic said. He went on to describe how Ervil never understood the concept of "working capital," using profits from the business to reinvest into the business. Ervil, Vic said, would keep taking all the money out of the till, which left the business unable to operate.

The most important thing to come out of Vic's testimony was the comtempt he seemed to harbor toward Ervil. He came across as being only lukewarm in his support for the church and that it was primarily because of his family's involvement. His contribution to the church was on a financial, rather than a doctrinal, level. So ended Thursday's round of testimony.

Neither Ed nor Mark testified. Since it was well established Mark wasn't at the April 20 meeting and for other reasons decided by the attorneys, it wasn't felt his testimony would be necessary.

On Friday morning, March 16, our attorneys put Alex Zarate Chynoweth on the stand. Alex, the son of my father's wife Noemi, had two key things to say in our defense: that Mark wasn't at the meeting and that Don Sullivan was a violent, military-type person. He was asked by our attorneys what the Dallas meeting was about and Alex said it was mostly religious and business. Vic's talk about the police, he said, had to do with the fact that some of our people were illegal immigrants. He was living in the warehouse at the time and, a few days after the meeting, he said he overheard a conversation between Don and Lloyd about going to Utah and killing someone. During cross-examination, Yocom tried to punch holes in his testimony but Alex held in there very well.

The next witness was Detective Gary Pedersen of the Murray Police Department. He was questioned about a photo lineup he took Richard Bunker through on July 1, 1977. During John's questioning, it was established that Bunker identified features in some pictures of suspects that matched those of Don Sullivan. His testimony didn't last very long, maybe ten or fifteen minutes. Everyone was anxious to get to the next and final witness in this nine-day-long trial — me.

I was sworn in just after Pedersen stepped down and, being a witness in my own defense, John was the first to question me. Five months after our first meeting, he knew me and he knew the case well enough to know what questions to ask me on the stand. Finally, I was reaching the culmination of a two-year-long ordeal of anguish and anxiety.

Being a defendant, I didn't have to testify. But it was felt to be to our advantage if I did. What I would have to say could very well determine the direction of the case. My fate and that of three others in the courtroom all came down to how I would handle myself on the witness stand — not to mention the fate of the child I had and the other I was carrying. Eight jurors were sitting on the side, waiting to weigh my words, determine my guilt or innocence, and decide the course of my future. It was the very height of courtroom drama, the kind portrayed in movies, except this was for real.

Anyone who has spent seven hours on a witness stand, on trial for his or her life, knows what a grueling ordeal it is. Anyone who hasn't can scarcely imagine what it's like. There is nowhere to go and no time to think. Nothing else in the world exists but that small space you occupy and the time you occupy it. You are the center of attention. The eyes of everyone in that courtroom are on you. The eyes of thousands — perhaps even millions — will be reading or watching news reports of what you have to say. They will be watching to see how your composure holds up under the withering cross-examination of a determined prosecutor trying to trip you up. Newspaper and TV news artists are sitting in front of you, sketching your picture to run in the late editions and on the 6:00 news. You are up there in front of all these people, both inside and outside the courtroom, and all else has ceased to exist.

John began by asking me some basic questions about my life and my background, leading up to the meeting in Dallas and the events of the next three weeks. I denied any discussion of murder at the meeting in Dallas, and said my reason for going to Denver was to help Nancy pack and move to Dallas. I testified that while in Denver, Nancy said Don called her from Salt Lake and asked her to buy a gun. He also asked Nancy to deliver it, but since she was in the middle of packing she asked me to do it. I agreed, but I didn't want to drive the 500 miles each way alone. Ramona and her two-week-old baby came along for the ride. That was my reason for being in Salt Lake on the day of the Allred murder, according to my testimony. I delivered the gun to Don, he yelled at me because it wasn't the type he wanted, and then he left. Ramona and I went to a motel to rest.

When John asked me about the Allred murder, I denied killing the doctor or that I'd ever been in his office. I said I'd never even heard of him and, after being shown a photograph of him, I said I didn't recognize it. He had me try on the blue parka found in the dumpster and it didn't fit. Then he asked me about the gun and I denied any knowledge of how to shoot it. On my arrival back in Dallas, I never admitted the killing to anyone — Don, Jack, John Sullivan, or anyone else, as they claimed in their testimony.

I then said I drove a truck Lloyd had bought in Dallas to Jackson, where he met me and Erin and I stayed at Mom's house. We were there when we learned about Nancy's arrest. Lloyd got scared and insisted that we leave immediately. He and his wife and daughter drove Erin and me to Indiana, where Don called and told him I needed to return to Dallas. I told the court Don wired me the money and I flew back and, when I got to Dallas, I stayed indoors for two weeks because he was afraid of the police. After that I went to Mexico.

Bob took over the questioning and asked me if Mark was at the April 20 meeting. I said no. I was playing the piano at the meeting and this is something I never did when Mark was around because he was a much better musician than I. Bob then asked me questions about Don — his personality, his "military orders," and whether we were afraid of disobeying him. I answered that Don was paranoid of the Church of the Firstborn and the police and he was extremely violent and short-tempered. We were all afraid of him, I told the court.

Steve asked me a few questions about Ed and the condition of the inside of the red El Camino he was driving when I first moved to Dallas. "It's a pig," I replied.

Then it was Yocom's turn. He was, I'm sure, eagerly awaiting this moment to grill me and try to trip me up. Even though he was just doing his job, I found his personality and his approach to be irritating and it ground on my nerves. At one point, while he was questioning me about purchases I'd made at Deseret Industries, I accused him of putting words in my mouth and told him, "I don't like it too much."

This kind of verbal dueling between us went on for a while until John finally came down heavy on me during a recess. My attitude on the stand was making me look bad before the jury, he warned. I took his advice and resolved not to fight with Yocom anymore.

When Yocom asked me about Phyllis Rindfleisch, the woman

at Deseret Industries who had identified me, I remarked that she had "a very strange memory." It amazed me, as it had amazed our attorneys, that she could distinguish my face out of so many others she must have seen, and could still remember it two years later.

John had entered a copy of the Bible as an exhibit for the defense. He used it to quote from in an effort to assist the judge and jury in better understanding the basis of our beliefs. When Yocom was cross-examining me, he took the same Bible off the table in front of the judge's bench where it was lying with all the other exhibits and slammed it down. I don't know what anyone else thought about it, but I thought it was shocking and irreverent. Here was this book, the oldest recorded history of mankind and the basis of faith for billions of the world's people, and this prosecutor was treating it like a piece of garbage. Of all the things said during and about this trial, that one incident stands out the most in my memory.

During the trial, there had been so much talk about prophets that when Yocom's questioning turned to monetary *profits*, I was confused and thought he was talking about the same thing. He was questioning me about our business in Dallas and he asked, "Where were the profits when this business was going?"

"He was back and forth as usual," I replied, thinking he was talking about Ervil.

Nearly everyone in the courtroom started laughing, except Yocom and the judge. Yocom apparently didn't catch the double meaning right away.

"Pardon me?" he said.

"He was back and forth," I repeated, still thinking he was asking about prophets.

The laughter continued and, when Yocom caught on, he began laughing too. Finally, the judge broke in and issued a warning. He threatened to clear the courtroom of all spectators if order wasn't restored immediately. That was the only humorous incident I recall during the entire trial.

Then Yocom's questioning turned to the April 20 meeting and what was discussed there. I was asked about "false prophets" and whether or not Ervil preached that they should be killed. I defended it on the basis of what it said "anywhere you want to turn in the Bible." He pressed me further and asked if I personally believed it and, again, I fell back on what the Bible said about it. But, when he asked me if I considered it a crime in God's eyes to kill a false prophet, I replied, "In God's eyes [it is] not, but that law is not being enforced right now . . . if you went out and did it, then it wouldn't be too good of an idea."

Then he asked me if I believed I would be punished by God for killing a false prophet. I replied that if people started taking the law into their own hands, "then I don't think God would approve of it." That ended his line of questioning on that subject. He had tried to get me to admit I could justify killing someone based on God's law, but I didn't.

Following that, we went into a lengthy exchange over my dealings with Don — from the time we left Dallas for Albuquerque through my stay in Denver and my delivery of the gun to him in Salt Lake. I was asked why I didn't question what Don needed the gun for and I replied we just weren't in the habit of questioning military orders when they were given. To support my statement, I said that Don physically hit me once and I asked Ervil to intervene and put a stop to it. Then Yocom asked when I found out I was being sought in connection with the Allred murder and I said it was after I crossed into Mexico, sometime around July 4, 1977. When he asked me why I didn't turn myself in if I had nothing to hide, I said I didn't think I would get a fair trial, considering all the bad publicity we'd gotten in the media and among the Mormons who were opposed to us.

Yocom ended his first round of questioning by again bringing up Ervil's doctrine about the higher laws of God. He asked me if I believed in them. I replied, "He teaches it the way it says in the Bible, so, yes." Did I believe that Ervil was a prophet of God? "Yes, I do," I said.

John came back and asked me a few questions about the Ten Commandments, then Yocom returned briefly to pick up the ball. He asked me if I thought violation of any of the Ten Commandments warranted the death penalty and I said it would if that law

279

— God's law — was "in effect right now, which it isn't." That ended my testimony for the day.

It was late Friday afternoon when I finally stepped down from the witness stand. I was relieved. For long, grinding hours Yocom had been grilling me, perhaps even hoping for a Perry Mason-style confession from the witness stand. But I didn't betray anyone — not even Ervil, who many people thought should have been up there instead of us.

The weekend was one of agonizing anticipation. In three or four days the verdict would be announced. Our fate would be decided, one way or another. That weekend I made no notes in the little Hallmark datebook I kept during my jail stay between January 1 and the date of the verdict, so I have very little recollection of what was going through my mind at that time. I do remember feeling numb, emotionally drained, and thankful that my ordeal was nearly over, but I was apprehensive about the outcome. Mom, Nancy, and John and maybe a few others came by to buoy my spirits. My fellow prisoners, the matrons, and even the bailiff who took me back and forth from jail to court every day were all very supportive. The bailiff would tell me it was going to be all right, things would work out okay, and I was surprised to see she was on my side. I certainly didn't expect that sort of reaction from someone working for a system I believed was persecuting me.

On Monday, March 19, the day for closing statements, the courtroom was packed as usual. It had been that way every day of the trial and the room had a capacity of about seventy-five spectators. Occasionally, at various times during the trial, I would look behind me for familiar faces, but I saw very few. I know Mom was there after she testified and there was no need to continue sequestering her. Glen was there part of the time. He brought his two oldest daughters, Wendy and Jody, with him once or twice. I saw the media sketch artists at work, drawing pictures of us, the judge, the prosecutor, and our attorneys. The other spectators were probably just there to witness the action; perhaps some of them were followers of Allred's sect. I spent much of the time looking directly at the members of the jury. John had advised me on the importance of eye contact and how it was essential to look at people directly, whether speaking to them or not, to show that I had nothing to hide.

John called me back up to the stand for a few minutes to establish whether I was righthanded or lefthanded. I explained that I use both hands for different things, but I was basically a lefty. Yocom came back with a few questions, trying to catch me one last time. He was asking me about my basketball and volleyball playing and which hand I used most often and, after I told him, he asked me which hand I ate with. Then he asked me, "And you shoot with your right hand?"

Thinking he was off the subject of sports, I replied, "I haven't been around guns that much."

"I didn't say anything about guns," he said.

I asked him what he was talking about and found out he was talking about which hand I shoot baskets with. After I told him, he then asked me which hand I shoot guns with.

"I don't know. I haven't been around them," I answered.

That was his last question. I was allowed to step down and John rested our case. There were a few legal maneuverings by our attorneys and Yocom, and the jury was asked to leave for a few minutes while motions relating to the charges were discussed with the judge. After the discussions were finished, the jury was brought back in and a one-hour recess was called.

After the recess, the judge gave instructions to the jury on how they were to deliberate on the counts as they related to Vic, Mark, Ed, and me. Then closing statements began. Yocom got up first with the closing argument for the prosecution and he laid out the full scenario of the plan as he understood it, from the meeting in Dallas to the events in the Salt Lake area. He said the composite picture John entered as evidence for us more closely resembled me or Ramona than it did Don or Noreen. He also noted how the stories of Isaac, Jack Strothman, and Don and John Sullivan were all basically corroborated, despite the fact they had all gone separate ways and had no contact with each other right after the Allred killing.

Then he zeroed in on the credibility of our witnesses — Mom, Nancy, Alex, and, of course, Vic and me — accusing all of us of lying. Toward the end of his closing argument, Yocom accused Ed of being "involved up to his ears," despite Ed's decision not to testify. This prompted Steve to ask the judge for a mistrial since the prosecution is forbidden to pass judgment on a defendant's failure to take the stand in his own defense.

The judge denied Steve's request and then John made a motion for mistrial on account of some remarks Yocom made against Vic. That motion was denied also. However, the judge explained to the jury, which had been out of the room when the two mistrial motions were made, that nothing in the prosecution's statement should be construed as evidence. He also reminded them that the failure of a defendant to take the witness stand is not to be taken as an admission of guilt.

Then John's turn came to give his closing statement. He made quite a point of discrediting the Sullivans' and Jack Strothman's testimonies, playing up the immunity issue, and implying it was inviting them to lie in order to protect themselves. Don, he said, was getting "the red carpet treatment, this hero treatment," in exchange for his testimony and a reduction in the charges. "When you tell a murderer you'll let him go if he blames somebody else, you're asking for trouble. You're asking for him to lie. You're putting the gun in his hand," John said.

He accused the prosecution of prompting the Sullivans and Jack to "make some modifications" in their stories to fit the State's theory of the murder. "And they became the good guys. And their story, I suppose, is particularly attractive because it had great media appeal. I mean, it was just the sort of thing that the *National Enquirer* goes bananas over." He went on to say that the prosecution "poisoned the well" for any chance my story had of being just as believable as that of Don and the others who testified for the State.

John also dwelled on the point of "reasonable doubt" and reminded the jury that, regardless of what they may personally believe as to someone's guilt or innocence, if the State failed to prove its case beyond a doubt, it was grounds for acquittal. The religion and polygamy issue, John argued, should not be considered a factor in trying to decide the outcome of this case. Just because polygamy is illegal doesn't mean people will stop practicing it. What it does, he said, is "drive it underground where people do not have the protection of the law. It makes a world where the wolves prey on the sheep . . . because nobody wants to talk to the police."

John also had some rather unkind things to say about Ervil. He repeatedly explained he was not there to defend Ervil. "Frankly, I rather despise the fellow if for no other reason that he leaves me to defend his wife instead of coming forward himself to do some explaining. I think he's a coward, and I don't care who knows about that." He went on to paint Ervil as a weak leader who had no power to control our minds, which is contrary to what the state had been contending.

Then he discussed our beliefs in regard to what the Bible says about false prophets being put to death. Just because I said in testimony that I believed it should be done, he said, didn't mean I would just go out and do it. If I could be judged guilty for holding to a fundamentalist belief in the literal words of the Bible, then twenty million Americans would be just as guilty.

Continuing, John made quite a point over the fact no one had positively identified me as having been in Rulon Allred's office the day of the murder. They'd had opportunities to do so from the lineup and from photographs and still failed to pick me out, although some of them got closer to identifying me as the trial itself got closer. In the case of Alfred Tucholski, John said, "for some reason as time went on his memory got better, or did he get swept up in the team spirit of let's convict these people that killed the doctor?" He also noted that these eyewitnesses were not certain whether they saw men or women in and around the doctor's office at the time of the murder. In addition, testimony had brought out the fact that I was lefthanded and the killer held the gun in the right hand.

John's final words to the jury were, "The law presumes her to be innocent, and the State has failed to prove otherwise, and I think there's a simple explanation for that, ladies and gentlemen. It's because that is not only a presumption, it's a fact. And all the lying accomplices, and all the fancy charts, and little models, and the rest of this stuff can't do a thing against that."

Bob was even more vehement in his denunciation of Don and the testimony he gave. He called Don "probably the most morally despicable person who has been in this courtroom who has testified, and who has certainly acted in a fashion which is more heinous and onerous" than anything the guys or I might have done. Bob also brought up the issue of Jim Jones and the Guyana tragedy and tried to convince the jury to disassociate what happened there from what was on trial here.

Then he took aim at Isaac's testimony, implying that he had been coached by the prosecution as to what he would say on the witness stand. As to Mark's part in the conspiracy, Bob said he wasn't at the April 20 meeting and that Mark was doing work for a customer at a time the prosecution said he was at a conspiracy meeting in Albuquerque. As for Vic, Bob maintained that the discussion about not talking to the police without counsel present was a constitutional right to which everyone is entitled.

Steve didn't have too much to say since Ed never took the stand, but he did emphasize that Ed's decision not to testify should not be counted against him. Like the other two attorneys, he attacked the testimony given by Don and John Sullivan, Jack Strothman, and especially Isaac, who most clearly implicated Ed in the April 20 meeting. He contended that no one other than the "accomplice witnesses" — Don and Jack — could place Ed in Salt Lake City around the time of the murder. The reason the soda can had Ed's fingerprint on it was because Don was driving Ed's car at the time and he happened to throw the can, along with other garbage, into a dumpster.

As far as the testimony of Don, John, and Jack went, Steve claimed that Lloyd had coached them on what to tell the police and they "had plenty of time . . . to get their stories straight."

Yocom was given one last chance to get a few more remarks in and he tried to put down what our attorneys had said in their closing statements. He defended his decision to use Don as his star witness. He said Don was not granted immunity but actually pled guilty to a second-degree felony that could put him away for up to fifteen years. However, he added that the State would recommend the sentence be light. He also said Don made his statements at the time of his arrest, in March 1978, before the immunity issue was even discussed. He criticized John's use of the immunity issue in regard to Don, John, and Jack, saying the State made allowance for it in the law.

Then he tried to further discredit my testimony in the same mocking, snide tone that I found very irritating throughout my dealings with him. He made it seem as though John "had to convince this poor, poor little girl, this poor, littlest victim of this great, great conspiracy against her by Don Sullivan, John and Jack Strothman . . . that she'd get a fair trial in these [American] courts." He also had a few unkind things to say about the other defense witnesses, especially Mom, Nancy, and Alex. In closing, he told the jury that the events went down exactly as he laid them out, despite the fact they might sound strange and bizarre.

After Yocom was finished, the jury left the room to deliberate. I was taken back to my cell to sweat it out. Those few hours that passed between the time I left the courtroom and the time I returned to hear the verdict are a complete blank in my memory now. When I was led from the courtroom, neither I nor anyone else could have known how long it would take for the jury to reach a verdict. It could be a few minutes or it could be the next day. Although I don't recall what I did during that time, it's safe to assume I prayed a lot.

Word got to me in about four hours that a verdict was in. I was led down the hall, into the elevator, through the tunnel, and back into the courtroom. My heart was pounding furiously the whole time during that long walk back into the court. When I got there, John was there already and he seemed a little concerned. He confided to me that when a jury reaches a verdict that quickly it's usually not a good sign. Seconds seemed an eternity as Judge Banks went through the formalities. He asked the jury if they had reached a verdict and the foreman said they had. The foreman handed the piece of paper to the bailiff and the bailiff handed it to the judge.

"Now, I'll not tolerate any outbursts from the crowd as I'm reading this verdict," the judge said. At that point I was squeezing John's hand so tightly my knuckles turned white. My heart was now pounding in my throat. Then the judge started reading off the counts against us in full, beginning with the murder count.

"Not guilty," he announced.

Then he read off the next count, conspiracy to commit the murder of Rulon Allred.

"Not guilty."

I eased up on John's hand, but I was feeling numb. Two more counts to go, as the judge read on.

Then the third count, attempted murder of Verlan LeBaron: "Not guilty."

Finally, conspiracy to murder Verlan LeBaron: "Not guilty."

It took him a few minutes to read all the counts and the not guilty verdicts for each one and this only heightened the suspense. Then, as the final acquittal was announced, I went limp. A profound sense of relief swept through me. I was in a daze, thanking God that it was finally over.

For the first few seconds I couldn't believe it. It took a little while to sink in. Then we hugged all around and congratulated our attorneys. Mom came up to the barrier that separated the front of the courtroom from the spectator section and hugged all of us. She was relieved and thankful. This whole affair had been as hard on her as it was for the rest of us. Having two sons and a daughter on trial, trying to keep the family together and watch over my child at the same time, had taken a heavy physical and emotional toll on her.

As for our own initial reactions, we weren't jumping up and down and screeching. It was not the way they show it in the movies. No TV cameras or mikes converged on us at that moment. I had to go back to my cell and wait for the judge to officially process me for release. Mark and Ed had to do likewise. Only Vic, who was out on bail, was free to go.

The verdict was announced in late afternoon and it didn't look as if the paperwork for me was going to be processed that day. When I got back to my cell I took a shower, put on my night-clothes, and started getting ready for bed, fully prepared to spend one last night there. But then the word came: my papers were signed and I would be released that night. I got dressed, gathered up my clothes and what few possessions I had, and said my good-byes to those around me. My hair still wet, I was walked through a tunnel leading to the street and the sweetest freedom anyone could ever have known.

CHAPTER 21

As I emerged from the tunnel onto the street, John was there with Mom, Vic, and Nancy. I was in quite a daze and found it hard to believe it was all over. I remember seeing some TV cameras and reporters following me, but I didn't give any statements to them. Things happened quickly and I don't recall many details.

Mom and I were ushered into a car (I don't know whose) and as we took off, I looked all around me at everything outside the windows. Even though it was dark, I could still see the snow-capped mountains that tower over Salt Lake City. They never looked more beautiful. I gazed around at all the lights. I inhaled clean, fresh air, and took in all the sights and sounds of the world I had been removed from for the past five months. Then we arrived at a nearby pub partly owned by Steve McCaughey. I was only twenty at the time and the legal drinking age was twenty-one.

As I stepped inside the door of the pub, I heard a loud cheer go up and saw all these people smiling and clapping and chanting, "Not guilty! Not guilty!" All my pent-up emotions just let go and I started crying tears of thankfulness and humility. Ed, Vic, Nancy, and John were there. It was great to be alive and to have family and supportive friends cheering for us. But the strangest thing was that this party was organized by some defense attorneys, people I didn't know. Our case was the largest not guilty verdict in the state's history, taking into account there were four defendants charged with a total of fourteen counts. This group of attorneys was celebrating our attorneys' victory, which was like a victory for *all* defense lawyers in Utah, they felt.

There was also a reporter there from one of the Salt Lake TV stations, Martha Radatz, who interviewed us live. It was the first time I had ever been allowed to talk to a reporter. She was the only reporter present. Apparently, someone had promised her an "exclusive" and she got it.

Our little celebration went on for about an hour, and we were celebrities for the evening. I felt a little timid in front of all those partying attorneys. I really didn't belong in a place like that. We left there, along with John, while the other lawyers continued to party.

Vic treated Bob Van Sciver, his wife, Nancy, Mom, and me to a Chinese dinner, and after that we went over to the TV station Martha Radatz worked for. As we entered the studio, she introduced us to Kathleen Sullivan, the anchorwoman at the time, and then she showed us the tapes of our live interview.

I spent the night in Mom's hotel room. The next day I got up early and walked around the city a little bit, staring at the buildings and the people. It felt so good to be "out in the world" again. Mom and I had some final loose ends to tie up, some kind of paperwork as I recall. Then we headed up to Glen and Kathy's house in Ogden and I got to see their new twins for the first time. Erin had already flown back to Oklahoma City with Alex, so I didn't see her until I got there.

After another day or two in Utah, Mom and I got on a plane and we were off to Oklahoma. As the plane's wheels lifted off the ground, I gazed out the window. I watched Salt Lake City get smaller and smaller below me. Finally, it disappeared from view and I breathed a sigh of relief. I was leaving captivity and a horrible chapter in my life behind me. The last time I had been at that airport, it was the exact opposite. I was being flown *in* — as a prisoner.

I don't remember much else about my flight to Oklahoma, but the reception I got on my return was very memorable. Dad was there, along with Lillian, her kids, and, of course, Erin. She was happy to have her mommy back and fascinated with the prospect of soon having a baby brother or sister.

It was nice seeing Dad again. It had been six months or more since I had seen or heard from him. Over the past four years he had bounced around quite a bit, going from Las Vegas to Denver, then finally to a small town deep inside Mexico where he lives today. While in Vegas he had his wife Annalee Barlow with him and they later had another wife, Chela Zarate, brought up. Each of his wives had two kids when they all moved to Denver, and after a couple of years working for Lincoln Auto II, they made the final move to Mexico. I had last seen Dad when Ervil and I were in Catemaco, shortly before I was arrested. Dad and his wives and kids were on their way to their new home and they passed through our village. Both Annalee and Chela were pregnant at the time.

It was hard to gauge Dad's reaction to the whole mess in which we found ourselves embroiled. Tears in his eyes told how tenderly he loved us all. He just wasn't much of a talker. He never had been. At some point, and it's difficult to say when, he got disgusted with Ervil and the church and quietly broke away from it. He was getting up there in years and just wanted to live the rest of his life in seclusion and tranquility with his new family. Nonetheless, the rest of us were his first family, and that meant a lot to him. When he came to Oklahoma, it was his role to be supportive and do whatever he could for us. And, he got to see the two boys he'd had with his now deceased wife Noemi — Harvey and Paul — in addition to her own children, Alex, Judy, and Johnny, whom he loved as much as his own children.

After Dad left, and the initial euphoria of freedom and acquittal wore off, I had to get used to settling into a new life in a new locale. Over the years I had bounced around so much and lived in so many places, Oklahoma City seemed like just another waystop on the road to somewhere else. Around me in this one house, besides

Mom and Noemi's five kids, there were Lillian and her three kids, plus my daughter, plus a few other children of Ervil's various wives — Anna Mae's daughter Celia and Lorna's daughter Tarsa. The house was in a commercially zoned area of the city so no one could complain about so many people living together. There were four bedrooms and a basement, and we spread out as best we could.

The spring of 1979 was a confusing time for the remaining, surviving members of the Church of the Lamb of God. We were all scattered about, confined, or splintered. Mark was still up in Salt Lake, having to answer charges of jumping bail, and he had to work out some method of repayment. Vic had gone off to live in another state. Duane left Mom and Alex in charge of the appliance shop in Oklahoma and went off to join Vic. Dan, having been released from jail in Ensenada, was back in Denver with his wives and children. Five of Ervil's wives — Linda, Rosemary, Anna Mae, Teresa, and Yolanda — were also in Denver. They were all working in Michael's Appliance under horrible conditions. Vonda was in a San Diego jail, awaiting trial for Dean Vest's murder. I don't recall where Ed was. The Sullivans were no longer among us. Lorna and Arthur were down in Mexico with Ervil and probably Ramona, who was no longer in any real danger of being convicted.

Four of us had been through a long confinement and trial and were struggling to adjust to a seminormal life again. We realized full well that only the grace of God and a few sharp attorneys had gotten us off the hook for some serious capital crimes. I don't think anyone among us was too eager to go through that again. The seeds were being sown for the Chynoweth family's split from Ervil LeBaron, the man who had led us down this road to near ruin.

In Oklahoma, Mom managed to keep the business going that she and Duane had started. Alex Zarate was a good technician and he helped her out a lot, even though he was only in his mid-teens. I was eight months pregnant but still did what I could to help out around the house. I didn't want to feel like a burden to anyone and I took over the cooking chores. My five months in confinement had left me feeling kind of weak because I didn't get very much exercise. In Oklahoma, I was able to rebuild some of my strength and even took to trimming some of the pine trees around Mom's place. I was obsessed with keeping busy all the time. I pushed myself constantly.

While I was in jail I'd pictured all the nice little things Erin and I would do together when I got out but, unfortunately, it wasn't to be that way for a while. I was so driven by my need to be useful again that she and I didn't go out too much except maybe to the store or on some other errand. I wished I'd had time to take her to the park or other nice places, but I was just too busy. What little time we did have together, though, was something I really treasured. It was wonderful having my daughter back with me again.

I remember the culture shock I felt on going into a Safeway or a department store and seeing items on the shelves and racks I hadn't seen or used in nearly two years. I had been a fugitive in Mexico for sixteen months and in jail for five months, and it was a strange feeling being free and roaming around in an American city again. I would go into a supermarket and spend hours just looking at the items on the shelves. The employees must have thought I was either nuts or that I was casing the joint for a theft.

In that house in Oklahoma City, on Sunday, May 6, 1979, the latest addition to the Chynoweth clan came into the world. About five or six months earlier, while I was in jail, Lillian had asked if I would let her deliver the baby (assuming I was free at the time) and I agreed. She had assisted in a few home births before and had taken some midwife courses. I felt confident letting her do the delivery. Having this baby in a hospital was never an option for me. My experiences when Erin was born in a hospital in Denver were so horrible that I resolved I wasn't going to put myself through the same thing again.

Vic was down with us on some kind of business and he was staying in the room where Erin and I usually slept. I was sharing Mom's room, and that's where I went into labor. My contractions began around 1:00 or 2:00 in the morning and I would simply let them pass and go back to sleep. Finally, about 6:30, I knew it was getting near time and I woke Mom. She woke Lillian, moved Vic out of my room, and that's where the delivery took place shortly thereafter. It went really fast and smooth and, with Mom assisting and Celia and Tarsa watching, John Ryan (J.R.) Chynoweth emerged into the daylight for the first time.

I had told John O'Connell that if it was a boy it would be named after him, and he was one of the first people I called with the news. He was honored and flattered, of course, and he offered his congratulations. Ryan was just a name I happened to like, so I gave it as his middle name. J. R. was beautiful, and he let out such a forlorn cry that I just wanted to hold him and let him know he was safe. He wanted to be fed right away, so I held him to my breast and let him nurse. Shortly after that we took him to a doctor to get him checked out and register him with the official records office. Lillian signed that she delivered him and, though Ervil Le-Baron was listed as the father, the name John Ryan Chynoweth is what appeared on the birth certificate.

Before May 1979 was over, several more momentous events would take place in our lives. On the fourteenth, Vonda was convicted of Dean's murder in San Diego and would soon afterward be given a life sentence. This was unexpected and shattering news to us. Then, about three weeks after J.R.'s birth, we took the first steps toward moving to Houston, which would become the most permanent and stable home most of us would know since our early years in Utah. And, around May 25 or 26, Ervil was captured in Mexico.

The circumstances surrounding his capture have never been clear to me. In Mexico they're not obligated to adhere to the police and judicial procedures that are constitutionally mandated in the U.S. If they don't like you down there, they don't have to have a reason to arrest you. They don't have to have a search warrant or an arrest warrant or show just cause before a judge. They can put you in jail for as long as they want, beat up on you, or even torture you to get a confession. Apparently, this was the case with Ervil. It seems that the Mexican authorities just simply wanted him out of the country, despite the fact that he was a Mexican citizen.

Lorna was with Ervil when he was arrested, and they took both of them to the same building in which Dan and I were held in Mexico City. They were even put in the same cell as I was (they saw my name and the date I had scratched on the wall). Ervil was the big fish the authorities were after, perhaps because of the embarrassment they suffered in arresting Dan on the mistaken identity deal seven months earlier. It has been reported that Dick Forbes had a hand in his capture through some connection he had with the American consulate, an attaché or someone like that who was also a Mormon from the Salt Lake area. There were some reports that Ervil had masterminded the kidnapping of a public official's daughter, though I doubt their validity.

Ervil and Lorna were held in the jail for a few days and Lorna later told us he was beaten up pretty badly right in front of her. With Lorna standing there, they would ask Ervil questions and hit him when he answered them. She said they asked him how many wives he had, as if she didn't know and it was supposed to shock her. And then they hit him again when he told them. He was asked to name each one of them, and they slugged him each time. They broke a few of his ribs and cracked a couple more. Lorna was later released and went back to wherever they had been when they were captured.

Then, just like Ed and I before him, Ervil was carted up to the border and forced to walk across the Rio Grande bridge at Laredo, right into the conveniently waiting arms of the FBI. On June 1, 1979, the notorious Ervil LeBaron was safely in the custody of the American authorities he had eluded for so many years. Through some legal maneuverings, he was made an American citizen so he could stand trial in the U.S.

We were upset that Ervil had been captured, but we also felt like it was in the Lord's hands now. We were confident God would take care of him. We were not able to go see him when he was being held in Laredo, since he was flown to Salt Lake not long after that. When he got there, Dan Jordan jumped in and started handling the details relating to Ervil's defense. He even talked to John O'Connell about possibly taking Ervil's case.

By this time, Mark had gotten his mess straightened out in Salt Lake and came to Oklahoma to join the rest of us. Looking for a better location to set up shop, he and Lillian went to Houston to check the area out. They found a place, paid the rent on it starting from June 1, and returned to Oklahoma a week later. They had glowing reports of the business possibilities there. Houston was a fast-growing boom town in the late 1970s and plenty of people there had money to spend. The price of gas and oil was at an all-time high, and though it meant higher prices at the pumps, it also meant higher profits for the oil companies, many of which had their headquarters in the Houston area. The petrochemical industry was the mainstay of Houston's economic base, and tens of thousands of employees were enjoying record-high wage levels. It was the ideal time and place to go and make some money, so off we went.

Mark and I went down first, taking enough machines with us to get started, and we settled into a fairly large two-bedroom house. We placed ads in the paper, fixed up the machines, and launched the business. Lillian and her kids came down a little later and I shared the house with her and Mark. The house had an extended kitchen with more space than we needed, and we blocked part of it off to form a separate bedroom for Erin, J.R., and me.

As always, we all worked really hard to get the business going and we didn't think much about the past. We didn't want to. The past was history, and this time we would be allowed to conduct our business our own way. No Ervil or Dan or Arthur or anyone else to get in the way. Later that summer, I found a house for Mom and her adopted Zarate kids and she came down, bringing Ed with her. Then Duane and a very pregnant Laura arrived a month later. On September 6, Lillian delivered Laura of a baby girl, and she was named Jenny for one of my mother's sisters.

Our family was growing fast. The Chynoweths' thundering herd had invaded Houston — not that anyone else would have noticed, among the two or three million other people in that booming metropolis.

The rest of 1979 passed rather uneventfully but happily. The business flourished and we continued to expand. This was the first real taste of freedom our family had known since we left Utah in the mid-1960s to join Ervil and Joel's followers in Mexico. Even though there had been other times when Ervil was jailed, he had still been able to maintain a certain amount of control over us during those times. We stayed in frequent touch with him while he was jailed in Salt Lake, but we were now having doubts about things he had done. We continued to revere him, though, until after his trial and conviction which came a year later. That's when the more serious questioning came in.

In Houston, we were beginning to lead normal middle-class American lives for the first time. We still kept our beliefs and held meetings to reinforce them, but we also interacted freely in society. Our children attended public schools and Mark was our moral and spiritual leader during this time.

On November 10, a Saturday night, I went to Gilley's, the famous nightclub outside Houston, with Mark, Lillian, Duane, Laura, Ed, and a few others. "Mr. Rose-Colored Glasses," John Conlee, was playing that night. I remember being impressed by the size of the place and all the goings on around me, with a thousand or more people under the same roof. You could have housed a small Mexican village in a place that size. I had not been to many bars in my life and certainly never one even close to this big. Ed and I danced together, and it was the first semblance of a "date" I'd had with anyone in quite a number of years.

But we were not completely free of Ervil — at least not at that point, anyway. We made no secret about where we were and he knew how to get hold of us. He would call us once or twice a week — collect — and try to keep us in the fold with his pep talks. Sometimes he would ask for money, either directly or through Arthur, and we would send him what we could. We still believed in what Ervil had to say and we weren't trying to break from him spiritually. We just didn't want him trying to control us from jail or telling us how to run our business, which he knew nothing about. We had zero confidence in Ervil's business ability, and it was very irritating to have him meddling in our affairs. We made it clear to him it was *our* business, and we were going to run it our own way.

Toward the end of the year Lorna and her flock descended upon us. With Ervil gone there was nothing to keep her in Mexico any longer. But having her around was a bad scene in many ways. Over the years, she had become quite bitter and there was no way of making her happy. Not only did she and I not get along, she was still intensely loyal to Ervil, whereas the rest of us were beginning to pull away. We were asserting some independence and thinking twice before acting on everything Ervil told us to do.

Then she started ripping us off. We wanted to help her make some of her own money rather than trying to support her in a welfare-like manner, so we let her take the pickup calls at her home. We would pay her for taking the calls, and we helped her out in other ways if she needed more. She was supposed to turn the pickup cards over to the guys so they could go out and buy machines, but she began keeping some of the cards for herself. She would have her oldest son, Andrew, pick up the machines, fix them up, and resell them, keeping the money for herself.

Finally, Mark, Duane, and Ed caught onto what Lorna was doing and they confronted her. An angry scene erupted. They threw her and the kids out of the house they were paying the rent on and loaded her belongings into an El Camino they'd bought for her. Lorna cursed them out as she drove off and had a few choice words for me as well. I told her to go fuck off, the first time in my life I'd ever used that word. After so many years of taking abuse from her, listening to her calling me a whore or a tramp, and having her turn her kids against me, it felt kind of good to finally say it.

Lorna headed for Salt Lake, where she could be close to Ervil. That was the last time I ever saw her. I heard that Ervil was trying to make arrangements for her to become his legal wife, but I don't think it ever came to pass. I don't see what good it would have done either of them. Perhaps it was her way of staking her claim to him, after being neglected for so many years.

The one we really felt sorry for through all her misfortunes was Vonda. She had been convicted of Dean Vest's murder on May 14, even though she did the same thing a jury saw fit to acquit us for. She was merely following what she believed to be God's will through Ervil. Steve McCaughey, who had done such a good job in defending Ed twice, suddenly let up on his efforts. We had been paying him a lot of money to defend Vonda and all he did was enter a plea of *nolo contendre*. He didn't build a defense and he didn't put anyone on the stand who could help her. In short, he made none of the effort that he put forth for Ed in Utah to discredit the prosecution's case against her. It was no contest. Vonda was left to the mercy of the State of California.

Vonda was given a life sentence. Today, in 1990, she's still in prison, in Frontera, California. Appeals have failed and every time she has come up for parole it has been denied. Most of her six children are grown and out on their own. From the letters I get from her, I can tell that the conditions around her are horrible. When we were writing to each other from jail, Vonda's letters sounded hopeful and cheerful. They had cute little pen and ink drawings on them in lively colors. She was very much into the scriptures, the *Book of Mormon, Doctrine and Covenants*, and other doctrinal writings. She even got some of her cellmates to take part in Bible study groups. Until her conviction, she seemed optimistic that she was going to get off. And she took a lot of encouragement from the verdict reached in our case.

Today her letters sound bleak and the poetry she writes is haunting — the words of a woman with little hope. She still conducts Bible study groups and counsels other inmates, trying to keep busy and make life better for those around her. I know that long ago she realized what she did for Ervil was not a command from God, as she believed at the time. However, every time another person is killed and it is linked to Ervil's group, that gives the parole board an excuse to deny her release. I'm convinced that Vonda has more than paid for her crime.

CHAPTER 22

Throughout the last half of 1979 and for the first five months of 1980, Ervil sat in the Salt Lake County Jail, awaiting trial. A preliminary hearing in mid-January determined that the State had enough evidence to bind him over for trial. Other states and localities were watching the proceedings in Utah, possibly hoping to get their turn when David Yocom and his people were done. Ervil could have been charged with ordering Dean Vest's murder in California, Robert Simons' murder in Carbon County, Utah, or Becky's murder in Dallas, but Yocom had first crack at him because none of these other places had Ervil's name on an indictment. Ervil was faced with the same charges the four of us had been acquitted on — murder and conspiracy to commit murder on Rulon Allred and attempted murder and conspiracy to commit murder on Verlan LeBaron.

Of the nine of us listed in the original indictment, Ervil would stand alone when his own earthly day of judgment finally came. Arthur, who had been arrested in Miami in July 1979, had the charges dropped against him. He was only Ervil's driver, even though he knew what the mission was all about. Charges were also dropped against Ramona after the rest of us were acquitted. She had jumped bail but the prosecution saw no sense in trying to make a case against her. Don and John Sullivan had gotten off lightly in exchange for their testimony. That left only Ervil, the mastermind of the whole plot.

Ervil wanted John O'Connell to defend him, but the circumstances here were a lot different than they were with my case. John had been assigned by the court to defend me, in the absence of an available public defender. He got paid through the system set up by the State. When Ervil's turn came to face the charges, there were some public defenders available and Ervil was broke. John did meet with Ervil in jail several times and it looked initially like he might defend him, but he wanted to be certain of getting paid for his services. Besides, John did not have a very high opinion of Ervil and indicated to me he would have turned the case down no matter what.

Consequently, Ervil had to accept three court-appointed public defenders: John Hill, Bruce Lubeck, and Fred Metos. They were all good attorneys, but this still put Ervil at a severe handicap. The three attorneys were simply not as familiar with the case as John was, or the man who would be prosecuting him. Yocom had stepped down from the county attorney's office shortly after we were acquitted and returned to private practice, but because of his expertise, he was appointed a "special prosecutor" to try Ervil. One of the reasons why it took a year to get Ervil's trial under way was so the attorneys would have time to catch up on their reading of transcripts, police reports, and all the other documents Yocom apparently knew by heart.

Ervil had not helped his own case too much by talking freely with Dick Forbes and several other investigators right after his arrest in Laredo. Mostly he talked about doctrine and reportedly rattled on for hours and hours about civil law and how he was supposedly destined to rule the world with everyone tithing to him. But in the course of his rambling he may have said some potentially incriminating things. He reportedly admitted authorship of letters to President Carter that had been interpreted as being threatening. Much of the case that was prepared against him had to do with his interpretation of doctrine and how he could justify the ordering of capital crimes such as murder in God's name. He had told us never to talk to police and yet here he was, doing just that, even before consulting an attorney. I don't know what he expected to accomplish besides drawing the noose tighter around his own neck. He undoubtedly thought he could convert these people who were out to put him away permanently.

Ervil continually wrote to us and called, asking us to help him — usually with money. He always needed money for something or other. Naturally, he expected us to come up and show our support for him, but we were too busy trying to get our own lives back in order. The appliance business in Houston was going strong, and we felt good about ourselves and what we were doing. Besides, we had no desire to hang around his jail cell, listening to him give us orders on how to conduct our lives and business while he sat back and pulled the strings. The jails of Salt Lake already held enough unpleasant memories for us; we were not about to subject ourselves to the same indignities again voluntarily.

So, for most of that time, we stayed in Houston and helped Ervil any way we could from a distance. We still respected his basic teachings and allowed him some human faults and failures, but we were going to be more careful and questioning about what we did for him thereafter. He had made some grave errors and we were now seeing what they were.

I did go up to Salt Lake once, in April 1980, to talk to Ervil's attorneys and give them some background on the Sullivans and their involvement with Ervil's church. I told them about how Lloyd Sullivan had tried to get me to divorce Ervil and marry him. I even mentioned the "revelation" Lloyd claimed in which we were supposed to go up on a mountain and marry each other in the sight of God three years earlier, when we were on the run. The defense was trying to build its case around undermining the testimony Don and John would give, in addition to the statements they had from Lloyd before his death.

I don't remember what else I might have discussed with them, but I was informed that I would not be needed to testify for Ervil's defense. For some reason they did not want any of the other defend-

300

ants to testify. I would have done it if they had told me I was needed, but apparently they didn't feel we would help the case they were trying to build.

I did not go to see Ervil. I simply didn't want to. The thought of seeing him in person again made my skin crawl. He knew I was coming up with J.R., and he begged me to come see him and bring the baby. But I wouldn't. It may sound cold-hearted, denying a father the right to see his own son, but I felt that he had no claims to J.R. other than the fact he managed to impregnate me. I had carried this child alone, through five months of imprisonment, without any kind of a paternal support system. What purpose would it serve to try to establish one now? John Ryan Chynoweth, the last of the fifty or so children of Ervil LeBaron, would never get to see his real father. This was the way I preferred it.

But someone very important did get to see my baby for the first time. John O'Connell was delighted with this healthy, chubby eleven-month-old boy who was named after him. I spent a night with John and his family and, of course, he felt honored to have a namesake. John thought it was rather cold of me not taking J.R. to see his father, but I still couldn't bring myself to do it.

I spent a few nights in a hotel and a few days and nights with Glen and his family, and then it was back to Houston for us. Before leaving Salt Lake, I bought a suit and tie and some shirts for Ervil to wear at the trial and took them to his attorneys to give him. It must have hurt him knowing I was there yet not coming by or even calling, but that was my decision. I knew I wouldn't have been able to handle it. As far as I was concerned, I had done what I could for him. The rest would be up to the courts and to God.

Ervil's trial opened on May 12. I stayed in Houston and kept abreast of it through Mom, who had gone to Salt Lake to testify for him. Lorna, who had moved to Salt Lake to be near him after we threw her and the kids out of the house in Houston, also testified for the defense. She had been one of Ervil's most frequent visitors while he was in jail there and was constantly complaining to him about how badly the rest of us had treated her. She even told him I was embezzling money from the business. This really upset me, since she was the one who had been doing it. The only other defense witnesses were Alex Zarate Chynoweth and Guillermo (Bill) Rios, who were at the meeting in Dallas when the Allred hit was discussed. No one else — not Vic or Ed or Mark or I — could help him out since his attorneys had decided against it.

When Ervil's trial got under way, Yocom produced a few surprise witnesses who hadn't been at our trial, most notably Verlan and Conway LeBaron and Ervil's older sister, Esther. They all gave testimony claiming to have heard death threats Ervil made against various CFB leaders and others who reportedly didn't go along with what he said. This was the sort of hearsay testimony that had been thrown out on appeals of his two previous trials in Mexico, but the judge in Salt Lake apparently allowed it to stand. It must have served to create a frightening picture of Ervil in the minds of the twelve jurors selected to sit in on his case.

Carol Jensen, mother of Ervil's sixth wife, Christina, who was forced to marry him at a young age as I was, also testified for the prosecution. She claimed to have heard Ervil plotting to kill Verlan and Allred during a meeting she had with him sometime in 1975.

Don and John Sullivan and Jack Strothman also testified against Ervil and told what they had seen, heard, and done between the meeting in Dallas and the failed attempt on Verlan's life. Don told the court he left Ervil's church because he had failed in the Verlan hit mission and feared Ervil was going to have him killed. Ervil's son Isaac told about what he saw and heard at the Dallas meeting, including the mention of my name as one of the two women assigned to the Allred hit.

Bob Torkelson, the man who found the evidence thrown in the dumpster, told the court what he found in the bag. Dick Forbes got up on the stand and related Ervil's lengthy discourses on doing away with false prophets while Ervil was being held in the Laredo jail. Merlin Kingston and Allred's brother, Owen, testified about Ervil trying to shake their organizations down for tithing. And, in the biggest surprise of all, Richard Bunker was now claiming to have recognized me as the woman he saw in Allred's office just after the shooting and who pointed a gun to his own head when he grabbed Ramona. According to the reports of the trial, Bunker was shown the same photograph of me he had been shown before and was now swearing it was my face he saw. Fortunately, I had already been acquitted and couldn't be retried.

In all, Yocom called more than forty witnesses against Ervil before resting his case ten days after the trial opened. Yocom himself, from what I understand, was more subdued, less flamboyant and fiery than he had been while trying to convict us. There was no picking up and slamming down of Bibles on the exhibit table. It was all very low-key, without the courtroom theatrics that characterized portions of our trial.

Lorna was the first defense witness. Because she wasn't present when the Allred-Verlan hit was planned, she couldn't refute the charges Ervil was facing. She was more or less there as a "character witness," to make Ervil look like the one being led — by the Sullivans and others — instead of the other way around. Mom, Alex, and Bill were asked about the details of the meeting in Dallas and Mom and Alex repeated pretty much what they said under oath in our trial, that it was a business meeting.

Ervil never got up on the stand. I'm sure his attorneys felt it would be destructive to their case if they allowed Yocom to get his teeth into him. And Ervil was a man who just couldn't keep his mouth shut. Of all the members of our church who could have blown it for him, no one could have done more damage than he might have done to himself. He was the loosest cannon we had on the deck.

On May 28, following the closing statements, the jury went out to deliberate on a verdict and came back with one after only three hours: guilty of first-degree murder of Rulon Allred; guilty of conspiracy to murder Verlan LeBaron. His sentence, which was handed down a few days later, was life imprisonment in the state prison at Draper, Utah.

I remember very clearly what my reaction was to Ervil's conviction because I have a copy of a letter I sent him on June 15, 1980, that describes it. More than anything else, I felt that justice had been done. We had killed and conspired to kill on his direct orders: now the real guilty party was being punished for his crimes. The first page of my nine-page letter read as follows:

Dear Ervil,

I haven't known what to say to you before so I just didn't write. Now I think I do have some things that need to be said.

I am really sorry about you getting convicted and it was a shock but I thought about it and now it makes more sense to me. Obviously, if the Lord had wanted you out then he would have seen to your getting acquitted. Since the rest of us did everything within our powers to see that you would be, it was His doing. I personally spent hours and hours with the lawyers spilling my brains for every possible bit of info that might be useful, and so did a lot of other people. So I feel the blame lies not with us or with the lawyers. As far as I've heard they did the best they could. So that leaves only one person to "blame" or whatever word you choose to use. The Lord knows best and I'm willing to trust Him in this matter . . .

In the letter I went on to tell him we were surviving and doing well on our own. I advised him to send any instructions for us through Dan, whom we acknowledged as his most logical successor in our secular affairs, or through Mark, who was the unofficial head of our group in Houston. I also cautioned him against placing too much stock in the lies Lorna was telling him about us, and me in particular. I assured him I wasn't sleeping around, despite Lorna's vicious allegations to the contrary.

Ervil's conviction was the catalyst I needed to step up my efforts to divorce him. I had been considering it for a long time, and now I was more determined than ever to go through with it. I didn't want to remain wedded to a man condemned to spend the rest of his life behind bars. I had two children who would never have a father around to help rear them, and I just didn't want to be sealed to him for time and eternity anymore.

Never, at any time during our five-year marriage, did I feel that Ervil really needed me — at least not in the way a husband normally needs his wife. It had been a big ego trip for him and he loved to flaunt it. Of all the men and boys who had sought me, it was him — the big, all-powerful leader — who got me. Then, when he "got" me, he couldn't figure out what to do with me except to try to keep me in tow. Now, with him in jail for life, what kind of demands was he going to make on me? I did not want to stick around and find out.

When I began looking into what it would take to get a divorce, I decided that the logical person to seek that advice from was Dan Jordan, the man who had married us. But Dan didn't give me any help or encouragement at first. He reiterated what Ervil had said: that a celestial bond was for "time and eternity." It could not be annulled in this life or in the next.

This left me no alternative but to go to someone else with my problem, someone I really disliked — Leo Evoniuk. Leo didn't have much of a part to play in Ervil's church until the very end, but the part he played then was a significant one. With Ervil on the lam and his church fragmented in the late 1970s, there was a vacuum among Ervil's chief counselors. Lloyd had defected and Dan was quite a distance away in Denver. While in Mexico, Ervil had only Arthur and the Rios brothers around him as aides he could trust. Leo saw an opening and rushed in to fill the vacuum. He became a combination of Dan and Lloyd to Ervil in exile and later while Ervil was serving time in Utah. He was loyal and faithful and, as a reward, Ervil gave him one of the Rios-Mendez daughters in marriage.

As I mentioned earlier, Ervil met Leo while in jail the second time in Ensenada, in 1976. Leo was doing time for running drugs, a livelihood he took up to help pay for his daughter's wedding, or so he claimed. Up to that time he had been a marine salvager, but apparently didn't find that line of work lucrative enough. His wife left him while he was in jail and Ervil converted him. When he was released, Leo went to Catemaco, where Ervil and I were living at the time of my capture. I found him to be obnoxious, and though I was cordial to him, I also tried to stay out of his way.

Leo fancied himself as quite a writer and scriptorian and, like Ervil, he wrote voluminously. But, also like Ervil, his writings were convoluted and very difficult to make sense out of. Nonetheless, I decided to ask for his advice on getting divorced from Ervil. As I would soon find out, I was going to the wrong person. Aside from Arthur, Leo was Ervil's staunchest loyalist and he wasn't about to let me divorce his boss. I had no choice but to go back to Dan.

Those not familiar with what we believed may well wonder why this question of a divorce should have been such a traumatic dilemma for me. Legally, under the laws of man, I was never married to Ervil. There were no papers on file showing that a marriage had been performed and there was no joint property in question. There was nothing with both of our names on it except J.R.'s birth certificate. Even that did not say we were married. There was never any question of child custody, especially now that he was in prison. So why did I feel this need to get a divorce from a man to whom I was never legally married? Why couldn't I just simply declare myself free to marry anyone I chose?

It needs to be understood that I, like the others in my family, still believed strongly in the Mormon doctrine of "celestial marriage" that Ervil taught us. It was for time and eternity. He may have been physically removed from our midst, but he and his teachings were still very much with us spiritually. We were still members of his church. He remained our prophet and our patriarch and, as such, we adhered to the doctrine he taught us, especially as it related to plural marriage and the celestial bond it entailed. These laws, we felt, came directly from God and ranked higher than the laws of man. We could not, of our own accord, simply set them aside and do as we pleased.

In the context of what we believed, we were fulfilling one of God's highest laws when Ervil and I got married. We would always be expected to adhere to the higher laws of God and, if we wanted a dispensation from them, such as a divorce, we had to go through the proper channels. At least this is the way it seemed to me. Since I was married by someone who held a priesthood, I could only be divorced by one who held the same high office.

This is what I believed and I wanted to go about it the right way, but I didn't know how to do it. I don't think *anyone* did. There was nothing written about celestial divorce anywhere — in the scriptures, in *Doctrine and Covenants,* in the *Book of Mormon,* or in any of our other written guides. There were volumes written on marriage and what it entailed, but all the writings on it pointed in the same direction: "What God hath joined together, let no man put asunder." Marriage was not only for this life but the eternal one that lies beyond. We simply had no precedents to go by. A few of Ervil's other wives had left him in the past, but all they did was declare themselves free with no man-made legal papers to constrain them. I did not want to do it that way.

I had many good reasons for wanting to divorce Ervil. By mid-1980, I had still another reason. His name was Ed Marston. Behind our house in the 7800 block of Bryonwood Drive in Houston was a small outbuilding — the "bachelor pad," we called it — shared by Ed and Alex. Ed was working with us in the business and, like the rest of us, he was trying to adapt to a normal life without Ervil or the others hanging over us. Ed and I had practically grown up together in what we believed and what we experienced. We had been through a lot together, including what very few other people have endured: a murder trial stemming from religious beliefs we strongly held.

Without Ervil around, and knowing that I was going to divorce him, anyway, Ed and I just naturally drew closer together. It seemed a logical, natural sequence of events. We believed in the same higher laws as taught to us by the same man, we had been through the same trials and tribulations our nomadic lifestyle entailed, and we were enjoying the same feeling of freedom and experimentation with a new lifestyle at the same time. We could relate to each other on so many levels. And, on top of that, Ed loved children — especially *my* children. What could have been more perfect for two people of the opposite sex only a few years apart in age? Given our backgrounds, who would have wanted either one of us?

In all of the newspaper and magazine articles and other books written about the LeBarons, Ed has been portrayed as a blood-thirsty killer. None of these people knew Ed as intimately as I did. Underneath the hardened features shown in all the wanted posters that the books and newspapers picked up on was a kind-hearted, soft, gentle, young man who was very confused and unsure of himself. As I've said before, he was treated as the unwanted stepson, not only by Ervil, but by Anna Mae — his own mother — who felt the kids she had by Ervil had a higher calling than those fathered by Nephi, her previous husband. This, and the scandalous manner in which Anna Mae left Nephi for Ervil, resulted in emotional scars on both Ed and his sister Ramona. Ervil wouldn't even let Ed go to his own father's funeral, despite the fact he was old enough to know what was going on. Ed never had the benefit of a good education, being continually carted around from one locale to another, and his reading and writing abilities were seriously deficient.

Ed may have killed a few people and stalked others targeted for murder, but these are not actions he would have done on his own. He was commanded to carry out these horrible deeds by someone much stronger than himself, and he was left with little choice but to obey. I and some of the others did the same thing, but none of us would have pulled any triggers acting on our own accord. Like the rest of us, Ed was a victim. He was victimized by a doctrine that had been twisted to justify acts of out-and-out murder in the name of God. He hated Ervil intensely for the way Ervil had always treated him, but he didn't dare question him. He felt deeply sorry and ashamed of what he had done.

When he lived behind us in Houston, Ed grew a full beard that he trimmed and kept neat and he wore tinted glasses. These did a lot to soften his otherwise hard-looking facial features. But, for many years, he had almost no self-confidence and little, if any, self-esteem. His experiences with the opposite sex were limited, at best.

I worked hard on his image of himself. I did my utmost to make him realize what he had going for him and all the good qualities he could offer the right person. It took me awhile, but I was successful to a large degree. He finally started developing a sense of pride in his abilities and the confidence he needed to make it on his own — quite an accomplishment for a young man who, in his first twenty-three or so years of life, never had the opportunity to think or do things for himself. As his confidence grew, so did his personality, and a cute sense of humor began to emerge.

From there, the natural progression led toward Ed and I getting married. There was no doubt that we loved each other and we openly spoke about it. The game plan was that he and I would marry as soon as I secured my divorce from Ervil. I stepped up my efforts to get it. In my June 15 letter to Ervil, I concluded by saying:

> . . . I intend to divorce you. I'm sorry if that hurts you but
> . . . I don't love you the way a wife should love her husband and
> I never will. I do respect you in a lot of things — but it takes love,
> respect and admiration to make a marriage. I have been thru a

lot because you told me years ago that I *couldn't* divorce you and I have fought many internal battles over that. I believed you and thought I really was stuck but, now that I've studied and asked around and found out that I really can, it was a relief. You have made me suffer a lot, Ervil, and I know I put you thru a lot too. I forgive you and hope you will do the same. I learned a lot, but now I want to marry someone I can love, admire and respect and who will return those feelings and who has a few things in common with me. Someone with common goals, of course, and who fears God and wishes to do right always in His eyes. I'm not playing games, Ervil. That's not my style. I'm serious. I'm sorry if this hurts you, but for me, it's like being released from a prison. You deserve better than someone who feels imprisoned. Cherish the love from the women you have who *do* love you.

But Ervil was not going to allow himself to be shaken loose quite so easily. His pride wouldn't allow it and he felt he had to keep the hold on the rest of us that he knew he was losing. His letters to me, which actually began before I sent the one above to him, were full of doctrinal justifications for us never being able to get divorced, such as this quote from a letter he wrote dated June 3:

> ... You might as well understand that under no circumstances can you be tied to one of my own sons on an everlasting basis. You might as well give that up right now. If you have been involved in wicked or degrading stuff, such as that which you have been accused of, you will be forgiven eternally if you will straighten up promptly and pull yourself back together ...

And then he tried the "I love you" angle which he had never seriously professed before. Another quote from the same letter:

> ... I need you no matter what, and will always love you. I love you too deeply to be willing to let go of you under any type of circumstances that I can dream of ...

This is the way most of his letters from prison were, all fifteen or so that I still have in my possession. They were full of doctrine and professions of love for me and the children he barely knew or didn't know at all. But there were a lot of inconsistencies in the things he was saying. Or maybe it was his half-hearted way of offering a compromise. In one letter he would say how much he loved me and that I belonged to him in the hereafter. Then, in the same letter, he'd say he would understand if I went to someone else in this life. In a letter postmarked June 10, he began:

> My Darling Angel Rena,
> You are making one of the most egregious errors of your whole life, in announcing your intent to withdraw from my family, so I hope that you will hold off for a while until you get what was promised to you when you gave yourself to me . . .

Then he went on to say, in the same letter:

> . . . After you obtain the blessings, however, if you can not endure to belong in our family during the remainder of this life, you may be sealed for time to someone else, if that is arranged according to the laws of the true priesthood . . . Don't worry the least about being coerced to stay with me. I love you tenderly and dearly, with all my heart, but will do anything possible to make you happy with someone else, if you will do the right thing about our two sweet angel children . . .

In short, he was trying to have it one way if he couldn't have both. Though I might have someone else for the rest of finite time (meaning until the end of my life or my spouse's), I would be his for the much longer period of time in the celestial kingdom. That did not satisfy me. I wanted it both ways too. I didn't want to spend eternity having to listen to him or look at his face. He might have granted me the divorce if I agreed to those terms, but I couldn't. And so I continued to pursue other channels.

Overall, Ervil was trying the hardest he could, in his limited circumstances, to hold all of us together under his wing, but we were holding together under *our own* wings. He had a lot of trouble understanding that. He continued to treat us as if we were his children — even Mom, who was seven years older than he. Ervil couldn't fathom the reality of us being able to survive and prosper without him being around. In fact, we were doing much better on our own than when he was among us. It must have hurt him even worse to know that.

310

CHAPTER 23

Sometime during the month of August 1980, Dan Jordan came down to Houston to meet with us on a business matter. After appealing to him for some time to divorce me from Ervil, my determination finally prevailed. Dan was also in the process of breaking away from Ervil, and so that might have been the reason for his change of heart. He was told I needed to have this done so I could marry Ed, and he agreed.

Dan took me aside and, prior to granting the divorce, did something I never would have expected from him. He said, "Rena, I'm sorry for the part I played in your unhappy marriage to Ervil." He was very apologetic for having confronted me in the car that day in Yuma five and a half years earlier and threatening me with my salvation if I didn't marry Ervil. He was only doing what our leader commanded him to do in the name of God. I was very touched by his apology.

Then he laid his hands on my head and spoke the following words: "By the powers of the Melchizedek priesthood which I hold, I hereby dissolve the celestial bonds between Ervil Morel LeBaron and Rena Lei Chynoweth in the name of Jesus Christ Our Lord,

311

Amen." That's all it was. No more than that. Three years to get about two dozen words that would terminate my "time and eternity" obligation to a man my family and I had followed for most of the first two decades of my life. I felt relieved. The cross I had borne for so many years was lifted from my shoulders. I was free!

During that short time Dan was in Houston, he seemed more mellow, more subdued than I'd ever seen him before. For many years, he had been a real ogre and martinet. He and I had fought over the management of our first business in Denver and he threw me out of the shop. He continued to treat me like dirt after that, and treated others the same way, especially Ervil's other wives and children. Now I could see signs of softening in him, a change for the better. We had been through a lot together for the same leader, despite our differences. We had both killed "false prophets" for him and we were arrested the same night, with Dan allowing the authorities to believe he was Ervil so Ervil could escape. But his determination to break away intensified after visiting Ervil in prison. A life sentence was not sitting well with Ervil and he was becoming irrational. The great patriarch was flipping out, and Dan wanted no more part of it.

So I was divorced by the same man who married me. Dan Jordan had come around full cycle in my life, but he wasn't finished with me yet.

Dan got on his plane and left soon after that. Immediately, Ed and I began celebrating and making plans to get married in a week or so. Our joy was short-lived. When Dan arrived in Denver he called Mark and Mark called me at Mom's house, where I was living. Dan was flying back and had to talk to us immediately, Mark said. We were to meet him at the airport as soon as he arrived. Apparently, on landing in Denver, Dan felt something was amiss and got right back on a plane bound for Houston. Ed and I, Mark and Lillian drove up to Houston Intercontinental Airport and met Dan as he was deplaning. We all went into one of the nearby coffee shops, sat down, and Dan spoke.

"I'm sorry," he said, looking straight at me. "When I got home the Lord told me that you and Ed are not to get married."

The four of us looked at him, stunned. Naturally, we wanted

an explanation and the one he gave us was very nebulous at first. He said there was someone else for me "just up the road," but he didn't elaborate on that. We pressed him further for a better answer and finally we got it. It was just something the Lord told him He didn't want done. It would have been "incestuous," since Ed's mother and I were both married to the same man. In the celestial kingdom, Ed would be sealed to Ervil as a son, and I couldn't marry someone who would have been considered my son too. The logic was preposterous, of course, since it is biologically impossible for a woman to have a son two years older than she, but in the hereafter that is still the way it would have been perceived, Dan said.

Nothing more was said about it. Neither Ed nor I protested. Dan grabbed the next flight out and returned to Denver. All the way home the four of us rode in silence. I kept thinking, "Please, God, say this isn't true." Only a few hours earlier we had been on top of the world — free to be married at last. Now our chance at happiness was being denied. All this time we had waited, hoped and prayed, and God was saying no again?

Ed and I fasted and prayed over it, hoping that would give us some answers. We debated whether or not Dan had interpreted God's command erroneously and toyed with the thought that maybe he had made the whole thing up, but we could see no reason to think Dan would do that. The same conclusion kept coming back at us: we had no choice but to end our relationship.

Ed moved out of the bachelors' den and into a little office-like room at the business' warehouse and we tried to stay away from each other. The kids wondered why Ed was staying away more, and I had to try to explain to Erin that Ed and Mommie couldn't get married after all — that God had said "no." It was a very trying and difficult time.

In the early part of September 1980, Ed had been coming by the house to watch the four-part miniseries, "Shogun." In the finale, when the hero lost the woman he loved, it hit me like a ton of bricks. It was so sad and so like our situation. This feeling of futility swept over me. God was denying us happiness together, but I didn't care what God wanted anymore. I was going to grab a little happiness — and damn the consequences.

I gave myself to Ed that night and for a few hours we blocked out all thoughts of the world outside those four walls. During the week or so that followed, he came to my room twice. After the third time, I told him I couldn't handle the guilt of our illicit relationship and that it couldn't happen again.

A few weeks went by and I was late for my period. I told Ed and we talked about what would happen if I were pregnant. We were both kind of excited. A big part of me hoped I was. That way, they would have to let us get married. The other part of me was afraid of the consequences — being stripped of celestial blessings for giving in to the lusts of the flesh, and so on. When my period finally came, it was as if God was saying, "I'm not going to let you off that easy." Soon afterward, my brothers decided Ed and I were not getting over each other fast enough and that they needed to put some distance between us. Ed moved to Phoenix, and as I had been forced to do in the past with other men I loved, I wrote him a "Dear John" letter. In it I told him the relationship would never have worked, we were fooling ourselves to think we were ever in love, and we were merely using each other to lean on after all we'd been through. In order to make it as final as possible, I told him I didn't even want to be friends because to keep any kind of connection between us would just prolong the situation. He wrote me several letters in late 1980 and early 1981 that were pleading in nature, and he continued to hold onto his love for me. Shortly after he was murdered, more than seven years later, Lillian revealed to me that Ed had recently told her I was the greatest love of his life. To this day, it hurts me to think I had once again led someone on, only to have it end unfulfilled. It had become a sad pattern with me, however inadvertently these things might have evolved.

All the while this was going on with Ed, Ervil persisted in his writings to me. After my June 15 letter to him, I wrote him one more, on July 30, then I stopped answering his letters and refused to accept his collect phone calls. Still, his letters kept coming, each time getting more desperate, more irrational, and sometimes even threatening. On more than one occasion he told me that I and the others would be cursed if we didn't help him out in the appeal he was planning to file, as well as in the mission he wanted us to perpetuate. The great blessings we had obtained in carrying out his will and God's would be taken from us. At other times he sounded like an angry father, scolding me for not testifying for him.

In addition, he knew about the relationship between Ed and me and he was furious over it. He was even more furious when he learned about my divorce from him. He would criticize me for spending more money on leisure activities and material possessions than he was spending on his appeal. He would say how much he loved me and beg me to come up with our kids, especially J.R., whom he had never seen. He wanted me to type up some pamphlets he was writing and do some other "great work" which he never specified. And, as always, they were full of his doctrine and were critical of me for upsetting the patriarchal family balance he had charted out in the celestial kingdom.

The declarations of love were those of a desperate man locked away in prison, not those of a caring and loving husband and father which he had never been. I didn't need to take this kind of abuse or listen to his threats. Yet, despite my refusal to answer his letters, he wrote through the end of November. Since he didn't seem able to take the hint I was trying to get across, I finally began returning them to him unopened.

On Saturday, January 10, 1981, while working in Mark's shop, I answered a sales call from a man named John M. He wanted a green washing machine to go with the green dryer he had at home. I told him about a nice Maytag I had that was the top of the line and he said, "Fine. When can you deliver it?" That was very unusual, to have someone buy a machine without seeing it first. Mark came down and got the machine and was ready to deliver it. But I tried calling John back at the phone number he gave me and didn't get any answer. We were closed on Sundays, so on Monday I called all day and finally got through to him in the evening.

"Well, hi," I said. "You're a hard man to get hold of."

"Who is this?" he asked.

"This is Rena, the lady you bought the washing machine from. Where have you been?"

He seemed a little taken aback with my forwardness, which

comes out more on the phone than in person. He hesitated a little and then said he took his daughter skating. I thought about that for a few seconds and it struck me as a little unusual. I had grown up in a male-dominated society where most men didn't do things like that for their kids. I don't know what prompted me to ask John about that but I did.

"Well," he began, "I'm divorced and I'm raising my fourteen-year-old daughter and we do everything together."

That really clicked with me. I had always wanted a man who loved kids and wasn't too busy to spend time with them. Again, it wasn't something I had seen much of, except with my own brothers.

As John and I talked further he told me he was searching for his other daughter, whom his ex-wife had run off with. He had spent a lot of money on attorneys and private investigators trying to find her, but his ex-wife kept one step ahead of them by moving around constantly. He was fighting for custody of his youngest daughter. At one time, while he was managing some huge, highly productive citrus orchards in the Rio Grande Valley, he was worth several million dollars. He walked away from the business to follow his family to Houston after his wife left him. She had caused not only his financial ruin, but his emotional ruin as well, for a while. Now he was working some modest-paying job, trying to raise one daughter alone, and seeking his other daughter. All of this impressed me.

He asked me about myself and I told him I had been officially divorced for five months, was living with my mother, and raising two kids of my own. We talked for quite awhile and finally I arranged for Mark to deliver the machine to his apartment that night. The next day John called me and we talked some more. He said something to the effect that he would like to get to know me better and Mom, who was standing close by, began giving me dirty looks that all but said, "You're making plans with a man you don't know who's not one of us?" I left the possibility open without agreeing to anything definite.

The day after that I went house-hunting for a place for Anna Mae, who was moving in from Phoenix where she was staying with

Ed. I had just walked in the house and the phone rang. It was John. He asked me if I wanted to go out and have a drink with him — "no strings" — and I surprised myself by saying okay. I was never much for bars or drinking, but I felt kind of reckless that day. This was a chance to get out of the house and meet someone new.

We were still a very insular group which didn't mingle too much with outsiders, except during the course of conducting business. I had not gone out with anyone outside our very closed circle since Michael Barnes six or seven years earlier, and Mom was shocked. I guess I was a little shocked myself. If I had thought before speaking, I would never have agreed to go out with this stranger.

John came over to pick me up about an hour later. When I opened the door, there stood this tall, thin man wearing shiny patent-leather boots, a cowboy shirt, and a cowboy hat. He looked at me and said, "Wow! You're beautiful!" and I really got flustered. I wasn't used to this kind of flattery. I brought him in to meet Mom and then we went out to a little place called The Chapparal where they played jukebox music.

We talked and he laughed a lot, but it was obvious we were both very nervous and tense. We danced a few numbers and it was almost comical. He was shaking like a leaf and I was stiff as a board. We stepped on each other's toes frequently. When we sat down he showed me pictures of his daughters and talked so lovingly about them. He spoke of his ex-wife too, and I could tell she still held a special place in his heart. He asked if there was anyone in my life and I replied that there had been, but I didn't elaborate. We changed the subject and then, later in the evening, he proposed to me.

He was kind of joking when he asked, but he was serious at the same time. I didn't know what to make of it — a cowboy proposing to me on the first date. I had never been exposed to this type of person before. I was extremely worried about what my family would think and the hell I was going to catch from Duane and Mark. In Ervil's absence, Dan had remanded me to the custody of my brothers, and they watched over me like hawks. I kept saying, over and over, "I can't believe I did this. I can't believe I'm here. My brothers are going to kill me!"

John asked me why I was so worried about my family's reaction, and I tried to explain that we were a very close family. Our religion didn't permit such close association with outsiders. He asked me about our religion and I told him it was based on the Ten Commandments. If he wanted more information, he would have to talk to Mark. I couldn't explain it very well. He expressed interest and indicated that he would talk to Mark about it.

After a few hours in the bar, he drove me back home and, as we got to the house, he still seemed a little nervous. I don't remember what his exact words were but he said something to the effect that he felt like a "cradle-robber" after learning I was only twenty-two. Then I said, "Well, my ex-husband was even older than you are." His jaw dropped and he was temporarily speechless. John, I would learn, was sixteen years older than me. He found it unbelievable that I had been married to someone seventeen years older than him.

By the time he walked me up to the door, I'd had time to think over the implications and they frightened me. I told him, "Well, it's been nice knowing you. This is the last time I can see you."

The events of that evening left me scared and confused. I was very worried what my brothers, my mother, and the rest of our family would think. Since he didn't belong to our religion, it would create a bad situation. I would be leading him on. I had been through this before with Michael, so I knew what it was like. I tried to put John out of my mind because I didn't want to get hurt again.

But John was not going to be deterred by my initial rejection of him. He was puzzled by my words after we'd had such a pleasant evening out, and he was determined to find out what was going on in my head. He was also curious about our religion and he called Mark the next day, asking if he could meet with him and find out more about it. Mark called me immediately.

"What's the deal with this John guy?" Mark asked.

My heart jumped to my throat. "What do you mean?" I asked, trying to be calm and casual.

"Well, he called me just now and wants to meet with me to

find out about our religion," Mark said. "What did you tell him about? What's going on?"

I could tell by the sound of Mark's voice that he wasn't angry. Perplexed, maybe, but not angry. I felt a sense of relief as I tried to make light of it. "I don't know. He's just some guy I met," I replied.

Mark gently warned me that I needed to watch my mouth and my step. We didn't have a church and we weren't looking for converts because we didn't even know where we stood at that point. Not much more was said and we hung up. I sighed with relief that his reprimand wasn't as strong as I feared it would be.

John called Mark a few more times, trying to get together with him and find out more information about us, but Mark kept hedging and putting him off. Finally, the following Sunday, Mark reluctantly agreed to meet with him at his and Lillian's house. For several hours, Mark talked to him about civil law and the Ten Commandments. John thought it sounded like something he could live with and live by. Mark didn't mention anything about Ervil LeBaron during their first religious discussion. By this time, what we believed differed considerably from what Ervil was now preaching. We had gotten back to the "basics" of what he originally taught us, the teachings we had always believed in. Unfortunately, they had gotten overshadowed by his later teachings when he began taking the law into his own hands. We weren't going around preaching "death to all false prophets." John had no trouble accepting that since he had been raised in a Christian home already.

Most men would have said to me or someone in a similar situation, "To hell with your family. You're an adult and you can make up your own mind." John did not do that. As soon as he saw what the system was and what the ground rules entailed, he made up his mind to work within them. He didn't try to steal me away or dissuade me from what I believed in. He wanted to learn more about where we were coming from, spiritually, and play by the rules. He loved me enough to do that for me.

After John's first discussion with Mark, he began attending our Sunday meetings and trying to absorb all he could. Afterward, he would sit down with Mark for long periods of time and listen intently as Mark explained to him about our doctrine and the higher laws of God and the priesthood. He asked questions and showed a genuine interest in learning more. The teaching made sense to him. He gave it a lot of thought and decided he wanted to be a part of it.

Not only did John accept our teachings, he also accepted the authority structure we had in place. Being the independent sort of person he is, this was a major concession for him to make. He knew that, in order to court me, he had to work through Mark and he did. It was as important to him to make a good impression on Mark and the rest of the family as it was to make a good impression on me. Mark and everyone else in the family greatly impressed him, anyway, so that made his acceptance of the situation that much easier.

John was working as a machinist at the time. In his spare time, usually in the evenings and on weekends, he began helping out around the shop, rounding up and delivering appliances, and just doing whatever he could to be of service. He sat in on business meetings, offering advice and suggestions whenever he felt they would be useful and, since he had experience running businesses himself, his advice was well taken.

Once he learned more about what we believed in, he was allowed to participate in the men's priesthood meetings. This was not something that just anyone could come along and be allowed to get into. But John was not only accepted, he was loved. Mom loved him, my brothers loved him, and the kids loved him. He was no longer the "stranger and outsider" he had been initially. He was officially one of us. We were very happy together, and I don't ever recall being that much in love with someone before.

But while the future for me was looking bright with John, there was still a sword hanging over my head. Specters from my past continued hovering over me, haunting me, reminding me of a life I was trying so hard to put behind me. Ervil still couldn't let go of me. He had been apprised of the situation, yet he refused to accept it. I had divorced him, refused to answer or even accept his letters and calls, and made it clear in every way imaginable that I was through with him. I wanted nothing more to do with him — period. Having failed to reach me by phone or by letter, he took to having his remaining two faithful counselors, Leo and Arthur, deliver messages to me in person.

Leo, as I said earlier, fancied himself as a writer and doctrinarian. In January and February of 1981, he wrote a number of "position papers" on the subject of marriage and the celestial obligations it entailed. He quoted extensively from the scriptures, *Doctrine and Covenants,* and other Mormon fundamentalist treatises, and tried so hard to sound like an authority. Ervil had made him a high priest by this time, and he was filling the void left by Dan's defection. Leo's missives were typed on legal-sized paper and were as complicated and hard to follow as Ervil's writings themselves, indicating to me that Ervil had been teaching him the art of abstraction and double-talk very well. One of Leo's papers was titled "Fornication and Idolatry," and he tried to make a case for the two crimes being interrelated. It was pure garbage, as far as I was concerned, and had no meaning for me and my situation. Leo's bumbling and pathetic attempts to persuade me that I was still, and always would be, sealed to Ervil simply had no practical application as far as I was concerned.

But the best was yet to come — from Ervil himself. In a typed letter, also on legal-sized paper, he threw the whole book at me. If I didn't straighten up and come to him and do his bidding immediately, my blessings would come to an end and I would be consigned to the everlasting fires of hell. Also, of all crazy things, he wanted me to bring back to him his ninth wife, Debra Bateman, who left him in the mid-1970s after bearing two sons.

Ironically, the letter was dated February 22, 1981 — Ervil's fifty-sixth birthday and the last one he would ever see. It is significant enough to quote in its entirety, since it gives a true picture of the deranged man he had become toward the close of his life.

My wonderful daughter and handmaiden, even Rena LeBaron;
As I live, I will exalt you on high, and will bless both you and your sweet, wonderful and glorious children, both the ones that you now have, and the ones that you will yet have in the future, if you will return to me, by returning to my well beloved, and kind, and generous Patriarch, even to my great, and awesome, and most astounding mouthpiece, even my Prophet, Seer,

and Revelator, your wonderful and gracious, and kingly head, and your most excellent Lord and master, whom all Israel will now accept; because I have purified him completely, I have greatly and magnificently enlightened him, and I will now send forth my mighty word, even my exalted word, through him, to all the twelve tribes of Israel, and to all my people, in every nation, kindred, tongue and people.

Now, if you will not obey my word, and the voice of my Heavenly Father, who is now speaking to you from the heavens, and you will not keep my commandments, and you will not do my bidding, and you will not hear my voice, through my great and most glorious servant, even Ervil M. LeBaron, the man in mortality who will exalt you, and who feels for you, and who will never permit any charge to be levied against you in any matter, whatsoever, from this time forth and forever, no matter what you may do in helping to build up the Kingdom of God, even my great, and my most glorious and most perfect, and most godly and wonderful millennial kingdom, I will then turn all these wonderful, and marvelous, and great everlasting blessings to the fullest extent, into cursings and into destruction, both spiritual and temporal. This is my word, and the law of my great and glorious celestial kingdom, and all those who come into it, must leave voluntarily, they must guarantee that they freely, of their own free will and choice, renounce all and every single one of its great benefits and blessings, and never return, worlds without end, and take nothing whatsoever with them, not even one extra handkerchief, or item of clothing, and not even dream of taking with them an heir of my great, and most glorious celestial kingdom; for otherwise, if they do not do this, and will not, and do not observe my laws, and do not keep the laws of this kingdom, and do not intend to keep it. I will most assuridly *(sic)* destroy them, and will utterly destroy them, and uproot them, and will thrust them down to hell, even as I live, and even as my great and glorious Heavenly Father lives; And this great and important law, and proclamation, and edict, will stand forever, as the law of my Great and Glorious and Most Perfectly Ordained Kingdom, and this shall be an ensample to all citizens of my great, and most glorious celestial order, and everlasting kingdom.

Now, if you will go and bring my elect handmaiden, even your sister, and dearly beloved helpmate, and helpmate of my holy and tenderhearted, and bereaved Patriarch, even my beloved daughter, Debra Bateman LeBaron; and notify her, that because she was removed from my kingdom by force, under the guise of armed men, and with open threats of death and destruction, and of persecution, and of disparagement, even from my most valiant, and determined, and faithfully dedicated Patriarch, Prophet, Seer, and Revelator, my now great, and wonerful *(sic)*, and pure, and humble, and almost perfect servant, Ervil M. LeBaron, he will now accept her, together with all of her sweet, and lovely and darling sons and daughters, or whatever children she might have. This is an ensample in relation to honorable and lovely and sincere women, who are taken from honorable men by corrupt and elusive stratedy *(sic)*, by wicked techniques, by loathsome and under cover threats of nigardly *(sic)* violence, and by the power of wicked and corrupt men, who exercise the laws of man to disparage those who uphold only the law of the Lord of Hosts, and who will never stoop to employing this type of abominable practices, if it is possible to avoid it. Now this is the case, in all particulars, as it relates to my dearly beloved daughter Debra Bateman LeBaron, and I hereby command her to come with you, my handmaiden Rena LeBaron; and if you will go get her, and bring her to the home of my elect handmaiden Anna Mae LeBaron, my handmaiden Debra will most certainly depart from among those ugly hearted, corrupt and detestable apostates, and from the house of Satan, even from his kingdom. She did not want to depart from my kingdom when she did this abominable thing, and would not have done it if she had been given all things that were necessary for her exaltation and glory.

Therefore, because she was disparaged in so many ways, and was crippled spiritually by the most deceitful, and awesome and crooked son of perdition, that the world has ever known, she is now and forever forgiven of all her past faults and failings, and, inasmuch as she returns unto me, and to my great and wonderful servant, Ervil M. LeBaron, my Prophet like Moses, my awesome and loyal and dedicated Patriarch, she will now be crowned by my Heavenly Father, through this man, even this humble and most obedient servant in my household, of whom I spoke in my prophetic sermon. This is my word, and my law unto my handmaiden Debra LeBaron, my lost, and fallen and greatly mourned handmaiden. Even so, Amen. I am the Lord, your God, even

Jesus, the Lamb of God, Amen, and Amen.

It was the last letter I ever got from him. I didn't actually receive it until April, when Leo and Arthur brought it to me in person. It shook me up pretty badly, but like the rest of his letters from August 1980 on, it went unanswered. I was no longer his "handmaiden." Nor was I "Rena LeBaron." And even if I knew where Debbie Bateman was, I would not have brought her — or myself — to him in his prison cell. (She has since remarried.)

Around this time the group that was in Denver started fragmenting. Arthur left and headed for Phoenix, taking Ervil's wives, Linda, Yolanda, and Teresa, with him. Rosemary and Anna Mae and their kids moved to Houston and we had to absorb them. Ervil had told Anna Mae that she had to get away from Dan, who was questioning Ervil's state of mind. While they were living in Denver under his supervision, they worked long hours in Michael's Appliance for little or no money and were forced to endure Dan's inhuman, demeaning treatment of them. Nothing had changed in all those years.

The kids were really in bad shape. With little or no supervision, they were running wild. They were neglected, ragged, foulmouthed, and disrespectful of God. Some of them were involved in smoking pot and a few of the girls were sleeping around. It was our job now to take them in and try to civilize them. Those who were having problems with their health or their teeth had to be taken care of. We did our best with them and tried to convince them they were worthy of the same chances for a better life that any other kids might have. We set up Bible study classes and youth meetings and gave jobs and other chores to the older kids. In short, we were determined to show them they weren't the "worthless pieces of shit" Dan had called them.

John and I did not go out alone together for quite awhile. Since I was under Mark and Duane's "protection," and I was being watched closely, John and I saw each other only at meetings or in the shop or in social situations where there were other people around. We were not even allowed to call each other, though we did anyway when we could sneak it in. This was another one of many inconveniences John accepted throughout our courtship period of eight months. He wasn't particularly happy with the rules as they were laid out to us, but he was more patient than anyone could ever have expected.

Dad came to Houston in April to do his taxes and he, too, took a liking to John. Having been a bishop, Dad still ranked high in the priesthood, even though he had long since split with Ervil and everyone else who was not direct family. He baptized John, then laid his hands on him and ordained him an elder. By that time, John had studied the doctrine intensively, reading up on it every night for months previous. Anna Mae had brought him a lot of Ervil's pamphlets and he even read those. Later he was even allowed to teach the kids. That, of course, speeded up John's acceptance among the men who also held priesthood offices — and paved the way for us to get married.

Finally, God had sent me the man I had wanted for so long. He fit nearly everything on the checklist I had in my head as to what the man for me should embody. Even those he didn't fit, at first, he worked on until they were right, such as joining our church. He loved my children, even though they weren't his, and that was so important to me. He was a hard worker, level-headed and outspoken when he needed to be, and a strong, God-fearing, righteous man. I admired, respected, and loved him. I couldn't have asked for more.

Perhaps Dan Jordan was a prophet after all. When he forbade Ed and me from getting married the previous year, he said there was someone waiting for me around the corner. He was right.

CHAPTER 24

In his last few months of life, Ervil LeBaron was a desperate, irrational man. A year in prison, facing the prospects of spending the rest of his life there, was not at all encouraging to him. He still talked about the great work he had to do and, at first, seemed confident of getting out soon, perhaps failing to realize he wasn't in a Mexican jail this time. If he had been successful in getting his case to be appealed, it is highly doubtful the lower court ruling would have been overturned. No judge or panel of judges in their right minds would have unleashed him on the outside world again, knowing what he had done and what he was capable of doing again. His chances for release were about as good as those of Charles Manson and, deep down inside, he must have realized that after awhile.

Then he began having revelations of a miracle that would free him. He envisioned God's wrath striking down the prison walls like the walls of ancient Jericho, because the pagan temporal authorities dared to incarcerate God's Chosen Prophet and Revelator. Until the end, he continued to cling to this hope.

Not only was he saying and writing bizarre things, he was also doing bizarre things which flew in the face of everything he taught. Knowing that most of his flock had defected from him, he had very few men left to do his bidding. Since Lorna and her kids were the closest ones to him physically and he saw them the most frequently, he began elevating her sons to the priesthood. A few sons of the other wives were similarly "anointed" as well. This was done despite the fact that all of them were mere children or teenagers and were untrained and ignorant. They hadn't studied the doctrine, they were never taught how to fulfill their priestly functions or the duties of that office, yet he was ordaining them anyway. Lorna's sons, Andrew and Aaron Morel (Mo); Anna Mae's son by him, Heber; Rosemary's son, Doug; Linda's son, Richard; and God knows who else were ordained priests, high priests, or patriarchs by Ervil just before he died. He would have ordained J.R., who was only a baby at the time, had he been able to lay his hands on him.

This was the very same thing he had accused Joel of doing and one of the main reasons he said Joel had to be killed. Now he was doing it. Unqualified people were being administered the celestial blessings of the priesthood. It was obvious he was doing this only to draft them into his own personal army and make them soldiers of his will.

In April, while Dad was still in Houston visiting us, a momentous meeting took place at Mom's house. In desperation, Ervil sent Arthur, Leo, Alex, and Andres down to try to bring us back into the fold and, failing that, they were to take the children. At the time, we had all of Anna Mae's youngest kids and some of Rosemary's, plus some of Vonda's kids (whom Anna Mae had custody of) and our own. We all sat around Mom's living room with the kids, and the four men who had come down from Ervil's cell in Utah were reading to us all the "revelations" he supposedly had. It was at this meeting that Leo handed me Ervil's February 22 "handmaiden" letter, plus two or three other treatises Leo had written on the marriage issue. Up to this time I had not seen or known about Ervil's demand that I bring Debra Bateman back to him.

Before the meeting, Mark spoke to the children. He told them that Ervil wanted them up in Utah and they were free to make up their own minds after hearing what Leo and the others had to say.

The four messengers, especially Leo, went on and on about how we had to straighten up and come back to Ervil and do his bidding if we wanted to be blessed instead of cursed. It was all old hat to us by that time; there was nothing we hadn't heard before. The only thing different this time was that we were told it was our "last chance" for salvation.

There was an ominous feeling about their words — as if we would be held accountable for anything that might happen to us after that, violent or otherwise. We still refused to fall in line, though, and they pressed their demands to let them have the children. They especially wanted Craig, Vonda's oldest boy, and Rosemary's oldest son with Ervil, Nathaniel, who were in their mid-teens.

John, who knew about much of our past by this time, was at this meeting. On three separate occasions that he can recall, he was tempted to speak up and challenge Leo. Being the outspoken person he is, it took quite an effort to restrain himself, but he finally couldn't hold back.

"Leo," he said, "how much of this garbage did *you* write?"

Everyone in the room went into shock, especially Dad. A loud, collective gasp was heard, followed by a tense, momentary hush. All eyes turned to John as if to say, "You're dead!" There was an unspoken knowledge among the rest of us who had been around the group longer that these guys were potentially dangerous. They might have been armed at the time; we had no way of knowing. You simply did not openly mouth off to someone holding a high priesthood who was under Ervil's direct control. Yet here was John, a newcomer, doing just that. Other people had been blown away for less.

Leo glared at him for a second or two. His only comment was that John had no business saying anything, since he was a newcomer. But he didn't push the matter, either, and what could have been an explosive situation was averted. But, at that point, Leo saw he wasn't getting anywhere with the adults and began directing his remarks exclusively to the young people. He told them that Mark was apostate and was leading them astray and they needed to come up to Utah to be around their father and get the doctrine directly from him. But, despite his threats against their salvation and appeals to their paternal loyalty, every one of those children refused to accept Ervil's authority over them. Not a single one offered to go with Leo and company.

To this day, John feels that his remark and the rapport he had established with the kids may have helped them make the decision to stay. There is good reason to believe this was the case. He had the courage to stand up to Ervil's bullies, and this gave the kids and the rest of us the courage and resolve to do likewise. John had been in dangerous situations before, having had run-ins with the local Mexican mafia back in his hometown. He wasn't going to let anyone scare him, and he wasn't afraid to call their bluff.

The upshot was that Leo, Arthur, Alex, and Andres reported back to Ervil empty-handed. They had come down looking self-righteously down their noses at us defectors and "traitors," but we remained firm. As far as they were concerned, our fate was sealed in the fires of hell. We were "going to be destroyed both spiritually and temporally," and it would be up to Ervil to decide the actual method of punishment. It was all very scary.

Mark and Lillian went to see Ervil in prison and came back with the consensus that he had truly flipped out. He was saying things that were totally irrational and acting bizarre. He was fighting with his attorneys instead of cooperating with them. On one occasion, when John Hill came in to meet with him, Ervil unzipped his pants and urinated all over John's briefcase. When Mark was up there, Ervil wanted him to go on a mission with George (Jorge) LeBaron to make converts of everyone in Utah — the stronghold of Mormonism — and this struck Mark as being totally off the wall.

Even though Mark had planned to go back and see Ervil on other occasions, Ervil began condemning him. Mark was called a "son of perdition," a "snake" (always Ervil's favorite description), and even "worse than a snake." Finally, it was "No Name." He was very unfair to Mark, who was only trying to convince Ervil that he should limit his role to that of a spiritual authority figure only.

We still believed in the basics of Ervil's doctrine and continued to look toward much of his written works and teachings for spiritual guidance. He just couldn't continue holding onto *all* the reins of power, we felt, especially in the economic sector. He was not a businessperson and had no business claiming to be one. We did not want him trying to dictate the course of our personal affairs and enterprises. He was not on the outside world with the rest of us and didn't know the realities involved in our day-to-day lives. If he could have accepted this arrangement and confined himself to ministering to our religious needs only, he might have been able to salvage some measure of our loyalty. But, as with all things, Ervil wanted it both ways. We couldn't accept that, and so the schism between him and us became final.

While earnestly trying to reach a compromise with Ervil, Mark was also attempting to get John onto the list of people allowed to visit Ervil in prison. This wasn't easy because prison policy placed strict limits on the number of people allowed to see any prisoner, and Ervil already had so many wives and family members on that list. Nonetheless, Mark tried because John insisted on it. John was anxiously looking forward to meeting Ervil, face to face, as two men. He wanted to see in person the man who held so much sway over us for so many years. He planned to tell Ervil he was in love with me, that he intended to marry me, and there wasn't anything Ervil could do but give us his blessing if he so chose.

John did not plan to be arrogant or boastful about it. He was simply going to tell Ervil I had gotten legally divorced from him, that he was now one of us, officially baptized and ordained by a bishop of the church, and everything was being done within the context of the beliefs we all held sacred. John sincerely wanted to get Ervil's blessing for our union because that would have put everyone's mind to rest over the "legality" question, especially mine. But he also planned to make it clear to Ervil that a failure to obtain the blessing would not have stopped either of us from going through with it. If Ervil refused, John could at least have come back saying he honestly tried.

It never happened, though. John never did get to meet Ervil. Even if he had, it's doubtful any good would have come of it. Ervil was irrational and unstable and would never have accepted the thought of me being married to someone else unless he, personally, arranged it. Even that was unlikely. There were no men left among his few remaining followers who couldn't be considered my brother, son, uncle, or nephew except Leo, and I would have fought any suggestion of that to my death.

Somewhere around this time, or perhaps earlier, Ervil began writing the pieces for his most infamous work of all, the *Book of the New Covenant* — the "hit list," as it has come to be known. None of us had any way of knowing this was going on since we had broken off contact with him, and much of what we learned about this book came only in later years. Before he died, Ervil was writing voluminously and getting his so-called revelations outside the prison through his few remaining loyalists. Leo was chiefly responsible for compiling these revelations and, after Ervil's death, he did the writing that put the book into its finished form. He was living in California at the time and had help from Kathleen LeBaron, the oldest child of Anna Mae and Ervil. The book had 500 pages, and was possibly larger than all of Ervil's previous writings combined.

The *Book of the New Covenant* was a list of names of all the people Ervil wanted eliminated, along with the reasons why. Those on the list were mostly defectors and others who had run afoul of him in some way or other. His "reasons" went well beyond the bounds of sanity, and many of the descriptions that followed each person's name defy belief. No one knows for certain how many copies of the book were printed or who might have copies of it. I have seen only one copy, which is safe and secure in the files of the Salt Lake County Attorney's office. When I went to Salt Lake to give a statement following the murders of Mark, Duane, Jenny, and Ed in 1988, Dick Forbes arranged for me to look at it for about fifteen minutes.

And there was my name, along with page after page of absolutely loathsome descriptions of me and the "crimes" I had supposedly committed. I was called a "whore" and an "adultress," despite the fact I never committed adultery. I also saw the names of Mom, Mark, Dan, the warden of the prison where Ervil was being held, Ervil's attorneys, Dick Forbes, the investigators who had tracked him down and interrogated him, and hundreds more people. Of course, Verlan was in it as the fountainhead of all his wrath — probably the one living person he hated more than anyone else.

The book was even indexed, alphabetically. For everyone's name there, descriptions were listed. There were index entries for "Snake," Ervil's favorite epithet for people he hated the most. If this piece of work could ever be termed a "book," in my opinion it would rank right up there with *Mein Kampf* as one of the most hateful, venomous, despicable, and vile collections of words ever written in human history.

Some of those listed in Ervil's *Book of the New Covenant* were called "the worst scum of the earth," and if they didn't return to him, "their eyes are going to fall out of their sockets" and "their limbs are going to rot and fall off." Their "crimes" went on and on in some cases; mine literally took up a whole section. The theme was always the same, whether the people listed were defectors, detractors, "false prophets," law enforcement officials, or whatever — they were to be punished and struck down by the Lord's wrath, killed by those foot soldiers he had recruited in his blood covenant with them, using this book as their blueprint.

Ervil was not having "revelations" by the time he got this list of names into the hands of his followers: they were hallucinations. He was a man possessed by demons. It was never "God's work" he did when he ordered us to do all the past killings for him, even though he had us believing that it was. This *Book of the New Covenant* was the work of Satan, who had taken control of his mind long ago and was only now manifesting itself openly. The same strain of insanity that had befallen his brother Ben and his sister Lucinda had taken full control of his actions. As a normal, rational, thinking individual he was finished the moment he began plotting Joel's death, ten or eleven years earlier. It just took the rest of us that long to find out.

A few of our people got to see some of these "revelations" before Ervil died. Mark got copies of them when he and Lil went up to see him, a few months before Ervil's death. Mark secluded himself in a hotel room and fasted for several days so he could study and pray. He came to the conclusion that they were indisputably false and the work of Satan. Ervil was either crazy or possessed, Mark concluded.

Mark showed them to Duane, Mom, and Anna Mae when

they came to visit him. Duane read about two paragraphs, threw them down, and said, "This is bullshit!" Mom read them more in depth, for about three or four hours, and came to the same conclusion. Even Anna Mae, who had never been known to question anything Ervil had ever said or done before, said "This doesn't make any sense. This is crazy!"

Sometime during the morning of August 15, 1981, I was in the kitchen at home when I got the news: Ervil was dead. Mark called to tell me that he died in his cell earlier that morning. I was in shock. I didn't feel any real remorse; it was just so unexpected. He was only fifty-six years old and hadn't been in particularly bad health. The newspapers reported it, initially, as a suicide, but by the next day's editions the official cause of death was listed as a heart attack. One of the guards had reportedly seen him doing push-ups in his cell in the early morning hours, sometime around 1:30 A.M. Later on he was seen lying on the floor and they thought he had fallen asleep there, but when they went to wake him, they couldn't. He was dead.

Several mysteries surrounding the circumstances of his death still remain unanswered. There were supposedly some suicide notes written to one of his wives, but they didn't mention any names. Those notes never resurfaced after they were allegedly seen by whoever found his body. None of us ever saw them or copies of them. One of the notes supposedly said, "I have gone to meet my Maker." It was also reported that he was heard talking about seeing a woman in the hereafter "in a few days," which may have been Marilu Vega, his second wife who had died in 1975. She was the only one of the wives to predecease him. Some investigators have theorized that he had a "suicide pact" with Vonda, who was supposed to kill herself at the same time. In my opinion, that was a ridiculous theory.

Though the "official" cause of death was given as a heart attack, John talked to one of the investigators afterward who said there were indications Ervil suffered a powerful blow to the throat, in the vicinity of the Adam's apple. One of the newspaper articles even quoted an investigator as saying all of the muscles in Ervil's neck had hemorrhaged after being struck and supposedly he took an overdose of drugs prior to that. Whether that blow, if there was one, was self-inflicted or inflicted by a guard or a fellow prisoner was never determined. It was not investigated, nor was it felt there was any need for a thorough inquest. The man who had been directly responsible for the murders of at least eight people in two countries was dead. That was all that mattered to them. The manner of death was unimportant.

To this day, Mom insists that Ervil never would have taken his own life, but no one will ever know. In his frame of mind, anything was possible.

At the time of his death, Lorna and anyone else who might have been with Ervil in Utah had disappeared. Years later, Thomas Anthony (Tony) LeBaron, Linda Johnson's oldest child, told us Ervil said "something big is supposed to happen" in Salt Lake, and he cautioned all his followers to leave, which they apparently did. Lorna was gone, none of us knew where, and she didn't find out about Ervil's death until much later. The "something big" that was supposed to happen remained just another one of many mysteries surrounding Ervil in his final days of life.

We made arrangements with the Salt Lake County Coroner's Office to have Ervil's body flown to us in Houston for burial. I was initially put in charge of making those arrangements. I had sold a washer and dryer to a family who owned a funeral home and I consulted with them on how to get the body transported from one state to another. They asked who the deceased person was and I told them it was my ex-husband. It was hard for me to explain that he died in prison and there had to be an autopsy before the body could be released, and so on, but once I found out what needed to be done I turned it over to Anna Mae. She wanted to make the actual funeral arrangements and Rosemary helped her. They were still married to him when he died, and I gladly stepped aside.

The rest of us pitched in however we could. We had three separate business operations going throughout Houston at that time, and we all pooled our money to pay the funeral and burial expenses. When we got the body into town, the coffin was laid out and opened while those of us present paid our last respects. Ervil's body was dressed in a suit and tie, the one I bought for his trial, and though he was lying at rest, his features still looked somewhat hard and intense. There was only so much the embalmers could do to soften them. Only three of his wives (Delfina, Anna Mae, and Rosemary) were there, plus one ex-wife (myself) and a good number of Ervil's children. In addition, there were Mom, Duane and Laura, Mark and Lillian, John, Ed, and a policeman we had become friends with named Jim Coate who headed up the funeral security. Dan came down from Denver with Elsa, Ramona, and some of his other wives, and he gave a eulogy for Ervil. Mark spoke also. In all, there were about fifty people in attendance.

There were fears of possible violence and none of us wanted to take any chances. Also, we felt that the media, which had been hounding us for years, might try to crash the funeral. Jim thrust a gun into John's belt and asked if he knew how to use it. John, of course, did. The two of them stood guard outside in case of any violent incidents, as well as to keep the press out.

In addition to helping out with security, John was also one of the pallbearers. He had never met Ervil in life and was only now seeing him for the first time, in death. He was my pillar of strength that day because, despite all the problems I'd had with Ervil over the years, he was still someone who had once meant a great deal to me as a spiritual leader, if not as a husband and father of my two children. I left J.R. with a babysitter and brought Erin, who was five at the time. As she was talking to some of the other kids in the funeral chapel, she said to one of them, "I'll share my new daddy with you." I didn't hear those remarks but Mom did, and she was very touched by them.

I think, more than anything, I felt bad for Ervil's kids because they loved him and, in spite of all his other flaws, he loved them in his own way. As Ervil's body lay in his open casket, I watched some of his daughters — Kathleen, Celia, and some of the others — come up and gently touch his face, and they were crying. This made me cry too.

I didn't really want to go up close and see the body but I did anyway, very briefly. I felt no real grief for myself. What I wanted, the man I truly loved, was standing next to me, not lying in front of me. Whether Ervil and I were really divorced, a condition Ervil contested until the end, was now a moot point. I was released from any earthly obligations to him. As far as the hereafter is concerned, hopefully Dan took care of that when he laid his hands on me a year earlier. John and I could now get married without any barriers preventing us.

Mom was very stoical about it all, despite feeling sad and shocked by the suddenness of Ervil's death. She felt strongly, as did the rest of us, that death was not the end but only the beginning of a better, happier, and more rewarding life that went on for eternity. Her mind flashed back over the whole history of her long association with Ervil and all that she and her family experienced as members of his faithful flock. Whatever good or bad he had wrought on this earth was behind him now and behind the rest of us as well, or so we thought.

Ervil was buried in Houston's Resthaven Cemetery. Later on, a headstone would be placed there with just the simple words:

BELOVED FATHER
ERVIL M. LeBARON
BORN FEB. 22, 1925
DIED AUG. 15, 1981

That was it. The mortal life of Ervil LeBaron was over; ours would continue. Maybe now the violence would end and we could settle down to normal, peaceful lives. At least we hoped so, anyway. Little did we know that a 500-page book was being compiled that would result in still more bloodshed. Ervil Morel LeBaron wasn't finished with us yet.

CHAPTER 25

John and I got married on August 28, 1981, less than two weeks after Ervil's death. To ensure legality under the recognized laws of the State of Texas and the United States, we had a brief civil ceremony in the private chambers of a Houston judge. Then we had the religious ceremony at Mom's house, with Mark officiating, and the rest of the group in attendance.

This was a *real* wedding, unlike the fumbling farce Dan had performed for Ervil and me six and a half years earlier. I wore an off-white dress and an orchid corsage John had given me. My hair was done up nicely, and I looked and felt like a real bride. We put a bunch of chairs together in the living room and formed an aisle between them as in a church. Craig, Vonda's oldest child, played some semblance of the wedding march on the piano, which he messed up and quit playing about halfway through. Duane walked me up the aisle to the front of the room on his arm and gave me away. John wore a suit and tie and had his oldest daughter, Sandy, with him. She sat up front with Lillian and Mom and my kids, who were soon to be her brother and sister. Jim Coate was our official photographer.

337

Mark, who had conspired with Ervil to get me to Yuma so Ervil could marry me and who had been one of the only witnesses to that marriage, performed the ceremony. This time we were all going to do it right. John put a ring on my finger and we were married according to the principles of our faith. It was a beautiful ceremony. Afterward we cut the wedding cake Rosemary baked and Anna Mae, Mom, Lillian, and the older girls helped out. Everyone kissed and hugged and they were very excited and happy for me. I was just floating around, not really knowing up from down. As we drove off, they threw rice at us and wished us well.

We drove to John's apartment, which was about three or four miles away, and his daughter spent the night with one of her girlfriends. Mom kept my two kids so that John and I could enjoy our wedding night alone together.

When we got to John's apartment, he carried me over the threshold. Before going to bed we knelt and prayed. I thanked God and asked him to bless our union and our lives together. Then, soon after that, I found out how fulfilling a true relationship was. The thought that went through my mind was, "So, *this* is what it's supposed to be like." It was the perfect ending to a perfect day.

Sandy was living with John and, with the addition of me and my two kids, the apartment became rather small in a hurry. Mark and Lillian moved to a bigger house soon after our wedding and we moved into the one they were vacating. John continued with his job in the factory and helped out around the business in his spare time. A year later, John officially adopted my kids after meeting all state requirements.

Two days after Ervil's death, Verlan was killed in an automobile accident outside Mexico City. From what I've heard and read, he was on his way back to Colonia LeBaron to settle down in his leadership role over the colony without the spectre of Ervil's vengeance hanging over him. He had spent the better part of nine years constantly on the run, taking precautions for his life, and keeping one step ahead of Ervil's assassins. How ironic and sad that, after all those years of living in fear and finally having that fear lifted, he was never able to enjoy the life of peace he sought. If nothing else,

Verlan went to his reward with the satisfaction of having survived Ervil, though not by much.

Immediately following Ervil's conviction and imprisonment there was a feeling among us of, "Where do we go from here?" After his death the feeling intensified and took on new dimensions. No one expected things to continue the way they had been under him, but no one was fully prepared to take command over all the followers, either. We were fragmented, with one group in Denver, another wandering around somewhere, either in Mexico or the Southwest, and the rest of us in Houston. We were divided by differences in doctrinal interpretations, and it is doubtful all of us could have united under a single leader. So, each group sort of became its own self-sustaining entity. Dan Jordan assumed full leadership of the group in Denver, Arthur and Leo led the hard-core Ervilites in Mexico or wherever it was they were, and Mark officiated over those of us in Houston. It was basically the same setup as it was while Ervil was alive and in prison, except now he was no longer a factor.

This central leadership void went on for several months before Dan tried to coalesce everyone under his wing. He presented himself as the logical choice as Ervil's successor, having been his right-hand man from the very beginning of the schism between Ervil and Joel and now being the highest-ranking living member of the priesthood. Of course, we weren't going to accept Dan and give up what we had to follow him. As Mom put it, "I wouldn't follow Dan around the corner." Even though he had mellowed somewhat for a while, he started reverting back to his old, domineering ways. Besides, we knew his track record as a businessman and a leader left too much to be desired. We were quite content to remain where we were, conducting our own lives and businesses, raising our own children, and living the closest thing to normal adult lives any of us had ever known. We trusted God to guide us in what was right.

When this was made known to Dan, he left us alone and didn't try to force the issue. He continued to lead only his small group, consisting of his seven wives and many children, and eventually a few of Ervil's wives returned to his fold.

Within our group, Mark and Duane and John continued on as the leaders. They administered the family affairs and spiritual matters. Anyone who wanted to stay or move in with us was given a home and all the necessities of life everyone else had. They were given an opportunity to work and earn an honest living. Anyone who didn't like it was free to go elsewhere.

It was the third contingent where the problems were bound to arise. Arthur, as Ervil's oldest son, would have been the logical person to assume the mantle of leadership, if indeed there was any mantle to be passed down or any credibility to the claimed succession that began with Joseph Smith and Benjamin Johnson.

Added to the problem was Arthur's own schizophrenic personality and lack of leadership ability. He was no Ervil. With all his flaws, Ervil had been able to command a measure of respect and loyalty. Arthur had none of those traits. He had none of Ervil's charisma or knowledge of the doctrine and scriptures. He was hot-tempered, erratic, condescending, and hostile to a large degree. The only justification anyone might have had for following him was a hereditary one, based on the fact that he was Ervil's oldest son, and he did attract some followers for that very reason. Four of Ervil's wives — Lorna, Yolanda and Teresa Rios, and Linda Johnson — and their children followed Arthur's contingent to Mexico.

Everyone expected trouble within Arthur's group. Leo was among them, and he was the more domineering of the two. He was also quite a bit older. He had understudied intensely under Ervil in just the few short years he had been with the group, and the doctrine he learned was the twisted, violent teachings of Ervil's later years. What was worse, he knew how to twist it to its most violent extreme, another useful skill he learned under Ervil's tutelage. A personality like his was not one to accept anyone else's authority over him, and he was not one who could share the reins of power. A power struggle between he and Arthur was inevitable.

Isaac LeBaron was the first known post-Ervil casualty. On June 18, 1983, he committed suicide at the age of twenty. Four years earlier, he had been a key prosecution witness against us and a year later against his father, and he had been on the run ever since. During the trials he had been very nervous and afraid, especially when he had to look down at Ervil from the witness stand. Fearing for his life that Arthur's group was out to get him, he became very paranoid and manic depressive. He kept a loaded gun on his person constantly and sometimes barricaded himself in a secluded room for long periods of time. For a short time, Mark took him in, along with Delfina, Delia, and Paul, but Isaac didn't feel safe there and moved into his own apartment.

All the fear he was experiencing caused him to have a nervous breakdown. He had just gotten out of the hospital and was at Mark and Lillian's home the next day where, in a back bedroom, he placed a .22-caliber rifle between his knees and fired a fatal shot to his head.

The next post-Ervil casualty was probably Lorna. She had followed Arthur to Mexico with her eight children when Ervil told them something dreadful was going to happen in Utah, shortly before his death. They and some of the others settled in a place they called Rancho La Joya in the Mexican state of Sonora. Tony (Linda and Ervil's son) had been one of that group, and he told us Lorna became disenchanted and wanted to return to the States with her kids. Arthur gave her the okay to go up by herself and find a place and she was assured the kids would be sent up when she got settled in. She was driven to the bus by her oldest son, Andrew, and by Andres Zarate, but she never got on that bus. Officially classified as missing, since her body was never found, Tony is certain she was taken out in the desert and murdered. One of the people at the ranch confirmed that this happened sometime in 1983, probably toward the latter part of the year. Her younger kids remained on the ranch to be cared for by the other women.

Sometime in 1984, George (Jorge) LeBaron, Ervil's son by Marilyn Vega, disappeared. He was last seen in the Dallas area and little if anything is known of the circumstances surrounding his disappearance. It can only be presumed that he is either dead or deep in hiding, but he is probably dead. It is known that he was strongly disliked by Heber LeBaron, the oldest son of Ervil and Anna Mae, and Heber was just beginning his rise to power around this time. George had been one of Arthur's followers after Ervil's death, as had Heber.

One of the Houston newspapers, in a lengthy article about the LeBarons, mentioned a woman named Brenda Lafferty who was stabbed to death along with her fifteen-month-old daughter in Utah in July 1984. The article went on to say she and her daughter were killed by her brothers-in-law, who were believers in Ervil's doctrine. Supposedly, she had been killed because she opposed polygamy. I don't know how the newspaper made this connection, since none of us ever heard of her before. Her brothers-in-law could not have been more than marginally involved with Ervil at most, but even that is doubtful. Perhaps, because the LeBaron story continued to be "hot" in Utah, they might have concocted this motive using Ervil's name.

In the meantime, some difficulties arose under Mark's leadership of the Houston group. Mark was strict and firm in trying to keep our affairs and the kids' upbringing in order and some of them couldn't handle it. But there were certain rules that had to be abided by and they grew stricter as time went on. To his credit, he was trying to get the teenagers — Anna Mae's and Vonda's kids — straightened out because they had never had any real guidance in their lives. They were used to running wild and doing as they pleased. However, he and Lillian got carried away with dictating how people should conduct their personal and family lives. A "dress code" was imposed, primarily for Anna Mae's rebellious, flirtatious daughters, and other rules were added as they went along. At one point Lillian tried to get John to get rid of our TV set and a ban on going to the movies was also considered. They even tried to restrict Sandy's dating privileges, which John and I felt they had no business doing.

John and I were stuck in the middle of all this. These rules were initially intended to apply to the kids and the teenagers, but they were soon expanded to include us. We were in a very difficult predicament. After all, they were family and we were not only living in their house but also working for them. John and I wanted the freedom to think on our own. We understood what Mark was trying to do, but we just couldn't agree with the extreme measures and methods he was using to get there, and we made our feelings known to him.

One day in April of 1982, while John and I and the kids were out of town attending John's grandfather's funeral, Mark and Lillian moved us out of the house we were renting from them — lock, stock, and barrel. We were opposing them and challenging their authority, so that was their way of showing us who was boss.

Mom also took issue with some of Mark's actions and he began challenging her for her share of the partnership in the business. Mom was so shocked and hurt she just said, "If he wants the business so badly, I'll just give it to him." And she did. She signed her half over to him and got nothing for it. Mark was convinced he was doing the right thing and following priesthood authority, but he ended up turning everyone off. The business went from three outlets to just one. Eventually, Anna Mae and Rosemary and their kids left to rejoin Dan because they'd had their fill of Mark's dictatorship. Dan must have convinced them that Mark was out of line and that he (Dan) had the "true authority" to be the leader. Our group, which had held together so well up to that point, had begun to fall apart.

Mom and Duane started their own appliance business and John and I worked for them. But then disagreements arose between John and Duane and that was devastating to me. Everyone seemed to be at odds with each other and it was very stressful to have all this going on. Houston had become such a bad scene that I just wanted to get out of there.

John and I eventually left Houston and went off on our own. We moved down to the Rio Grande Valley and lived for a few years in the area where he grew up. We set up and worked a number of businesses which, for one reason or another, were not successful. But we were happy, for the most part. Like any two people living under the same roof, we had our differences and our problems, but we always worked them out. The most important thing was that we were a family, just like any other. We were just average, normal people. After so many years of living in turmoil, sometimes without a real home at all, it was a welcome relief for me.

During much of the mid-1980s I was going through a personal spiritual dilemma. I had broken with Ervil long before and religiously I was in limbo. I still believed in the Ten Commandments, but the issue of the priesthood continued to be a problem. While I was at work one day in our shop, around February 1984, a customer came in and started talking religion with John and me. He was a Mormon. We indicated an interest in learning more and having one or more of their missionaries come visit us at home. In an April 24, 1984, letter, I described some of this to Ramona, who had left Dan a few years earlier and was in Dallas working with her new husband and Ed. In the letter to her, I wrote, in part:

> . . . Well, two girl missionaries showed up a few days after that. We enjoyed their visits. I for one wanted to hear the Mormon approach since we've only heard the CFB and Ervil and Dan approach to things. So, they went thru the whole thing, just as they would have with someone who knew nothing about Mormonism.
>
> Now, there are some things I just can't bring myself to accept, of course. Like their belief in their President of the Church as being their prophet and I still just don't know *where* the priesthood is, etc.
>
> There are a lot of unanswered questions in my mind. They tell you to pray about it and the spirit will tell you what is right, but I personally don't think it's that easy.
>
> I know a lot of people in different religions who are really sincere and feel that God guided them or told them to do such and such or told or indicated they should do such and such . . . I don't think praying to find out if [Mormon Church] President [Spencer] Kimball is a prophet would be a thing I would do. We've *all* felt that God wanted us to do things and we can look around and see other people we think are totally off-base who feel that God guided them to do something we think God wouldn't have wanted done, or whatever . . . I guess I'm trying to say that I'm going to do a lot more studying . . .

As my letter indicates, I was flirting with present-day Mormonism, the church our family had renounced. But somehow I just couldn't bring myself to accept it totally. Ervil and Joel and the rest of them had planted too many questions and seeds of doubt in my head over the years, and these teachings were not going to be easily overcome. The Mormons don't teach the Ten Commandments, and that's what I had been raised on. So, in a religious sense, I continued to drift while trying to wean myself away from a twisted doctrine and a way of life that had brought about many hardships and tragedies. John was a tremendous help to me throughout this whole period, building my faith in myself, and basically working on me every day to put the past in its proper perspective and become my own person.

One of the most important things John convinced me of was that we weren't supposed to be so harsh and judgmental of other people. It was a new and foreign concept to me. Ervil built his whole prophetic career around judgments of others, and he passed those judgments on to the rest of us. And we accepted them. He was the judge of other people and we eventually ended up being the executioners, by following his judgments and orders. Even after our split from Ervil, we continued to judge.

In some instances we would observe people going into churches of other denominations and we would "feel sorry" for them because we felt that we alone held the true spiritual keys to the Heavenly Kingdom and the rest of the world was in "utter darkness." I now believe that there are a lot of good people in the world and many of them are doing the best they know how with the knowledge they have. God will reward them according to the amount of knowledge they had, as well as what their intentions were, however misguided those intentions might have been. We are all expected to do the best we can with the knowledge we have and not be so critical of others. This was just one of many things John taught me about tolerance of other faiths that helped soften my own hard-line attitudes. I'm still conservative in my views but much less judgmental and militant toward others.

Sometime around the early 1980s, Mark saw the need for a spiritual rapprochement with the Mexican contingent. Reports had gotten back to Houston about the "hit list." Rather than go into hiding and spend his life in fear, he decided to meet the problem head-on. He, Duane, and Ed met with Arthur and Leo and others from that group somewhere in southern Arizona and their confab went on for several days. Mark tried to drive home the point that the *Book of the New Covenant* Leo had compiled from Ervil's direction was not the product of a sane mind. He pointed out how radically inconsistent these supposed "revelations" of Ervil's were with the teachings and writings of his previous years. In short, he was trying to convince the hard-liners that the dead leader they continued to follow was not the same leader who had founded a church based on more rational premises. These "revelations" Ervil claimed in his final days of life did not come from the Lord, Mark explained.

But, in the end, the conclave did no good. The hard-liners were too set in their ways to modify their stance and they remained determined to fulfill Ervil's dying blueprint for vengeance. The road was left open for the tragedies that were still to come.

And in late 1983 they came on heavy. After two years of a shaky leadership coalition, the inevitable power struggle between Leo and Arthur erupted at Rancho La Joya. In addition to Arthur and Leo and their families, their group consisted of some of the Rios brothers and sisters (two of whom, Teresa and Yolanda, were Ervil's wives), their wives and children, Lorna's kids, and a few other people. The ranch was a veritable hotbed of hatred, militarism, and illegal activities. It was reputed to be an arsenal for many types of automatic weapons and the group was reported to be dealing in stolen cars and motorcycles from the U.S. It was a bad scene all around, according to some of the younger boys who defected from them and came to live among us.

No one seems to know what the final straw was that broke the back of the Arthur-Leo coalition. Some of the people we talked to think it had to do with Lorna's death, since one of them had her killed and the other avenged her. Others think it might have been Arthur's decision to marry another wife in a Catholic ceremony. Leo was furious and blasted Arthur in no uncertain terms about how he'd blasphemed and was sacrilegious. Perhaps there were indications that bloodshed was in the works and Gamaliel Rios, long regarded as the "peacemaker" of Arthur's group, set up a meeting to try to calm things down. In a phone call from the ranch to Mom on December 19, 1983, Gamaliel told her he was trying to bring Leo and Arthur together, face to face, to settle their differences peaceably.

The meeting appears to have been held sometime late in December 1983. Within the confines of this heated atmosphere an argument ensued — no one seems too certain what precipitated it — and shots were fired. Arthur was killed by bullet wounds in the back.

Retribution was swift. Yolanda Rios, who was suspected of being part of Leo's conspiracy to murder Arthur and assume leadership, was killed. According to Tony's account, Yolanda had taken all of the little kids into a trailer on the property and told them to lie down on the floor. The shots that killed Arthur were fired immediately afterward, leading others to suspect she knew the murder was coming.

Gamaliel, who was suspected of setting up the meeting as a ploy for Leo to get at Arthur, was murdered about the same time as Yolanda. Raul Rios was also shot around this time, and he died of his wounds. No one knows who murdered whom, but Lorna's oldest son, Andrew, plus Heber, Alex, and Andres are the most likely suspects.

Leo, who was living in northern California at the time, had founded a group calling themselves the Millennial Church of Jesus Christ. His following was small and his only converts were his wives and a few others. Three and a half years later, he was hunted down in Santa Cruz County, California, most likely by a group led by Heber. His body was never found but blood stains and bullet holes, along with empty shell casings, were found in and around his pickup truck, along with a pair of dentures that were traced to him. Investigators estimate that he was shot to death on May 21, 1987.

With Arthur dead, it appears that Heber and Andrew took on the leadership of the Mexican faction. Heber, who would have been around twenty-six at the time, had always been a troublesome youth and he resented all forms of authority. As a child he had been difficult to babysit and was almost impossible to control. Now it appeared that he was taking the kids — in effect, the second generation of LeBaron followers — and leading them down the disastrous path of defiance and violence. He was perpetuating his father's legacy of blood and vengeance. As one investigator put it, "Someone has picked up the sword and is off and running with it."

Whether it was Heber or Andrew directing the "military affairs" of the group, no one seemed to know. But what is known is that they had a copy of the *Book of the New Covenant* — Ervil's "hit list." One by one they began going down the list of names of those still living, beginning with the most visible. Dan Jordan would be the logical place to start.

One day, in the late summer or early fall of 1987, five of the younger LeBaron kids showed up on Dan's doorstep in Bennett, Colorado, a Denver suburb. They were Aaron Morel (Mo), his sisters Andrea Monique (Nicki) and Natasha (Tasha); Linda Johnson's daughter Cynthia and her brother Richard; and Norma, one of four daughters Ervil had with Teresa Rios. They told Dan they had escaped from Heber and Andrew and apparently won Dan's sympathy with their descriptions of alleged atrocities they were forced to live under there. Dan took them in and kept their presence a secret.

In mid-October, Dan took Mo and Tasha, along with a number of his wives and other kids, on a hunting and camping trip to Manti-La Sal National Forest in Utah. On October 16, as Dan went to the bushes to relieve himself, he was ambushed and shot to death. The kids who had come to him from Mexico were later suspected of conspiring in a setup to catch Dan in the open. No one has yet been brought to trial in Dan's murder, but Andrew is most strongly suspected. The younger children say he is bloodthirsty and they have spoken of him with great fear.

The fragmentation that resulted during Ervil's imprisonment and in the years following his death was splintered even further. The "first generation" leaders of the Mexico contingent — Arthur and Leo — were both dead, and now the "first generation" leader of the Denver group — Dan — was dead also. That left only Mark in Houston as the last survivor of the original group leaders. It was obvious that a pattern was being set and followed. These "second-generation" kids were going after the older church leaders and trying to centralize the power of what remained of Ervil's church in themselves, using Ervil's "hit list" as their road map.

If that was Heber and Andrew's original plan, they must have been thwarted somewhat by Mo's next actions. Just after Dan's funeral, Mo proclaimed himself as the new prophet and holder of the keys to the priesthood. Despite being a mere seventeen or eighteen years old, he ordered Dan's wives and whoever else remained in the Denver group to follow him, including one or two of Ervil's widows. Sharon, Dan's first wife, called the police. Mo was arrested as a suspect in Dan's murder, and the rest of the kids were put in foster homes from which they later escaped. Mo was released for insufficient evidence and went into hiding.

Lillian was the first one to call us with the news about Dan. Five minutes after we hung up, Elsa called. She was crying and distraught over her husband's death and we felt more sorry for her, the other wives, and the kids than we did for Dan. He had wronged me too many times over the years, and I found it hard to feel any sorrow over what happened. But of more immediate concern to me was our own safety. It became obvious to us that the infighting between the militant faction was now over. With both Arthur and Leo dead, those who remained were uniting and going down the list. That meant we were next.

We were all extremely worried about Mark. We knew that if the killers were going to hit someone after Dan, Mark would be the next logical target. About a year earlier, we had made our peace with Mark and Lillian and the unpleasant incidents of the past were forgotten. They had apologized for their "un-Christianlike behavior" and we renewed our friendships again. Now, in the face of what was happening, we had cause for common concern.

I knew, also, that my name was on Ervil's "hit list." Others had seen it and they told me about it. It didn't take a genius to see they would kill me if they knew where I could be found. I spoke about this fear in a November 17, 1987, letter to John O'Connell, one month after Dan's murder. I knew they were coming after at least Mark. By the beginning of 1988, they must have already had their sights set on Houston.

After all those years of following Ervil like the rest of us, Mark and his family had finally begun adapting to a normal lifestyle. He was highly visible and was conducting his appliance business in the open. The turmoil of years past was behind him now, and he had settled down to a stable and comfortable life. He and his family had joined a local nondemoninational Church of God, he was an organ accompanist for their Sunday services, he drove a bus for the Sunday school kids, and he even coached a YMCA basketball team. His phone number and address were listed, and he thought he had no reason to hide where he was or what he was doing. He had influential friends, a beautiful home, and was an upstanding member of the community.

Duane also had his own appliance business, with Mom, and he was beginning to do well too. They had some of the younger Zarate-Chynoweth kids working for them, which kept them active and productive. A few years earlier, Duane's wife Laura decided she wanted to be a free spirit and started running around with other guys. She was a rather shallow person and didn't want to be tied down with a husband and kids, so she and Duane split up. They got back together briefly and had another child, then, while the baby was still in diapers, Laura started running wild again. They parted for good and Duane retained custody of the kids. He raised the children alone, with the help of an elderly live-in housekeeper he hired.

The housekeeper left after about a year and, with no one to help care for the kids, one of the men who worked for him offered to bring his nineteen-year-old daughter, Lucy, up from Venezuela. Duane agreed to pay her way into the country in May 1987. Lucy was hired as Duane's housekeeper and she was great with the kids. Duane and Lucy fell in love and got married two months later. Although Lucy was eleven years younger than Duane, she was very mature. She loved the children as if they were her own. She had taken over the role of mother to Duane's four girls and they adored her. Unfortunately, his son Adrian was not happy with the situation. Duane never told his kids about Laura's infidelity, and so Adrian blamed his father for the absence of his mother. Adrian had gone to stay with Mom.

The eleven months between Duane's marriage to Lucy and his death were the happiest I had ever seen him. The hurt look in his eyes was finally gone, and it seemed as if he finally had everything he had ever wanted out of life.

Unlike Mark, who talked openly about our past, Duane was very subdued about it. He was trying to put it all behind him, as if it never existed. He wasn't as well versed in the doctrine as Mark, but he had a lot of common sense. Duane was always the one to call something for what it truly was. If he thought something Ervil taught us was bullshit, that would be the exact word he'd use to describe it. Like Mark, he had settled down to a normal life, conducting his business in the open. Both he and Mark were easy targets when the time finally came.

So was Ed Marston. He had moved to Dallas a number of years before and gained confidence in himself and his abilities. He opened an appliance business with Ramona's new husband, then went out on his own. He still hadn't married but he had a girlfriend. Like the rest of us, he had put the past behind him. It was a horrible nightmare he had finally conquered. Duane stayed in touch with him and, at one point, the two of them set out on a trip to the western states trying unsuccessfuly to find Lorna's children.

It started with anonymous threats Mark began getting on the phone in early 1988. He went to the Houston police about it and asked for some measure of protection or at least have them step up their patrols around his business and home. However, it didn't appear the police were taking the threats seriously, not being fully aware of the history of the cult and how Ervil's last "revelations" were being interpreted by the new generation of his followers. Not wanting to worry any of the rest of us, Mark didn't say anything about the threats to Mom or anyone else. Somehow the media knew about it.

We were visiting Mark and Duane in Houston toward the end of January 1988 when a front-page article about Ervil and the whole cult business came out in the *Houston Chronicle*. To this day it never ceases to amaze me that the press knew and understood the danger Mark was in better than the police. Normally, the media gets much of its information on crime stories from the police, but this was one case where the police could have gotten some valuable information from the media.

Mark and Lillian came to our home for a visit on April 26,

1988, and they stayed about two or three days. John and I and Erin and J.R. were living in another town. We had a very nice time and did a lot of fun things together. We went sightseeing, browsed through antique stores, and went to hear a free symphony concert at a nearby college. It was the first time any of us ever attended a classical music performance, and we were enthralled by it. On those two or three nights, after the kids were in bed, Mark played the guitar and we all sang songs from the '50s, '60s, and '70s.

In this visit Mark gave me some good insights into why we chose to follow Ervil rather than Joel. I had just turned thirty and, given the perspective of a mature adult, I could understand a lot better what our family's reasonings were at that time. After studying the doctrine intensely, Mark and Mom and Dad had concluded that Joel could not defend his doctrinal position. Mark described the Joelites as "a bunch of blind sheep following a blind shepherd, heading for a cliff." Mark also told me some other things I didn't know or realize about those early years and he answered many questions I had. He was closer to Ervil in some respects than I ever was. Ervil would either confide in him or have him along with the other men in priesthood meetings which were closed to everyone else. I'm glad I got this information from Mark because it would have died with him otherwise. When Mark and Lillian said good-bye and drove away, it was the last time I ever saw him.

Duane never received any threats that we're aware of. Although he had followed Ervil with us for the same length of time, he was never a central figure in the craziness that went on. He held the priesthood but never really exercised his role in that office. He wasn't a leader, but he wasn't a blind follower either. He did some horrible things for Ervil, like the rest of us, but he was not one who found himself in the limelight like my other brothers, Vic and Mark. Duane had kept his nose relatively clean and was never charged with any crimes, despite the hand he had in Becky's murder and the stakeout of Verlan in El Paso.

Duane carried a gun but said it was more for the protection of Mark, who refused to carry one. Unfortunately, when the day came he might have needed it, he was unable to save Mark. Or himself.

CHAPTER 26

The date was Monday, June 27, 1988. I had just finished clearing away the dishes from dinner between 5:00 and 6:00 P.M. when the phone rang. It was John's daughter Sandy who, several years earlier, married her high school sweetheart and lived in Houston.

"Rena," she said, "there's something on the news about an appliance store owner and his eight-year-old daughter being killed on Rena Street and there are police cars all around Duane's store."

I felt the bottom drop out of my stomach and my knees suddenly felt weak. A chill ran through me as I thought, "Oh, dear God! It's started again!" I told Sandy I was hanging up to find out what was going on.

My hands were shaking as I dialed the number of Duane's appliance shop. A man's husky voice answered and I thought at first it was Johnny, the second oldest of the five Zarate kids Mom had adopted.

"Johnny?" I asked.

"No. Who's this?" the voice asked.

353

"It's Rena."

"It's Rena," the voice repeated. In the background I heard Mom's voice say, "Oh, that's my daughter." Mom got on the phone and asked if I was okay.

"I'm okay, Mom," I assured her. "But what's going on? Sandy said she heard something on the news about a murder."

Mom took a deep breath and her normally soft voice became practically a whisper. "Rena, Duane and Jenny are dead and Mark is hurt, but I don't know how bad. I haven't been able to get any information. Lucy and the rest of the little girls are here with me, but we don't know where we're spending the night yet."

I asked Mom what happened and she told me what she knew. Duane had been lured out on a pickup call that set him up to be killed, and Jenny had the misfortune of being with him. The house at which he was supposed to make the pickup, on Rena Street, was vacant, but Duane didn't know it. A For Sale sign that had been in front of the house had been removed. The gunman who pulled up in a pickup truck killed them both.

My heart was pounding and I felt dazed as Mom told me the story. I don't remember much of our conversation after that, except for asking if she thought it was deliberate or a coincidence he was set up to be killed on a street that had my name. Was it supposed to be some kind of omen aimed at me? Mom definitely felt that it was.

Mom said she and Lucy and the remaining kids were being rounded up by the authorities and moved to a safer location. They were to be taken into protective custody, for fear the killers would attempt to strike again. Mom knew her name was also on Ervil's "hit list" after we all defected and, though Mom has never been afraid of death, if she could save herself she would. She asked me several more times if I was okay, and after giving her those reassurances, we hung up.

I spent the next several hours trying to get details. I called Mark's store and home repeatedly but never got an answer. Finally, later that evening, Elsa called me from Denver to say she'd heard from an FBI friend of hers that Mark was shot and killed in his shop right around the same time as Duane. Then she broke the news about Ed: I hadn't heard anything about that previously. She said Ed was lured out on a service call, just like Duane, to a vacant house in the Dallas suburb of Irving. There he was shot around the same time as Duane and Mark and later died in the hospital. In none of these shootings, either in Houston or in Irving, were the police able to make any arrests.

Knowing now that my family and I were in great danger, I called the local police. They were on my doorstep in less than ten minutes. Other backup units arrived, bearing uniformed and plainclothes officers. They quickly spread out and combed the vicinity of the house and the neighborhood, looking for suspects or anything that might be suspicious. With lights flashing and police radios crackling from the dashboards of their squad cars, there was commotion all around.

The neighbors came out and clustered a short distance away, wondering what was going on. We had never told any of them about our past and, until that night, we blended in with them like everyone else in the neighborhood. They never had reason to suspect anything unusual about us. All of a sudden, here we were hastily gathering up clothing and personal items and being hustled into waiting police cars. God only knows what they must have been thinking.

The decision was made at police headquarters to get us to a "safe house" immediately. We were taken into protective custody like Mom and the others in Houston. We would have been in too much danger if we stayed home, they felt, despite the fact we were distantly removed from the sites of the other killings.

John and I were certain that those who killed Mark, Duane, Jenny, and Ed were long gone by this time, but we went along with the protective arrangement, just to be on the safe side. After gathering up the possessions we would need to hold us over for a few days, we got into an unmarked patrol car and were driven off, with two or three marked units escorting us. They took us out into the countryside, making many twists and turns along the way to elude anyone who may have been following us. Then they dropped us off by a railroad bridge, escorted us across with their weapons drawn and ready, and we arrived on foot in the next jurisdiction. Another police car met us and drove us to a nearby hotel.

The police wanted to keep us there in protective custody for a few days, but we balked against that idea. I wanted to be free to make phone calls and stay in touch with the rest of my family. I had to know what was happening. Was everyone else safe? Were there any more threats? Any arrests? I had to stay on top of the situation as best I could. I was scared but I felt that if they were going to get me the way they got Ed, Mark, Duane, and Jenny, then they would have done it at the same time, assuming they knew where to find me. And I was a long way from either Houston or Dallas. I knew I wasn't going to live my life in fear like a hunted animal. After only one night in protective custody, we insisted on going back home.

John had arranged earlier to take his vacation on July 1–12. Instead of going to Mexico with the kids to see Dad and on to Cancun as we planned, we spent the time in hiding. The funeral for the four victims — Mark, Duane, Jenny, and Ed — was held in Houston on July 2, but I stayed home. John wouldn't let me attend. Ervil had been known to plot the murders of people he wanted eliminated at funerals, and it was feared his younger children and stepchildren, the most likely suspects in the murders, could be out there stalking us. I was inclined to go anyway so I could pay my last respects and be there with my family, but John would absolutely not allow it. He was not going to risk having anything happen to me. Instead of going to the funeral, we started packing our belongings and prepared to make another move.

The funeral was like an affair of state. Security was as tight for it as it would have been for a visiting dignitary. The Houston police delayed the funeral until the first available Saturday so they could call up some of their off-duty officers to work extra security detail, some of whom were SWAT team members. No less than fifty policemen were on hand, some wearing bulletproof vests and leading bomb-sniffing dogs around. Nothing was being left to chance and perhaps there was the hope that the murderers could be captured. Perhaps, also, they wanted to atone for their failure to take Mark's warnings and requests for protection seriously, several months prior to the tragedy, not that there was anything they could have done anyway. Whatever their reasons, the protective shield around the funeral home and the subsequent motorcade to the cemetery was extremely tight. Everyone entering had to identify themselves properly and every license plate number was recorded. Pictures were taken by police photographers of everyone who came. Plainclothes and uniformed officers, with automatic weapons in full view, surrounded the funeral home, allowing the mourners to pay their last respects in safety. During the funeral procession to the cemetery, the freeway was shut down to all other traffic in both directions as an extra precaution. Police blocked off all access ramps to oncoming vehicles until the procession had safely passed.

Mom went to the funeral. These were her sons and her granddaughter, as well as another young man who had been like a son to her. She was sure that the murderers were long gone and, even if they were lying in wait, she was not afraid to die. My brother Glen flew down from Utah to be with Mom and he delivered a eulogy which I heard was very beautiful. He spoke kindly of all four of them, not singling out anyone for more attention than the others. He even spoke kindly of Ed, who wasn't direct family and whom he barely knew. Glen had never joined us in all those years with Joel and Ervil and never showed any inclination to join us, but he was always with us in spirit and was always there when we needed him. At the funeral, he was a pillar of support for Mom and Duane and Mark's widows during this greatest single tragedy of our lives.

The crowd that came to pay its respects was enormous. Mark had become very well known and popular over the years, especially among his customers, business associates and their families, and the members of the church he and his family attended. One of his friends was a candidate in the Houston mayor's race. Mark had climbed a long way up the ladder of respectability and was climbing even higher when he was tragically and senselessly cut down.

Duane had a lot of friends and business associates as well. Like Mark, he was fair and honest to both his customers and his employees. His death was a great loss to the employees who depended on him for their living, including Lucy's father, who considered him a son. Jenny was a bright and sweet child and many of her friends and their families attended the funeral, along with many people who knew Ed.

David UnRue, the pastor of Mark's church, the Spring Branch

Church of God, led the memorial service. According to the media, he was wearing a bulletproof vest under his suit. Anna Mae had flown in from Denver and she sang a solo. Eulogies were given by other people who knew Mark and Duane.

The news media was out in force with TV crews that zeroed their minicams in on the mourners. Newspaper reporters and photographers crowded up to the police lines. The story that had been making headlines all week continued through the funeral and for weeks beyond. Not only were the Houston papers and TV stations covering the funeral and other developments in the story, the Dallas, Denver, and Salt Lake media were there as well. The story went out over the wire services and was picked up by thousands of papers, including the one in the small town where we lived. Glen's picture was on the front page of the Ogden *Standard-Examiner* the day after the funeral and Lucy's anguished face was on the front page of the *Houston Post* and the *Salt Lake Tribune*. I thought it was rather callous and insensitive showing people in such a bereaved state, but that's what the media people were there for.

Vic didn't go to the funeral. He wasn't going to take any chances. He knew his name was on the list and he was living in seclusion far away. Ramona stayed away, also. Her new husband was a good friend of Duane and Mark's, but she didn't feel safe either. All the family members living in the Houston area attended, including Lillian and both of Duane's wives. Though no longer married to him, Laura showed up to mourn him and her late daughter. She later took the four surviving kids, despite the fact Lucy had been raising them for more than a year. Lillian's brother, Paul LeBaron, who had taken a picture of Mark and Lillian minutes before Mark was shot, was one of the pallbearers.

It was a sad day for everyone, seeing these promising young men who had become respected productive members of society cut down in the prime of their lives. Ten beautiful children in two families were left fatherless, and a beautiful eight-year-old girl who had never harmed anyone was killed because she was unfortunate enough to be present when her father met his fate.

Several months earlier, I had started keeping a diary again, renewing the contact with "Pat," the imaginary confidante I hadn't written to in ten years. At first, my entries were those of a normal, average, middle-class young woman with the usual concerns in life — the kids' activities and illnesses, shopping, making money, paying bills, and other everyday occurrences. After the multiple tragedy, however, my mind and my entries were again focused on the bleak past I thought I had left behind. On June 30, two days after the shootings, I wrote, "There is absolutely no way anyone should question that I am a target. If they can find me, I'm next."

Suddenly, it was all part of my life again. We knew about the power struggles between Arthur and Leo that resulted in both of them being killed, and we knew about the murder of Dan. We feared that sooner or later they would be coming for us, but somehow, it still didn't seem real or possible. What could anyone have hoped to accomplish by killing us? Fulfilling a covenant that wasn't the product of a sane man at the time it was drawn up?

We had served Ervil for two decades as well and faithfully as anyone could have asked for or expected. The only "wrong" we could have done to him was trying to break away after it became apparent he was going to be spending the rest of his life behind bars and was out of his mind. For twenty years, my family and I had served him; now we were condemned to death because of one or two years in which we didn't. After he died, we pooled what little money we had to give him a respectable funeral and burial. Now his bloodstained hand was reaching up from the grave to pull more of us down with him. Why? Did he think that would hasten us to his side in the Celestial Kingdom?

I began having bad dreams, which shouldn't have been at all surprising, considering the anguish I was going through. The past that I had so successfully blocked out was coming back full force. In one of my dreams I was being followed by people from the CFB — Joel's people. I tried telling them that I, too, was a "victim," but they didn't believe me. I started shouting, "Fire!" and woke myself and John up. It was terrible what I went through those first few weeks of July when there was so much fear and tragedy going on around me.

The police, FBI, and investigators from many of the western states stepped up their investigation and search for the suspected

359

killers. Dick Forbes, the LeBaron expert whose investigation helped put Ervil away, was called upon to help out. Within days, it was announced the primary suspects were Heber, Andrew, Mo, and some of the younger kids under their control. By this time, it was known that they were in possession of Ervil's "hit list" and were going after the people on it. What scared me the most was that Mom and Lillian weren't taking any precautions for themselves or the kids, despite both being on the list. Mom just kept saying she had led a long, full life and wasn't afraid to go home and meet her Maker. John and I were more afraid for her than she was for herself.

In the meantime, I was called in to help any way I could with the investigation. I was shown pictures of Heber, Andrew, Mo, and the other children: Tasha, Nicki, Richard, Cynthia, and Norma. Doug Barlow was also known to be hanging out with them. The police also had recent pictures of Alex and Andres Zarate. I hadn't seen any of them since around 1980 or 1981 and, except for Alex and Andres, they were all just kids then. After seeing photos of them eight years later, I could barely recognize them, especially with the hard, cold faces they now had. And, after so many years, I still had trouble fathoming the horrible changes Andres had gone through. The sweet, kind, understanding boy who had been my confidante and long-time admirer was now a hardened criminal who had chosen to continue following the worst of Ervil's teachings. He had reportedly raped one of the younger girls when she was twelve years old.

I went through hell with the assistant district attorney. Despite having spent four hours with the investigators, telling them everything I could, he called up and said my family and I couldn't qualify for the Federal Witness Protection Program. He said I didn't give them any information that could lead to an arrest. I was furious. It didn't matter to them that my life was in danger; I had to be able to "give" them something before I could be protected. What more could I do? I didn't know anything. I hadn't seen those kids in many years. The investigators knew more about what was going on than I did. They had stayed close to it over the years, while I went about getting my life back in order and trying to forget.

The assistant D.A. then said he would put one of his investigators in touch with me to continue probing and see if I could come up with more information they could use. But when the investigator began asking me questions about things I was trying to block out and couldn't remember, he became suspicious that I was hiding something. He apparently thought I was covering for Heber, despite the fact that he might have been responsible for killing my brothers, my niece, and Ed. I was even asked if I had anything to do with the illegal theft and extortion ring Heber's group was running in Dallas and Mexico. I'm sure my frequent, "I don't know" or "I don't remember" answers must have made him suspicious, but if I was trying to hide *anything*, it was only from myself and my kids. My hesitation probably fueled their suspicions even further. It would have taken people with more perception and understanding to know what I was going through.

The police investigating Duane and Jenny's murder had a description of the gunman and the vehicle he was driving. Apparently, one of the people living nearby in the 6000 block of Rena Street saw a man in a dark late-model Chevy Silverado pickup truck drive up to where Duane was parked. The day after the murders, a composite sketch was released, showing a man in his late twenties or early thirties, about 6'1, weighing about 185, with short reddish-brown hair and a short, full beard. It didn't match the description of anyone we might have suspected, but it could have been a disguise.

I spoke to Lillian on the phone for more than an hour a week after the funeral. She suspected a plot by Heber and the others to kill off the remaining adults in our group so they could take control over our kids. Supposedly, Ervil had ordered the older boys to gather up all of his children and adopt them into his "spiritual family." Any adults who tried to stand in the way were to be eliminated. They were going to overthrow the government of Mexico and then the U.S., according to what Ervil reportedly told them.

John and I and the kids went deep into hiding. We picked up and moved to another area to live and work. After all the moving we had done over the years we should have been used to it, but that didn't make it any easier or more pleasant. We hated having to live our lives on the run like this.

John took a job in a nearby plant. He had to get up at 5:00 and be at work by 6:00 A.M. I would get up with him, help him get ready, then go back and lie down for an hour until it was time to get the kids off to school. John rarely called from work, so I thought it was very unusual when he called me at 8:00 in the morning on July 15. He was excited. Some of the guys at work had showed him the front page of the local paper, and on it was a report of an arrest made in Phoenix, Arizona. Heber had been taken into custody, along with Doug Barlow, Linda's son Richard and her daughter Cynthia, and my niece Tarsa.

John went on to say they were arrested at a motel around July 1 or 2, after a routine license plate check found their pickup truck was stolen in Texas. Inside the motel room where Heber and the others were first arrested, police found a false red beard and books describing techniques of theatrical makeup. They also found ledgers listing all the vehicles the group had stolen — over one hundred in the Phoenix area — along with three or four blue suits and empty shoulder holsters.

The five suspects were using false names, and it was eleven days before their true identities were discovered. Heber, who was twenty-seven at this time, had jumped bail after being arrested for robbing a bank in Richardson, Texas, a Dallas suburb, in November 1986. He also reportedly tried to kill a police officer who had responded to the call.

At first the authorities in Phoenix believed they had evidence of a stolen truck ring. Before the identities of Heber and the others were discovered, the Phoenix police released them on bail and followed them to see if they would lead to more evidence in the theft ring. Heber, Doug, Richard, Cynthia, and Tarsa were rearrested when they tried to cross the border into Mexico. Natasha and Patricia LeBaron had also been arrested initially, but when released on bail they drove in an opposite direction from the others and police chose to follow the vehicle carrying the most people.

Meanwhile, back in Houston, the team of investigators working on the Chynoweth murders had turned up an address in the Phoenix area that Linda Johnson had used at one time. One of the sergeants who knew someone on the force in Phoenix called and described the group of people they were looking for in their murder investigation — people who sold used appliances and stole vehicles. The next day, as word was spread around, an officer said, "Hey, that sounds like the group we have in custody right now!" Soon, Phoenix was faxing pictures and other information to Houston, and Houston was able to tell Phoenix the true identities of the people in custody. It was the first break in the case.

Although the authorities had found enough items to possibly link this group with the murders, there was not enough evidence to seek murder indictments against them. Instead, they charged them with operating an illegal enterprise and multiple counts of auto theft.

Heber was also charged by Phoenix police with unlawful flight to avoid prosecution. Houston and Dallas-area investigators were eager to question him as the prime suspect in the Chynoweth/Marston murders and the plot that went into them.

At first it was believed that the authorities in Phoenix had Mo in custody, but it turned out to be a false alarm. He and Andrew and the younger kids, mainly the girls, remained at large. It was believed that the one adult traveling with them and sheltering them was Linda Johnson. She was being sought on forgery charges, credit card fraud, and passing bad checks.

The stories that began coming to light were sickening. There was incest and rape and cruelty going on among that group of kids. Heber, the son of Anna Mae, was reportedly "married" to his own half sisters, Patricia, daughter of Ervil and Marilu Vega; Tarsa and Tasha, Lorna's daughters; and Cynthia, Linda's daughter. These kids were ignorant, uneducated, rootless, and living in poverty. Some of the older girls like Tasha have kids of their own who, when last seen, didn't appear to be physically healthy. Everyone is scared to death of Heber and Andrew, and all of them have been taught they will be killed if they talk against them or turn themselves in to the authorities.

Heber, Doug, Tarsa, Cynthia, and Richard remain in prison

in Phoenix, having been sentenced to varying terms for auto theft. Heber was sentenced to seven years in prison; Richard, three years; the others, varying terms ranging from three to five years. They are suspected in the murders of Dan, Ed, Duane, Jenny, and Mark, but indications are that unless someone talks or comes forward or further evidence is uncovered, these deaths will go unpunished.

In August I flew to Salt Lake City to testify before a grand jury looking into Dan's murder. I mostly provided background information on Ervil, his church, and doctrine. I also talked to Dick Forbes and other investigators. Mom, Tony, and Johnny were also there. It was during that visit that I saw the "hit list" for the first time, along with my name and my supposed "crimes." It is frightening enough to think that anyone could draw up such a venomous document, and more frightening still to think that other twisted minds are actually carrying out the so-called "revelations" it contains. I told Dick whatever I knew and flew back home after discussing my situation with John O'Connell. He was doing whatever he could to get us under the Federal Witness Protection Plan.

Mom and Johnny tried to keep Duane's business going after Duane's death, but it just wasn't the same. Johnny simply wasn't up to the task. Mom closed down the shop, cleared out the inventory, and sadly watched the business at which she and Duane had worked so hard come to an end.

Mark's business remained open until Lillian committed suicide in January 1989. It was sold after business began to slow down, perhaps because bad publicity kept customers away.

Laura laid claim to the four surviving kids she and Duane had. Because of Duane's insurance policy, she benefited handsomely. Lucy, who had cared for those kids so lovingly in the year before Duane died, got none of them. She took the small part of the insurance money she was awarded and put it away for use toward her schooling. The whole situation between she and Laura had gotten very ugly, and none of it was Lucy's fault.

On October 16, 1988, a story appeared in the *Salt Lake Tribune* that Andrew might be dead, a victim of one of the Rancho La Joya power struggles. The story went on to say he hadn't been seen since 1986. How much stock can be placed in the story is open to question. Some of the kids we talked to said they have seen him more recently than that. With Heber in jail, Andrew is regarded as being the most dangerous of the group that might still be out there. Since he is being sought in at least one murder case, it would certainly be to his advantage to stay incognito and allow the authorities to think he is dead. That would enable him to strike again, if he has indeed struck before. The only ones who might know his whereabouts are too scared to talk. Until we have confirmation Andrew is either dead or in custody, we have no intention of relaxing our guard or blowing our cover.

After Mark's death, Lillian was never the same again. Over the next seven months her behavior changed radically for the worse. She knew her name was on the "hit list" and she was scared, but she refused at first to take the kids and go into hiding. Sometime shortly after Mark was killed, she claimed to have received a threatening phone call from Heber, and she said it wasn't a long distance call. It had been many years since she had seen him or heard his voice, but she swore it was him and no one could tell her otherwise, even though he was in jail in Phoenix at the time.

Lillian began having other horrible visions as well. Her whole personality changed. The trauma of Mark's death triggered a chemical imbalance in her brain that developed into manic depression. She started doing bizarre things. She told people that Mom was trying to kill her and she hired a bodyguard to protect herself, as crazy as that sounds. She even had Laura and Duane's kids afraid of their grandma. Lil's state of mind was such that Mom finally left and came to live with us, bringing Harvey and Paul with her. With her own grandchildren afraid of her, Mom had nothing left to keep her in Houston.

Lil had become totally irrational, calling up people in the middle of the night and keeping them on the phone for hours. Several times she called Glen at 1:00 in the morning and kept him on the phone until he had to go to work at 6:00 A.M. At first, she almost had him convinced that Mom posed a threat to her, but Glen was able to sort out the truth and see how irrational she was. She succeeded in alienating nearly everyone else as well, especially in the church she and Mark and the kids had attended in good standing. Mark's insurance left her about $250,000 richer, and she started spending it freely. She took the kids, went to California, and got involved with some religious organization run by a charismatic evangelist. Then she began pledging and giving away money right and left.

After several months in California, Lil and the kids returned to Houston. She tried telling people she was sorry for all the things she had said and done. Finally, she sought professional help, but she was so depressed, ashamed, and lonely that it may have been too little too late. She wouldn't put her kids back in the church school they attended before, so she hooked up with a Baptist church school and sent the kids there. By this time, Lil had ceased her extravagant spending and had become almost miserly.

On January 28, 1989, at the age of thirty-three, Lillian committed suicide at her home in Houston. Investigators called to the scene found a .357 magnum on the floor next to her body and concluded that she pointed it to the right side of her head and fired one fatal shot.

Immediately after Lil's death, members of the church where she sent the kids to school offered to help out. In her will, Lillian named the people she wanted to act as guardians for the children, should anything happen to her. The six kids are now in a very stable Christian home. We hear from them often and they have adjusted wonderfully, due to the efforts of the nice people who took them in. We feel that this was the best thing for them, to be away from us and out of the "line of fire."

It was a sad end to a beautiful person. Despite occasional disagreements we'd had over the years, we were family. We shared many memorable moments together, and she brought my second child into the world. When I think of Lil now, I try not to think of her in the manic depressive state that marked her final few months of life, but rather the loving, normally cheerful, radiant personality she was. On my wall at home I often look at the pictures I have of her and Mark and the kids — a stable, monogamous family that held together for fifteen years in the nomadic whirlwind of a polygamous society.

It was a joy that should have lasted much longer, were they not victimized by a demented vengeance that should have died long ago. As long as that vengeance lingers, the joy that I and my family can realize will have to be subdued.

Epilogue

The tragic legacy of Ervil LeBaron continues to this day. Some of his youngest children and stepchildren are still out there, roaming. Their lives and the promise their youth should hold out to them are not being fulfilled. They are living in squalor and poverty with no responsible adult supervision or guidance, no education, and no skills. They could be easy prey to whatever misfortunes of being homeless may befall them. And there is the danger of them further "intermarrying" and producing mentally or physically deficient offspring.

On February 14, 1989, almost seven months after the Phoenix arrests, police in the Chicago suburb of Northlake arrested Mo and Linda after spotting their expired out-of-state license plate in a motel parking lot and becoming suspicious of the conflicting stories they were given by the pair. Inside the hotel room they found Lorna's four youngest children — Andrea Monique (Nicki), seventeen, Bridget Veronica (Jessica), fifteen, Jared, thirteen, and Joshua, eleven — plus Yolanda's son Danny, thirteen, Marilu's daughter Patricia, twenty-eight, and Teresa's daughter Norma, sixteen. All nine of them were crowded into one little motel room, sleeping on

367

the floor and eating in the room itself. It took the police a while to figure out who they had in custody, but once they did, Dick Forbes, the LeBaron expert, was called in, along with Sgts. John Burmester and Fred Carroll from Houston and many others seeking answers to unsolved crimes in their respective states and cities.

For the most part, the younger children knew little about what their older brothers and sisters had been involved in since they had been kept on "the ranch" in Mexico while the older ones were in the United States running their illegal operations. I was told that Dick Forbes was the one who informed Lorna's youngest child, Joshua, that the reason he hadn't seen his mother in seven years was not because she was working in the U.S. and sending money down to support the ranch, but that she was presumed dead.

Gradually, the story unfolded. After Heber, Doug, Cynthia, Tarsa, and Richard posted bond and started to head for the border in July 1988, Patricia and Tasha, who had also been arrested at the same time as these others, took off in a separate vehicle in another direction. The police who were following them opted to stay with the vehicle that held the most people. Therefore, they escaped being rearrested and made their way to wherever it was the others were staying. They warned Linda and the other kids staying there. Eventually making their way to Atlanta, Georgia, they set up an appliance business, sold defective equipment without serial numbers, and because of numerous complaints, police investigated and Tasha was arrested. The others packed up and escaped, making their way up to the Chicago area.

Mo was charged with a misdemeanor in the Chicago arrests and spent some time in jail there. He was then sent on to Utah, where he was in custody on other charges at the time of this writing. Linda has many charges against her: credit card fraud, multiple counts of grand theft, fraud, forgery, passing bad checks, and so on. She will hopefully be kept out of circulation for a while. The six minors were taken to Utah and eventually placed into foster homes. The State of Utah did its best to keep us away from these children and denied us custody, placing them in foster homes with people who had no way of comprehending what these kids had been through or what was going on in their heads. One Friday morning, instead of going to school, they escaped together. As of this writing they are still out there somewhere.

The surviving wives of Ervil LeBaron are scattered about, except for Vonda, who remains in prison. Some of them are also in hiding. One of the wives, Teresa Rios, was believed to have been a victim of the La Joya vendetta that claimed her sister and two brothers, but investigators tracked her down to a mental institution in Dallas. She was released in 1988 and no one has heard from her since.

In late 1987, just after Dan's death, I began giving serious thought to the suggestions people had been making to me for years to write a book about my experiences. Some of the most important people in my life, especially John O'Connell and my own John, urged me to begin "getting it all out," feeling that, if nothing else, it would be very therapeutic for me. They said maybe others could benefit from my family's experience of following charismatic leaders and ending up being led into breaking the very commandments and teachings that had originally attracted us to these men.

As I read my old diaries and letters, I became more convinced that I did, indeed, have a story worth telling. But I saw another reason for writing this book that was better than all other reasons combined: those kids out there. They deserve a chance.

I was given a "second chance." Maybe God wants to use me to reach those kids. Because I've been through years of intensive self-deprogramming myself, I feel I can help them through my own experiences and because I understand their very complicated background. They should also receive extensive professional help, guidance, and a chance to be around people who really care what happens to them. Simply putting the younger children in foster homes and hoping for the best is not the way to handle the situation. They will only run away and return to the lifestyle they always knew, breaking the law and posing a danger to people's lives. They should not be allowed to grow to adulthood without being given a chance to learn proper values.

These last remnants of Ervil LeBaron's flock are still a risk to the rest of society. They are the last ones who may still feel bound by his blood covenant that has claimed so many innocent lives.

They have grown up around violence and violent teachings, and there is grave danger that they will pass these values on to their own children. I want the killing to stop. Only by finding those still out there and getting them the help they need can we stop the bloodshed.

What John, my mother, and I envision is a ranch — a place where these young people can live with family who loves them, where they can finally have the chance to go to school and church, and be able to receive the counseling and guidance that will help them become assets to society. There are a few of us who are willing to do anything we can to give them a chance. If God is willing, and with His help, we shall succeed.

If anyone has information that would help us reach out to the LeBaron children, please contact:

Sgts. Fred Carroll or
John Burmester
Houston, Texas
(713) 247-5418